The Texas Model

Prosperity in the Lone Star State and Lessons for America

by

Chuck DeVore

Former California State Assemblyman
and
Vice President for Communications
at the

Texas Public Policy Foundation

Cover by Nancy Druart

The Texas Model is dedicated to the newest Texans: my wife and daughters.

Table of Contents

FOREWORD

Mirabeau Lamar's voyage from the mostly rural Georgia of the Old South to the wild frontier of the Republic of Texas was both extraordinary, for it was a life's journey fraught with risk and danger, and ordinary, for it represented the experience of so many of the intrepid and independent original Texians. When he was elected by acclamation the second President of the Republic in 1838, he began a tenure as the most frankly nationalist of the three Texas presidents. Sam Houston and Anson Jones both sought—and achieved—the annexation of the Lone Star Republic to the United States, but Mirabeau Lamar envisioned a Texas forever independent, and stretching eventually to the Pacific. Among other adventures, he funded an abortive Texian invasion of New Mexico in 1841, which collapsed when the expeditionary column lost its way.

But Lamar's record was not simply one of territorial expansion and imperial dreams. The Georgian-become-Texan wished to be remembered as the builder of a continental Texas: but he is instead remembered today for something vastly more consequential. It was, in fact, Mirabeau Lamar who set aside the land that became both the University of Texas, and Texas A&M. When he passed away in 1859, he was not remembered as the conqueror of Santa Fe, but as the Father of Texas Education.

"The cultivated mind is the guardian genius of democracy," said Lamar in his first address to the Texas Congress—and what was true in 1838 is true today. Modern Texas—a great state, now, within an indissoluble Union—boasts what must be adjudged one of the most successful democracies, in terms of objective outcomes, in the Western world. The record of the past half-decade speaks for itself. Where the world suffered under global recession, Texas comparatively thrived. Where immigration to the United States from sources like Mexico nearly stopped, Texas welcomed about a thousand domestic migrants a day. Where manufacturing declined in its historic regions, in Texas it increased. Where social strife engulfed cities from Oakland to Athens, Texas remained relatively calm and prosperous.

The "guardian geniuses" of Texas democracy are, indeed, doing well. From the start, our state has valued intellect and its fruits—not as substitutes for labor, but as enabling more and better labor—and now, at the dawn of the twenty-first century, the light of prosperity and liberty is increasingly that of the Lone Star.

Liberty proves its case in Texas—not just on moral grounds, but in real and measurable outcomes. If you want a good job, you increasingly come to Texas. If you want to found a business, you increasingly come to Texas. If you want world-class medical care, you increasingly come to Texas. If you want good education for your children, and world-class education for yourself, you increasingly come to Texas. If you want some of the cleanest urban air in the United States, you increasingly come to Texas. In short, if you want a future that looks like the old American Dream—still dimly remembered by those of us recalling men like Ronald Reagan in the American presidency—you increasingly come to Texas.

That is what this book is about. This book, authored by Chuck DeVore of the Texas Public Policy Foundation, explores exactly what the "cultivated minds" and "guardian geniuses" of Mirabeau Lamar's vision have been up to—and lays forth the results in clear prose that makes sense of some extraordinary data. The tome exists for two reasons: because it is important to explain what Texas has gotten right, and how—and also to make plain that these things are not unique to Texas.

We Texans are unique and proud, it is true: but as you read this book, remember that liberty used to prove its case, not just in Texas, but in a great and wonderful place called the United States of America. It still can. We Texans are the product of unique Texas history, yes: but our heritage of liberty is our inheritance as Americans. Our achievements now are products of that inheritance, and our fondest hope is not that Texas remains its most eminent repository, but that all of the states in time rediscover its promise and its glory.

Brooke L. Rollins
President and CEO, Texas Public Policy Foundation
December 2012

PREFACE

Why Texas?

My family and I made Texas home in December 2011. Tens of thousands of Californians made the same move over the past decade.

The reason why people move from one state or nation to another is usually tied to opportunity: they perceive that their ability to thrive in their new home is better than in the old. So, they pick up stakes, say "goodbye" to family and long-time friends, and migrate.

My family's history has touched Texas twice in the past 145 years.

Sometime in the 1700s, a German by the name of Keithley made his way to America. He had a son in Kentucky in 1789. That man farmed in Missouri, then a common destination for Kentuckians.

His son, Griffin Stith Keithley, got caught up in the Civil War and fought under the banner of General Joe Shelby's army at the age of 17. Shelby's Confederate force, severely outnumbered by the Federals, marched hard to make up for the lack of men. By war's end, they logged the most miles of any Confederate unit, marching from Arkansas, to Missouri and down to Texas.

After the war, Keithley married and settled down in Missouri. But, whether due to lingering trouble in Missouri from the late unpleasantness, an innate wanderlust, or the fertile lands he saw during the war, he packed up his family of five to farm on the south bank of the Red River near Denison, Texas. Two children were born in the Lone Star State, one of them my maternal great-grandfather, Walter Griffin Keithley.

The family soon migrated north to Idaho Territory, then not yet a state with fewer than 30,000 pioneers.

Moving out of state in 1876 was still an arduous undertaking. Today, we have freeways.

From 2000 to 2010 the U.S. Census Bureau tells us that a net of more than 5.5 million Americans decamped from California, New York, Illinois, Pennsylvania, Ohio and Michigan— six of the eight most populous states. Of the other eight biggest states, Texas and Florida saw a net influx of 2.1 million Americans.

Census data tells us that much of Florida's population boom can be attributed to retirees moving south from the Northeast. But Texas presents an entirely different picture, with working age people, families, and immigrants from abroad all flocking into Texas seeking work.

Clearly, something is going on here. People don't casually vote with their feet—it takes a lot of effort and an accompanying emotional toll to uproot and move.

For us, the move to Texas came after years of having a front row seat watching the internationally famous California Dream start a long fade to black.

I was an aerospace executive when I was elected to the California State Assembly in 2004, about a year after Hollywood action star Arnold Schwarzenegger became governor in an historic October 2003 recall promising to "cut up the state's credit card." I represented about 500,000 people in Orange County, including the communities of Irvine (usually listed as one of the safest cities in America), Newport Beach, and Laguna Beach.

Schwarzenegger's election was an improbable turn of events.

In 2000 and 2001, California suffered an embarrassing electricity crisis coupled with a state budget meltdown caused by overspending during the Dot.com boom that came to abrupt end in 2000, taking tax revenues with it. In spite of these travails, California's 2002 elections placed Democrats in control of all eight statewide elected offices with large majorities in the state legislature—the most complete one-party control the state had seen since the Watergate election year of 1974.

California had deep problems: it taxed too much, spent too much, regulated too much, and sued too much. These attributes took their toll as the state's budget deficit mounted and employers shifted jobs out of the state. Schwarzenegger, with his outsized personality and professed love for free market economist Milton Friedman, promised to "blow up the boxes" of bureaucracy and fix the state. As a conservative who believed in less government and more liberty, it was an amazing time to serve in office—albeit, briefly.

In November 2004, the 32 newly-elected Republican Assembly members (including Republican leader, Kevin McCarthy, now Majority Whip in the U.S. House of Representatives), met with Governor Schwarzenegger. We briefly introduced ourselves. When my turn came, I simply said, "I'm Chuck DeVore and I represent Irvine and Coastal Orange County." Schwarzenegger immediately responded, "Ahh, that means we don't have to listen to a thing you say," the implication being that Orange County is conservative and conservative opinions aren't worth listening to. There was scattered laughter in the room, some of it nervous. It was my first personal confirmation that the Governor from Hollywood wasn't as conservative as we were hoping he'd be.

Events over the next six years were to bear out my fears.

Schwarzenegger tried his hand at major reforms in a November 2005 special election that featured four not particularly well-coordinated ballot initiatives. But, government employee unions and their allies poured in $150 million to personally attack the governor and his reforms, sending them all to defeat. Chastened, the man who mocked legislative Democrats as "girlie-men" did a 180 and found his inner liberal.

Months after his special election initiative defeat, the governor called for borrowing $70 billion to go on a public works spending spree. He said at his 2006 State-of-the-State address, "Do you believe in California's economic future? Well then we must invest in it. If we do not invest in ourselves, how can we expect others to invest in us?" Concluding by saying, "…the state of our state is sound because our dream is sound. Let us commit to building California so that the dream can remain alive for this generation, for the next generation and for generations to come."

Schwarzenegger's well-paid coterie of advisors knew what they were doing. Some $42 billion worth of bond proposals made it to the November 2006 ballot. Legislative Democrats were positively giddy at the prospect of the new spending and made appearances with the governor up and down the state to the extreme chagrin of the hapless Democratic gubernatorial nominee, State Treasurer Phil Angelides.

Democrats captured the U.S. House and the U.S. Senate, but Schwarzenegger triumphed, winning reelection by 55.9 percent to 39 percent.

It was to be the hollowest of victories.

With his win fueled by borrowed dollars and sensing the leftward tilt of the national mode, Schwarzenegger promised a new "post-partisan" era of big government. His 2007 State-of-the-State speech cited a liberal laundry list of accomplishments from the prior year, praising the Legislature for acting, "…on infrastructure, the minimum wage, prescription drug costs and the reduction of greenhouse gases in our atmosphere…" then indulging in hyperbole with, "We are the modern equivalent of the ancient city states of Athens and Sparta. California has the ideas of Athens and the power of Sparta." He then stated that, "California, if a nation, would be the sixth-largest economy in the world."

Except that California wasn't then the world's sixth-largest economy and never was while Schwarzenegger was governor. California lost its rank as the sixth-largest economy back in 1999, had fallen to seventh by the 2003 recall, and was eighth behind the U.S., Japan, Germany, China, the United Kingdom, France and Italy when the speech was given.[1]

That few present in the audience of elected officials caught the misstatement or cared about it if they did showed the primacy of strongly held feelings over troublesome facts.

California has legislative term limits. This put a 2010 expiration date on my service in Sacramento. Surveying the state political landscape and looking for an opportunity to spread a message of liberty and prosperity across a state that desperately needed it I decided to run for office statewide. My object: the U.S. Senate seat held by liberal Senator Barbara Boxer.

But, as a State Assemblyman, I only represented a little more than 1/80th of the state (my district had grown a lot since the last redistricting). I wasn't a millionaire capable of self-funding a

---

[1] "California falls to world's eighth-largest economy," *Associated Press*, January 13, 2007.

campaign. I wasn't a well-known actor. And, I didn't have the allegiance of any powerful special interests. In short, it would be not an uphill climb to win, but an up Mount Everest-sort of quest.

From the start we decided to do things differently, looking at President Obama's 2008 win and his campaign's savvy use of social media and technology to reach voters. By early 2009 we were beginning to be noticed. Our campaign earned a "Shorty Award" for "Best Political Use of Twitter" and soon thereafter, the *Wall Street Journal* gave me front page treatment with their distinctive pencil point portrait.[2]

As our Internet-based grassroots campaign took root, a new phenomenon, the Tea Party, blossomed on the political scene. Born of opposition to the liberal excesses of big government and espousing a deep faith in the Constitution, I felt at home in the new movement and addressed scores of rallies and meetings up and down the Golden State.

A few months into the year, however, it was rumored that former corporate boss Carly Fiorina, once the head of HP until the board fired her, was interested in running for the Senate. If she did, promised to spend millions of her personal wealth. But, just as her campaign appeared ready to launch, she was sidelined with breast cancer.

My wife, Diane, is a cancer survivor. I wouldn't wish that diagnosis on any political opponent. As it was, Fiorina faced her illness with determination and aplomb and earned a degree of regard from voters who knew of her challenge.

While I was running for the U.S. Senate, I still had a job to do as a lawmaker in Sacramento and, with the recession taking its toll, California's deficit was soaring again by early 2009. Desperate for a deal to raise taxes, Schwarzenegger convinced a handful of Republican lawmakers to break their pledges never to raise taxes and join with majority Democrats to enact the largest tax hike at the state level in U.S. history. It was a two part plan with two years of taxes totaling $24 billion approved by the legislature to be extended by another two years in a special election vote in May.

I worked hard to stop the tax increase, appearing on television and talk radio up and down the state. For my efforts, Schwarzenegger was said to have referred to me as a "hitman" as well as another, less-kind epithet likening me to an unseen body orifice.

On May 19, Schwarzenegger's tax hike extension failed by two-to-one in spite of a $24 million-to-$1 million fundraising advantage. The next day was my 47th birthday. I claimed the loss of the tax extension as the best birthday present ever.

The growing strength of the Tea Party movement, my work against the tax hike and tens of thousands of miles on the road in America's third biggest state (good thing I didn't mind driving)

---

[2] "Playing Catch-Up, the GOP Is All Atwitter About the Internet, Republican Hopefuls Ponder a 'Tech Gap'; Chuck DeVore's 'Tweets' Raise Campaign Cash," by Christopher Rhoads, *Wall Street Journal*, January 30, 2009, p. 1, http://online.wsj.com/article/SB123309277668321299.html.

held my poll numbers up. A pair of polls in October and November showed the race to be a statistical dead heat with Fiorina as she was preparing to formally enter the race with her last chemotherapy treatment. Iconic South Carolina Senator Jim DeMint endorsed my campaign in November, going against the quiet, but very real unofficial endorsement of Fiorina by the National Republican Senatorial Committee. I was encouraged that my sweat equity and social media innovation had matched Fiorina's corporate fame—at least until she opened her checkbook in earnest.[3]

But in January, former Congressman Tom Campbell, a socially liberal Silicon Valley Republican, jumped into the race. Campbell was running for the Republican nomination for governor against billionaire former eBay CEO Meg Whitman (now head of HP, the firm that Fiorina once ran), but her willingness to deploy her immense wealth to win office persuaded him to switch to the Senate race, a seat he had sought unsuccessfully twice before. Campbell's superior name identification immediately boosted him to the top of the polls.

Fiorina's campaign, sensing an opening, successfully repositioned the former CEO as the conservative alternative to Campbell, in spite, or perhaps because of, her lack of a public record.[4] After spending $5.5 million from her own bank account, Fiorina handily won the nomination with 56.4 percent to Campbell's 21.7 percent. I netted 452,577 votes, placing third of five candidates with 19.3 percent. Our campaign raised $2.6 million from some 25,000 donors, matching Campbell's own fund raising total, and raising more than the combined fundraising efforts of the top four Republican candidates in the last cycle against Sen. Boxer. Importantly, we raised almost double the total of small donations than Fiorina and Campbell combined. Our Internet-based effort was successful in some aspects.

The Tea Party movement served to energize voters across the nation in 2010, flipping the U.S. House of Representatives back to Republican control after four years of Nancy Pelosi as Speaker. Republicans also picked up six seats in the U.S. Senate. Republicans won 680 legislative seats and netted six governorships nationwide.

But seven years of Schwarzenegger's philosophically erratic rule, combining large tax increases with equally large increases in debt and spending, left voters understandably weary and wary of California Republicans. Attorney General Jerry Brown, campaigning to reprise his role as governor from 1975 to 1983, captured the electorate's *zeitgeist* in a damningly effective ad labeling Meg Whitman as "Schwarzenegger in a dress." Brown won, 53 percent to 42 percent as the national Republican wave crashed at the eastern edge of the Sierra Nevada, leaving Democrats in California not only untouched, but strengthened and in control of every statewide elected position and with greater numbers in the legislature.

---

[3] "California's best years have passed, voters say," by Cathleen Decker, *Los Angeles Times*, November 8, 2009, "In a head-to-head matchup, DeVore and Fiorina each won the support of 27% of Republican primary voters."
[4] Prior to Tom Campbell's entry into the Senate race, Fiorina's was considered a "wealthy centrist"—seen as an advantage to her Republican backers in D.C. That her campaign could so quickly recast her as a conservative speaks to the adroitness of modern campaigns run by paid professionals with malleable principles. See: "Senator DeMint bucks Republican party, backs conservative in California race," by Reid Wilson, *The Hill*, November 4, 2009.

As my six years in office were coming to a close, my wife had to fly back to the small Hudson Valley village of Marlboro to attend to her ailing parents. We made the decision that they were incapable of living on their own in rural New York. Soon our modest Irvine house had four adults and two children living in it—and two of the adults demanded far more care than the two teenage children.

As I reentered private life in late 2010, California's unemployment rate stood at 12.3 percent, the second-highest in the nation. Home values were plummeting. And, aerospace, the industry that sustained me for 13 years before election in 2004, had a vastly smaller profile in California, the state of its modern birth.

As a lawmaker, I often invoked Texas and how its low taxes begat an economic dynamism that California would do well to emulate. Perhaps this constant refrain is what led Gov. Jerry Brown to remark defensively in his January 2012 State-of-the-State address, "Contrary to those declinists who sing of Texas and bemoan our woes, California is still the land of dreams…"

The month before, my 35-year California dream came to a close as I started anew in Texas, lured to the Lone Star State by its love of liberty and vitality.

Before I moved, I did my due diligence. I'm a numbers guy. In aerospace, I constantly worked with spread sheets. I'm a U.S. Army intelligence officer (a lieutenant colonel in the retired Reserve). As a lawmaker, I was vice chairman of the Revenue and Taxation Committee and was on the committees for Budget and Audit.

As I gathered information on Texas, the numbers certainly looked impressive. But, there were a few troubling indicators: the Texas poverty rate appeared to be high, per capita income wasn't particularly impressive, and, Texas had a long line of critics claiming the state was not at all a desirable place in which to live. I had to dig into these criticisms to satisfy myself that I was making the right move for my family.

Digging into the liberal critique of Texas is an important task. It not only shows the things they view as important, it also shows how they present numbers that make heavily urbanized, but liberal, areas of the nation look better than less urbanized, more conservative regions. Understanding this critique and answering it using logic and data formed a large part of my confidence that moving to Texas was the right thing to do.

A December 2002 report from the liberal Center for Public Policy Priorities,[5] based in Texas, cited the left-leaning Corporation for Enterprise Development's 16th annual "Development Report Card for the States."[6] This study assigned Texas a grade of "F" for the fourth year in a

---

[5] The Center for Public Policy Priorities was founded by an order of the Catholic Church in 1985 to advocate for increases to government spending for healthcare for the poor. It became a nonprofit corporation in 1999 with 78 percent of its funding coming from liberal leaning foundations.
[6] The data spread sheet from the Corporation for Enterprise Development's (CFED) 16th annual "Development

row for its "Economic Performance Index"—California earned a "C." Ironic, given that, over the following decade, Texas saw the creation of more than a million jobs as California lost more than half-a-million jobs. Clearly, the Corporation for Enterprise Development was using indices that had little to do with predicting success or failure.

This critique follows the same pattern as other studies showing Texas in a negative light. Common to all of them is a lack of contextual data. For instance, how the high cost of living in states such as California and New York that impacts indices such as the poverty rate. How the number of foreign immigrants and their nations of origin impacts educational attainment rates. And other important demographic factors, such as race, ethnicity and the average age of a state's residents and how these factors can drive per capita income. In short, whether purposefully, or out of ignorance, such studies from the left universally make Texas look bad—it's as if they have a stake in discrediting *The Texas Model*.

Lastly, there are the personal aspects of my family's move to Texas. Our Texas home is 70 percent bigger than our California home, with two ground-level bedrooms for my in-laws on 1.2 acres of land—it wasn't uncommon for land in Irvine, California to sell for one million dollars an acre. Further, people are just plain friendlier in the Lone Star State—perhaps because they can keep more of their hard-earned money due to the lower taxes and lower costs for things like housing, food, clothing, and gasoline!

Chuck DeVore
Dripping Springs, Texas

Report Card for the States may be downloaded here:
http://cfed.org/assets/documents/publications/drc/drcdata2002.xls, as accessed on June 12, 2012. CFED's assessment of Texas was lower in 2007 than it was in 2002, just as the recession was to prove how much more resilient Texas was as compared to the rest of the nation, see: http://cfed.org/assets/pdfs/2007_DRC.pdf. CFED ceased publishing its report card in 2007.

INTRODUCTION

Government, Morality, Liberty, and the Free Market

It's frequently said that, "You can't legislate morality." If what's meant by this is that by passing a law against murder, some people will still murder others, then it's true. Passing a law against sin won't stop some people from sinning. However, one can just as easily say that all laws, from laws setting tax rates to laws detailing speed limits, are the majority's version of morality at the time the law was passed.

For instance, in 2009 there were 10.8 million traffic accidents in the U.S. that resulted in 35,900 deaths.[7] Congress could act to save most of those lives by passing a national speed limit of 5 miles per hour. Ridiculous? Perhaps. That Congress doesn't pass such a law suggests that the people's representatives value freedom, convenience, efficiency, and time savings above the lives of drivers, passengers, and pedestrians that might be saved.

The above example was theoretical but we can easily link two recent federal motor vehicle policies to value judgment tradeoffs.

In May 2009, President Barack Obama used his presidential powers to put forward new Corporate Average Fuel Economy (CAFE) standards designed to increase fuel efficiency and reduce greenhouse gas emissions for new cars and trucks sold in America beginning in 2012. These standards, by forcing vehicles to be smaller, will increase traffic fatalities while limiting consumer choice and proscribing to auto manufacturers the kinds of vehicles they may sell to the public.

Next, imagine a government program whose very operation made it more difficult for the working poor to get to work—one might say such a program, if it existed, would be immoral. But, such an immoral program was approved on a bipartisan vote at the federal level in 2009. It was called the "Car Allowance Rebate System" otherwise known as "Cash for Clunkers." This $3 billion rebate program resulted in 690,114 used cars being traded in and destroyed for rebates of up to $4,500.

Cash for Clunkers hurt the working poor by drying up the market for less expensive used cars, causing an artificial shortage while rewarding the wealthy and middleclass for buying a car that met certain government requirements.

Rather than stimulate the economy the operation ended up with a net cost of $2,000 per car with total costs exceeding benefits by $1.4 billion.[8] The program likely just pulled vehicle purchases that would have happened anyway ahead a few months as sales dropped off significantly when

---

[7] Transportation: Motor Vehicle Accidents and Fatalities, table 1103 "Motor Vehicle Accidents—Number and Death," 2009, U.S. Census Bureau, accessed June 1, 2012:
http://www.census.gov/compendia/statab/cats/transportation/motor_vehicle_accidents_and_fatalities.html
[8] "Is CARS a Clunker?" by Burton A. Abrams and George R. Parsons, University of Delaware, The Berkeley Electron Press, Vol. 6 (2009), Issue 8.

the program expired. Further, contrary to the intent of the program, Japanese and Korean automakers expanded their market share at the expense of domestic automakers except for Ford. To add insult to injury, charitable organizations reported that auto donations declined sharply during operation of the federal program.

How could anyone have thought that using $3 billion of money borrowed from future generations of Americans not yet able to vote to destroy the value inherent in almost 700,000 functional vehicles leading to a shortage in affordable vehicles for the working poor was a good and proper use of taxpayer money? But, a bipartisan majority of Congress approved the measure and President Obama signed it.

Moving from the economics of transportation policy to the morality of what has become, in some eyes, an overgenerous welfare system, imagine a Texas single parent household of four. The mother, a college graduate, earns $60,000 per year. She's trying to teach her children that success must be earned and that diligence has its rewards. After paying taxes, health insurance costs, and childcare costs, her disposable income is somewhere in the range of $35,000.

Now, imagine this family's shock and dismay when they learn that a single mother of three working a minimum-wage job earns as much or more. Federal entitlements such as the Earned Income Tax Credit, Food Stamps, National School Lunch Program, Medicaid and Children's Health Insurance Program (CHIP), Section 8 Rent Subsidy, Utility Bill Assistance and other programs now add up to about $17,380 for each for every man, woman and child below the poverty line in 2011.[9] In fact, federal spending to alleviate the symptoms of poverty has tripled in inflation-adjusted per capita dollars since 1980. Not that every dollar reaches its intended recipient though, with one study suggesting that government overhead eats up 70 percent of welfare resources.[10]

Speed limits, federal vehicle mileage standards, using borrowed money to destroy used cars, and welfare spending are all, at their core, public policies that are driven by moral value judgments. Such policy decisions prove that, in fact, not only can morality be legislated, it's done all the time, usually without much notice from the public. So, the issue isn't that "You can't legislate morality," rather, it's whose morals are we using and to what effect? What set of values make it into law or regulation? What are the tradeoffs? Liberty vs. equality of outcome? Lives vs. convenience?

Sometimes these tradeoffs are easy to discern and bills or rules that overstep commonly-agreed upon bounds are never seriously considered for adoption.[11] Other times there are vigorous

---

[9] "Promises, Promises," by Charles Kessler, *The Claremont Review of Books*, Spring 2012, citing the testimony of Ron Haskins of the Brookings Institution before the U.S. House of Representatives Budget Committee in April, 2012.

[10] *Breaking the Poverty Cycle: Private Sector Alternatives to the Welfare State,* by Robert L. Woodson, 1989, Commonwealth Foundation, p. 63.

[11] For instance, the regulatory body responsible for improving California air quality, the California Air Resources Board (CARB), considered rules mandating that new vehicles sold in California be equipped with reflective paint or coatings to reduce solar heat-loading that would in turn, reduce vehicle air conditioning use. After public outcry the

arguments over what is proper and just. But, more frequently, bills and regulations are proposed and enacted that erode liberty and place burdens on the economy with little or no debate.

It is this latter case that should most concern lawmakers. It did the greatest observer and commenter of American democracy, Alexis de Tocqueville, who expressed his fear that a "soft despotism" would be the fate of America via a web of "small complicated rules." In *Democracy in America* de Tocqueville warned of the attraction of seeing government as a sort of "parental authority" that could wield "an immense protective power." Such state power would attempt to ensure happiness but simultaneously result in reducing the once-free American citizenry to a "perpetual childhood" free "from all the trouble of thinking and all the cares of living."

All of which brings us to the Lone Star State. Political observer Michael Barone, in a June 4, 2012 piece about national demographics, noted that:[12]

> *But Texas has been doing very well. If you draw a triangle whose points are Houston, Dallas and San Antonio, enclosing Austin, you've just drawn a map of the economic and jobs engine of North America.*
>
> *Texas prospers not just because of oil and gas, but thanks to a diversified and sophisticated economy. It has attracted large numbers of both immigrants and domestic migrants for a quarter century. One in 12 Americans lives there.*
>
> *America is getting to look a lot more like Texas, and that's one trend that I hope continues.*

Mr. Barone makes four main points about Texas in his article. Texas is producing lots of jobs. Texas has a diversified economy. People are moving to Texas. And, the rest of the nation is taking notice and becoming "…a lot more like Texas."

The Texas Model examines these issues. In the following pages we look at Texas' remarkable success, using objective data, usually from federal government agencies, to measure how Texas stacks up to other large states with diversified economies. We take stock of the critics who claim the Texas model shouldn't be copied. And we come to the conclusion that the case for the free market is fundamentally a moral one and that, to maintain Texas' nation-leading economy, Texas can't rest on its laurels since other states are carefully studying Texas to see how they might improve their own economies.

The Texas Model, the Role of Government and Taxes

What is the role of government? Is government's purpose to secure liberty? Or, is ensuring equality of outcome desirable? Should government take on more responsibilities, not only feeding the hungry and housing the homeless, but going beyond providing basic needs, even for the able-bodied? Are the poor incapable of enjoying the fruits of liberty without material

---

mandates are being held in abeyance until technology makes them more cost-effective.

[12] "Are We at a Demographic Inflection Point?" by Michael Barone, *DC Examiner*, June 4, 2012

abundance being given to them from the sweat of others, as some might suggest? Or, when high taxes take from the productive and give to the idle, does that steal time and property—liberty—from some to give to others what is not rightly theirs?

The proper role of government is central to every political dispute—other issues are secondary. For instance, the Texas model is frequently defined as low taxes, a light and predictable regulatory burden, and a business-friendly lawsuit climate that, taken together, encourages job growth.

Liberty, rightly understood, is the core principle of the Texas model; the benefit of the model is prosperity.

The role of government in prosperity can spark sharp political disagreements that often devolve into a discussion about the role of government in creating jobs—as if it's a given that that's the proper role of government. For instance, the debate over the federal American Recovery and Reinvestment Act in 2009 (aka, the Stimulus) was largely over whether or not borrowing $787.2 billion to spend on various government programs would generate jobs and help the economy or not. Largely lost in the discussion was whether such a program was a proper role of government.

In Texas, a similar debate can be had over state and local economic development programs. Some might look at a cost-to-benefit analysis of conditional tax breaks for business: do the tax cuts generate more economic activity in the long-run that may eventually "pay for the lost tax revenue to government." But, the discussion of costs and benefits and job creation misses the larger point which is, do economic development programs enhance liberty or constrain liberty?

When a governmental entity offers conditional tax incentives for business, for instance, if a firm were to hire certain categories of people or offer certain health insurance benefits, the government is telling business: act the way we wish for you to act and we will reward you. Such policies distort free markets, enlarge government power and open the door to corrupt, so-called "crony capitalism."

A pragmatist might say that the preceding paragraphs are theoretical, dealing with political philosophy—that liberty doesn't put bread in a man's mouth. Fortunately, for purposes of our discussion, we have the benefit of decades of data to compare various measures, such as economic growth, job creation, and the relative size of government between Texas, the U.S. and other large states. This data serves to prove or disprove notions that the Founders saw as self-evident through their personal observations and reading of history. Further, we can see if, in fact, Texas has lower taxes and less government and how those factors might affect economic growth and the wellbeing of Texans.

Figure 1 is the first of many data-packed tables and charts presented in this book, using facts to test various propositions. This figure provides high level detail, much of which we'll explore in greater depth in the pages ahead, comparing Texas to the seven largest states in the nation as well

How Texas compares to the U.S. and the 7 largest states	U.S.	California	Texas	New York	Florida	Illinois	Pennsylvania	Ohio	Michigan
Growth in the Economy, Jobs, and Per Capita Income									
Economic Output, 2000-11	18.71%	20.14%	**30.96%**	21.14%	23.32%	9.62%	13.16%	0.39%	*-4.94%*
Non-Farm Employment, Jan. 2000 to May 2012	1.70%	0.26%	**15.65%**	2.88%	5.40%	-5.28%	1.07%	-8.20%	*-14.55%*
Change in Real Per Capita Income, 2000-11	4.90%	1.65%	**6.03%**	**11.44%**	3.86%	3.22%	7.68%	0.53%	*-5.14%*
State and Local Government, Size and Taxation in 2009									
Government Spending as a Percent of Economy	21.17%	23.32%	**17.58%**	*25.24%*	21.78%	19.49%	21.45%	23.21%	23.32%
Personal Income of Residents Consumed by Taxes	9.8%	10.6%	**7.9%**	*12.1%*	9.2%	10.0%	10.1%	9.7%	9.7%
Population, Migration, and Foreign Immigration as a Percent of 2000 Population									
Population Growth, 2000-11	10.72%	11.28%	**23.13%**	2.58%	19.24%	3.62%	3.76%	1.69%	*-0.63%*
Net Domestic Migration, 2000-10	N/A	-5.80%	3.75%	*-8.27%*	**8.42%**	-7.09%	0.26%	-3.64%	-7.12%
Foreign Immigration, 2000-10	3.40%	5.73%	4.79%	4.72%	**5.74%**	3.47%	1.55%	*1.14%*	1.81%
Prosperity and Poverty in Real Cost of Living Adjusted Dollars									
Cost of Living Index	100.0%	132.0%	**90.2%**	*132.6%*	97.2%	94.7%	102.3%	93.2%	92.5%
Cost of Living Adjusted Per Capita Income, 2011	$41,663	*$33,703*	$43,895	$38,118	$40,698	**$46,601**	$41,523	$40,548	$39,516
Cost of Living Adjusted After Tax Per Capita Income, 2011	$37,167	*$29,691*	$40,055	$32,304	$37,161	**$41,391**	$36,924	$36,340	$35,663
Cost of Living Adjusted Poverty Rate, 2010	15.3%	23.3%	16.1%	22.0%	15.5%	13.3%	**12.6%**	14.2%	14.2%
Education Spending, Teacher Ratios, and 2011 National Testing Results for 8th Grade Reading, Math & Science									
Cost of Living Adjusted Per Pupil ADA Spending, 2009-10	$12,465	*$ 8,346*	$12,676	$11,830	$11,082	$13,007	**$16,094**	$12,204	$13,807
K-12 Student/Teacher Ratio, Fall '09	15.3	*21.4*	14.5	**11.8**	15.9	14.9	14.0	17.1	17.1
8th Grade Standardized Test Composite & (+/-) U.S. Avg.	225	*219 (-6)*	**233 (+8)**	224 (-1)	225 (0)	225 (0)	221 (-4)	228 (+3)	224 (-1)
8th Grade Composite White	243	*239 (-4)*	**248 (+5)**	243 (0)	*239 (-4)*	243 (0)	244 (+1)	245 (+2)	240 (-3)
8th Grade Composite Hispanic	220	*211 (-9)*	**228 (+8)**	214 (-6)	226 (+6)	221 (+1)	212 (-8)	225 (+5)	227 (+7)
8th Grade Composite Black	213	*207 (-6)*	**222 (+7)**	215 (+2)	211 (-2)	210 (-3)	*207 (-6)*	214 (+1)	*206 (-6)*
Transportation, Energy, Pollution and Crime									
Average Commute Time in Minutes, 2006 to 2010	25.2	26.9	24.8	*31.3*	25.7	28.1	25.5	**22.7**	23.7
Average Price for a Gallon of Regular Gasoline, 6/5/2012	$3.59	*$4.18*	$3.37	$3.80	$3.39	$3.77	$3.51	$3.54	$3.61
Retail Price of Electricity Cents per Kilowatthour, 2011	9.61	12.91	8.99	*15.38*	10.70	8.73	10.43	**8.72**	10.00
Cities in Top 20 in U.S. with the Worst Air Pollution, 2011	N/A	5	0	0	0	0	2	4	0
Cities in Top 25 in US with the Highest Violent Crime Rate, 2011	N/A	2	0	1	2	2	1	1	2

Sources: U.S. Census Bureau, U.S. Bureau of Economic Analysis, U.S. Bureau of Labor Statistics, the Tax Foundation, National Education Association, National Center for Education Statistics, U.S. Energy Information Administration, www.CaliforniaGasPrices.com, Forbes, and the Federal Bureau of Investigation.

Figure 1—By objective measures, Texas' model of maximum liberty and limited government delivers material benefits for Texans compared to other states with more government.

as the United States as a whole. The figure sets out data in five broad categories: economic performance, the size of government, population, wealth, and education. It adds to that three other important, measurable factors: transportation, energy costs, and pollution. The figure highlights the best numbers in bold and the worst in italics. There are 22 rows of objective data. Texas boasts the best data of the eight biggest states in 12 of the 22 categories and second-best in three more, placing last in none. California, the largest state, and the state most like Texas as far as demographics and natural resources, places last in 11 of 22 categories, including last in all six education categories, and second-to-last in four, scoring first in none.

The Texas/California comparison is all the more remarkable, given the drumbeat of criticism directed at Texas from elites on both coasts.

Texas has the smallest government and the lightest tax burden among the big states. On the other end of the scale, California has the second-largest tax burden, after New York while tying Michigan for the second-largest share of state and local government spending after New York.

Might there be a connection between less government and more economic growth? A pair of Swedish economists think so. Andreas Bergh and Magnus Henrekson, writing in the *Journal of Economic Surveys*, present evidence that yearly economic growth is depressed by 0.5 percent to 1 percent for every 10 percent of the economy consumed by government.[13] Beyond providing for the basics, public safety and rule of law and national defense, bigger government does two things: it consumes resources that, if left in the hands of individuals, would create more wealth; and, it pays for bureaucrats who regulate and, to borrow language from the Declaration of Independence, "…harrass our people, and eat out their substance."

All things being equal, we can expect that states with more government would perform less well over time compared to states with less government. Testing that hypothesis isn't easy in the real world however, as every state and time has its own unique circumstances. The previous figure shows that Texas' state and local government as a share of the economy was 17.58 percent in 2009 while California's was 23.32 percent. The Swedish economists would expect to see that Texas' economic growth rate would be 0.57 percent to 0.29 percent greater than California's over time, assuming that the share of the economy consumed by government remained the same as well as other key factors such as natural disasters or federal spending in the state.

Interestingly, according to the U.S. Bureau of Economic Analysis, Texas grew 4.6 percent from 2008, the start of the recession, to the end of 2011. California's economy grew 1.6 percent. On an annual, compounded basis, Texas grew 1.51 percent per year while California's economy grew by 0.51 percent. This is a 1 percent difference, almost double what Bergh and Henrekson predict at the high-end. Looking at the Texas and California economy from 2000 to 2010 we see that Texas' economy grew at a 2.4 percent compounded rate while California's grew at a 1.65

---

[13] "Government Size and Growth: A Survey and Interpretation of the Evidence," by Andreas Bergh and Magnus Henrekson, *Journal of Economic Surveys*, Volume 25, Issue 5, December 2011, Pgs: 872–897.

percent yearly rate, a difference of 0.75 percent and much closer to the economists' expected range, given California's greater state and local government spending as a share of the economy.

Government spends money on collective defense and law enforcement, transportation, education, parks, welfare, health care, and myriad other functions, such as regulatory costs. Proponents of government spending often use the word "investment" as a euphemism to justify spending more of the public's money. The term "investment" is often used to justify higher education spending in Texas. Education already consumes the largest share of Texas' public funds, as is the case in most states—and it will continue to do so at least until new federal Medicaid mandates crowd out other state spending over the next ten years.

Government spending on public schools is generally thought to be a needed function of government. Article 7, Section 1 of the constitution of the State of Texas specifies:

> *A general diffusion of knowledge being essential to the preservation of the liberties and rights of the people, it shall be the duty of the Legislature of the State to establish and make suitable provision for the support and maintenance of an efficient system of public free schools.*

Note the reference to liberty as justification for public education: that an educated public is a necessary condition for a liberty-abiding democratic republic. However, beyond the notion of a public school system that is "free"—in other words, supported by taxes—one key public policy question presents itself: is there a point of diminishing returns where higher taxes to support more education spending harms the economy more than it helps education?

Beyond the size of government, there are other factors at work that impact a state's growth rate, such as the tax code, right-to-work laws that determine the strength of labor unions, the lawsuit climate, the impact of foreign immigration and domestic migration, and federal programs such as the Troubled Asset Relief Program (TARP).[14]

Along with the size of government, taxes are easy to measure and analyze from state to state.

Taxes are a necessary evil to pay for needed government functions. Tax policy should be designed to produce the revenue required to fund the level of government needed to secure liberty, not to shape behavior to government's liking.

---

[14] TARP, otherwise known as the Bailout, sent some $431 billion dollars to financial institutions mainly concentrated in New York, which received more than $80 billion of U.S. Treasury money, a sum that likely contributed to New York's eight big state leading growth rate of 5.1 percent from 2009 to 2010, fully one-third of which came from the financial and insurance sector. North Carolina, the 10th-largest state, received $28.7 billion from TARP, the second-highest amount after New York, the Bureau of Economic Analysis shows North Carolina's economy growing 3.4 percent in 2009, enough to put it with New York in the nation's top quintile of growth for the year. TARP data from http://online.wsj.com/public/resources/documents/st_BANKMONEY_20081027.html accessed June 7, 2012.

Taxes shape behavior to the extent that taxes reduce the activity of what is taxed. Income taxes penalize income. Property taxes curtail property values by discouraging investment. Cigarette taxes reduce smoking by increasing the cost of the activity. This is economics 101.

Figure 2 overviews common taxes and their basic impact on the economy as well as their unintended consequences or secondary effects.

Why Texas Matters

So, if the lower level of state and local taxation and spending in Texas vs. the other large states positively influences its economic growth, job creation, and the overall well-being of Texans, might this fact have relevance to the rest of the nation?

This book addresses this question, taking a look at two important issues, both of which are vital to America, even if, at first blush, they appear to be matters of only regional importance: has the Texas economy been consistently over-performing the national economy; and, if so, why?

Tax	Primary Impact	Unintended Consequences or Secondary Impacts
Income	Depresses income	High income taxes encourage productive people to move to states with lower rates to avoid taxation, depressing economic activity and tax revenue; high rates also encourage resources to be put into tax avoidance strategies
Sales	Decreases sales	Encourages tax avoidance or evasion by increasing the cost savings by switching purchases from local retail outlets to out of state online retailers, thus depressing the local economy while increasing use of package delivery firms
Property	Decreases property values	Discourages investment in property, increases housing turnover by penalizing people who maintain underused properties, e.g., retired "empty-nesters" on a fixed income are more likely to sell a house with unused bedrooms
Tobacco	Decreases tobacco use	May encourage the use of other products that aren't taxed as much; may cause government funding instability due to declining revenue base; high taxes increase the incentive to smuggle
Inheritance	Increases use of tax planning	Encourages people with large estates to move out of states that impose death taxes reducing the available capital in that state; reduces transfers of family assets (bequests) between generations, resulting in pressure to break-up family businesses and farms
Gasoline	Decreases use of gasoline	Increases the cost of operating vehicles fueled by gasoline, encouraging the use of vehicles powered by untaxed fuels, thus decreasing tax revenue available to fund roads
Franchise	Discourages business	Increases resources put into tax planning, distorts business planning to the extent that tax breaks are available to firms of a certain size
Oil extraction	Reduces oil extraction	Increases reliance on foreign oil imports to the extent that taxes on domestic oil increase the cost of production, leaving more oil in the ground
Hotel occupancy	Reduces hotel use	Reduces spending by tourists on other items, such restaurants and local entertainment venues

Figure 2—The impact of taxes is simple to understand: you get less of what you tax.

Critics of the Lone Star State, and they appear to be growing in numbers, if not in the strength of their arguments, claim that the "Texas miracle" is a myth—that America's second biggest state in terms of both population and area owes its economic vitality to oil and low wages.[15]

Boosters of the Texas model, including its elected officials, economists, and limited government conservatives, assert otherwise. They cite Texas' modest taxes and restrained spending, light and predictable regulatory climate, and business-friendly lawsuit environment as the reason for Texas consistently outperforming other states.

Why does it matter to Americans whose argument is correct?

Because those who attack Texas, mainly on the Left, claim that its success cannot be replicated in other states because substantial amounts of oil are to be found only in select regions. Further, they say, even if the Texas model could be repeated, why do it, because most of the jobs created in Texas are low-wage jobs without health insurance, on which it is impossible to support a family.

Those who criticize Texas look instead to Big Government. They favor the interventionist model pioneered in big states such as California, New York and Illinois, and approve of its application nationally through trillion dollar Stimulus, Cash-for-Clunkers, national Healthcare, and other ambitious programs requiring more taxes and more government workers.

If those who admire Texas' success in creating jobs are right, then Big Government only serves to put a drag on productive economic activity—the very activity that generates the tax revenue that government itself relies upon.

Beyond the arguments over the nature of the Texas economy and the degree to which public policies there have helped create jobs, there are two more fundamental questions at stake. First, what is the nature of liberty in America today? And second, how much leeway should the states have to experiment with their own policies, free from Federal interference?

America's Founders created a self-governing republic whose purpose was to secure for its people certain God-given, "unalienable Rights, that among these are Life, Liberty, and the Pursuit of Happiness."

---

[15] In "The Texas Unmiracle" liberal economist and *New York Times* columnist Paul Krugman wrote on August 14, 2011, "...the alleged economic miracle in Texas, which, it's often asserted, sailed through the Great Recession almost unscathed thanks to conservative economic policies. ...So what you need to know is that the Texas miracle is a myth, and more broadly that Texan experience offers no useful lessons on how to restore national full employment. It's true that Texas entered recession a bit later than the rest of America, mainly because the state's still energy-heavy economy was buoyed by high oil prices through the first half of 2008." The piece was corrected 10 days later with the following note: "An earlier version of this column referred incorrectly to low-wage workers in Texas. Nearly 10 percent of hourly workers in Texas are paid the minimum wage or less, not almost 10 percent of all Texan workers." See: http://www.nytimes.com/2011/08/15/opinion/the-texas-unmiracle.html.

To better secure those rights, they enacted a Constitution to "form a more perfect Union."

Thus, the Declaration of Independence proclaims America's mission, "Liberty," while the Constitution provides the practical framework that moves liberty from theory to practice.

Knowing that men crave power, and fearing a concentration of it, the Framers of the Constitution purposefully drafted practical means of securing liberty. They created three, co-equal branches of government: Executive, Legislative, and Judicial. This acted as a system of checks and balances. They also devised a federal system, with a central government having specific powers, mainly in the realm of defense, foreign policy, and trade, reserving for the states the greater sphere of criminal and civil law and internal development. As James Madison, the Father of the Constitution, wrote in *The Federalist*, "The powers delegated by the proposed Constitution to the federal government, are few and defined... [T]he powers reserved to the several States will extend to all the objects which, in the ordinary course of affairs, concern the lives, liberties, and properties of the people, and the internal order, improvement, and prosperity of the State."

This arrangement worked well for many years, even surviving a great war that almost tore the new nation apart over the unsettled issue of slavery. By 1870, with the ratification of the 13th, 14th, and 15th Amendments, the Constitution had resolved the inconsistency between the Declaration's promise of Liberty and the compromises of 1789's Constitutional convention that made the new nation possible by bridging serious disagreements between the slaveholding South and the free North.

But, shortly after 1870, a new political philosophy arrived on America's shores: progressivism. With its beginnings in the precepts of the French Revolution[16] progressivism drew upon the writings of the German political philosopher Georg Wilhelm Friedrich Hegel. Hegel's theories emphasized the state at the expense of individual liberty. While Hegel set the foundation for Karl Marx, the more important contribution he made to American political science was the concept of the state as a means to its own end.

Thomas Jefferson was America's first philosopher king. Jefferson penned the Declaration of Independence, which provided the animating principle of the Constitution. In 1912, America elected its second philosopher king, Woodrow Wilson. Wilson was president of Princeton and of the American Political Science Association. He then spent two years as New Jersey's governor before becoming President. He reserved especial scorn for Jefferson's main work, saying, "...if you want to understand the real Declaration of Independence, do not repeat the preface." The first President to publically attack the Constitution, Wilson condemned it as, "political witchcraft." Rejecting the notion that the ideals of the Constitution were based on a practical appreciation for the unchanging aspects of human nature, Wilson instead advocated for an

---

[16] Edmund Burke's 1790 book, "Reflections on the Revolution in France" and Thomas Paine's 1791 rejoinder, "Rights of Man" begin a discussion of the nature of liberty and democracy that continue to this day, albeit, in generally less elegant forms. Ironically, Paine was arrested in 1793 by the same French revolutionary government he defended in his book.

"evolving" Constitution that "must be Darwinian in structure and in practice." Since the Constitution did not contain any fixed principles or set out a theory of government, Wilson argued that "Government is not a machine, but a living thing. It falls, not under the theory of the universe, but under the theory of organic life. It is accountable to Darwin."

With the practice of politics becoming increasingly unmoored from the principles that were to animate it, at least in America, the slow and often purposeful dissolving away of the Constitution's safeguards against a liberty-threatening concentration of power marched onward.

A new and powerful development in "scientific government" was the advent of the "administrative state." Created by broad, often vaguely-worded and sweeping legislative language, the administrative state takes form when a legislative body empowers an unelected bureaucracy to make, enforce, and adjudicate laws in its stead. For instance, President Richard Nixon created the U.S. Environmental Protection Agency (EPA) in 1970 to unify various bureaus with environmental rulemaking authority under the one roof. Today, the EPA uses the wide latitude bestowed on it by Congress to issue and enforce regulations dictating a wide range of economic activity in the 50 states. For instance, rules issued in 2011 threatened to restrict the use of lignite coal found and burned in one state, Texas, accounting for 11 percent of that state's electrical power generation—all without a vote of Congress. Chapter six details the EPA's broad sweep of power and how it impacts Texas.

With its enlarged writ of power, using legions of unelected experts to draft what amounts to law for the rest of us, the Federal government has expanded its book of rules from 2,275 pages in 1935 to 166,000 pages in 30 volumes in 2010, detailing how we are to live our lives in a one-size-fits-all ever-growing dictate from Washington, D.C.[17]

The Federal government's rulemaking, from which there is no escape and for which there is little recourse—at least for the average citizen without access to a top-flight D.C. law firm—amounts to a serious erosion of liberty, a restraint on the creation of wealth, and a harness on the many states, at one time proscribing them from action, while at another, dragooning them into doing the Federal government's work through mandates.

Alexis de Tocqueville, who, in many respects, knew us Americans better than we knew ourselves, foresaw how despotism could arrive on the wings of democracy. Had he glanced at today's 166,000-page *Federal Register*, he'd instantly recognize the, "network of small complicated rules" he warned about in *Democracy in America*, "…the species of oppression by which democratic nations are menaced is unlike anything that ever before existed in the world… (Americans are ruled by) an immense and tutelary power, which takes upon itself alone to secure their gratifications and to watch over their fate. That power is absolute, minute, regular, provident, and mild... seek(ing)… to keep them in perpetual childhood… spar(ing) them all the care of thinking and all the trouble of living… Thus it every day renders the exercise of the free agency of man less useful and less frequent; it circumscribes the will within a narrower range

---

[17] "Restoring Federalism," by former U.S. Senator James L. Buckley, *The Claremont Review of Books*, Summer 2011, http://www.claremont.org/publications/crb/id.1846/article_detail.asp.

and gradually robs a man of all the uses of himself. The principle of equality has prepared men for these things; it had predisposed men to endure them and often to look on them as benefits... **It covers the surface of society with a network of small complicated rules, minute and uniform, through which the most original minds and the most energetic characters cannot penetrate, to rise above the crowd. The will of many is not shattered but softened, bent, and guided; men are seldom forced by it to act, but they are constantly restrained from acting. Such a power does not destroy, but it prevents existence; it does not tyrannize, but it compresses, enervates, extinguishes, and stupefies a people, till each nation is reduced to nothing better than a flock of timid and industrious animals, of which the government is the shepherd** (*emphasis added*)."[18]

Likewise, in the "Occupy Wall Street" et al movement in the aptly-named "American-Autumn" de Tocqueville might see a measure of the "perpetual childhood" he feared springing up from the citizenry of a republic where the government "spares them all the care of thinking and all the trouble of living."

Some 104 years after the appearance of the second volume of de Tocqueville's "Democracy in America," a much smaller, but no less insightful tome was issued by Friedrich von Hayek: *The Road to Serfdom*. In it, the Austrian economist who, writing from wartime Britain, warned of the inherently undemocratic nature of centralized planning in which, "...the will of a small minority be imposed upon the people..."

Whether a "small minority" can work their will on the rest of us is what is at the heart of the growing attack on Texas and the ability of Texans, including the net of 781,542 Americans who moved to Texas in the first decade of the new millennium, to determine how to best manage their own affairs.

In this, Texas is a proxy for the principles of how we Americans *used* to govern ourselves, understanding that government was limited to securing our "unalienable Rights."

The clearest enunciation of a new form of liberty, a liberty free from want, came during President Franklin Roosevelt's 1944 State of the Union Address in which he called for a "Second Bill of Rights." Roosevelt's rationale was that the "political rights" enshrined in the Constitution's first ten amendments "proved inadequate to assure us equality in the pursuit of happiness." Roosevelt's "economic bill of rights" has been at the center of the argument over the proper role of government and liberty ever since. Roosevelt's new compact called for the right to: employment, with a living wage; freedom from unfair competition and monopolies; housing; medical care; education; and a social safety net. For it was only by being free from material needs that a person could engage in the "Pursuit of Happiness."

The principles behind Roosevelt's "Second Bill of Rights" explain what animates much of the negative commentary on Texas: Texas may have added jobs, but they're not at a "living wage";

---

[18] Alexis de Tocqueville, *Democracy in America*, Chapter VI, "What Sort of Despotism Democratic Nations Have to Fear."

Texas' lower taxes and light regulatory burden allows it to "unfairly compete" with other states; Texas has insufficient low income housing and weak tenants' rights; medical care in Texas is inadequate for the poor; education in Texas is subpar and the government should spend more to make college more affordable; and, the Texas safety net isn't robust enough.

So, criticisms of the Texas model aren't only about facts on the ground—whether or not things are really different in Texas because of public policy and to what extent those policies can be applied nationally—but, at a deeper level, these criticisms are about what course is right for America.

Former Speaker of the House Nancy Pelosi said on June 7, 2012, in words FDR would clearly recognize, that government provided healthcare is "about life, liberty and the pursuit of happiness for the American people," that "unlocks" them from the fear of having to work to keep their health insurance.[19] Speaker Pelosi's remarks are simply the latest chapter in the back and forth national debate over how big a role the federal government should play in the lives of Americans.

Just over 30 years ago, America confronted the malaise brought about by a burgeoning federal government. Only 12 days after Ronald Reagan's election to the presidency in 1980, his transition team authored a memo to him entitled, "Economic Strategy for the Reagan Administration" which said:

> *Many of our economic problems today stem from the large and increasing proportion of economic decisions being made through the political process rather than the market process. An important step to demonstrate your determination to rely on markets would be the prompt end of wage and price guidelines and elimination of the Council on Wage and Price Stability.*
>
> *To advance the entire regulatory effort—both to galvanize public support and to strengthen the positions of Administration appointees—we urge you to issue a message on regulatory reform in tandem with the budget and tax messages. The message should call upon state and local governments to launch similar regulatory reform efforts—as a few have already done.*

While America is in difficult times today, it is important to realize that we've seen worse and found our way through bad times and back to good.

Since Texas has had its own regulatory, tax code, lawsuit and budget reform efforts in the recent past, we believe Texas is a useful model for the nation.

The Texas Model aims to clearly set out the case for Texas by examining the causes of Texas' economic success over the recent past and especially since the start of the Great Recession. The

---

book looks at tax policy, government spending, the lawsuit climate, economic diversity, energy, regulation, immigration to Texas (both domestically and from abroad), and crime and punishment to make the argument that the Texas model isn't unique to Texas—it really started sometime around 1776 in America.

CHAPTER ONE—OF TEXAS AND FREEDOM

To understand the origins of Texas's success, one should learn about the origins of Texas. Colonizing Texas wasn't high on the list of priorities for imperial Spain. So, it wasn't until 1821, after Mexico won its independence from Spain, that the colonization of Texas began in earnest.

Instead of Spanish-speaking settlers, however, it was mainly Americans who sought opportunity in Texas. In less than ten years the government in Mexico City grew alarmed at the autonomy shown by the rising Anglo-American population, by now a majority. When Mexican revolutionary Antonia López de Santa Anna overthrew the Mexican government in a coup in 1833, he decided to crack down on the restive Texans. In response, Texans formed a provisional government in 1835, formally declaring independence in 1836.

The Texas war for independence from Mexico lasted seven months in series of sharp military engagements from 1835 to 1836 (fighting at sea lasted a few more years). The most famous battle took place at the Alamo where American legends Davy Crockett (a frontiersman and former Congressman from Tennessee[20]), James Bowie (of the hunting knife fame), William B. Travis and up to 254 others, faced down a Mexican army of 1,500. For 13 days they delayed General Santa Anna's advance, striking down some 400 to 600 Mexican troops before being killed to the last man.

As he arrived in Texas, Crockett wrote to his family in Tennessee, "I have no doubt [this] is the richest country in the world. Good land, plenty of timber, and the best springs. …I am rejoiced at my fate. I had rather be in my present situation than to be elected to a seat in Congress for life. I am in great hopes of making a fortune for myself and my family."

Texas was admitted to the union as the 28th state on December 29, 1845 after ten years as an independent republic.[21]

The nature of Texas founding, its size, ten years as a nation, and distance from Washington, D.C. all contributed to a strong sense of independence and self-reliance—traits that the American Founders expected of states in the federal system were in great abundance in Texas.

Texas may be in the news more frequently than usual because of its economy, but what is truly significant about Texas is not its rate of growth, but its persistent focus on liberty.

---

[20] Congressman Davy Crockett drew President Andrew Jackson's ire when he called him "a greater tyrant than Cromwell, Caesar, or Bonaparte" and opposed Jackson's Indian Removal Act. Jackson retaliated by working to defeat Crocket for reelection to the U.S. House of Representatives in 1834. Seeing the political forces arrayed against him, Crockett later wrote of that election, "I told the people of my district that I would serve them as faithfully as I had done; but if not ... you may all go to hell, and I will go to Texas."

[21] The other independent republic to become a state, California, lasted all of 26 days before bypassing territorial status, being ruled by a military governor, then becoming a state in 1850. It never had a functional government—perhaps a portent of things to come.

Davy Crockett was drawn to Texas in the hopes of providing for his family and improving his life. He was optimistic in the face of the difficulty of life on the frontier because he knew that hard work and freedom would allow him to pursue his own path to happiness.

Today's Texas is much the same—especially when comparing the liberty-restricting laws, regulations, and legal climate in America's other large states to Texas.

Make no mistake Texas doesn't have California's mild climate, beaches, mountains and forests or Hollywood, nor New York's prestigious international financial hub. No, something else drew 781,542 Americans to move to Texas from other states in the past ten years. Freedom—the freedom to work; the freedom to create; and the freedom to keep a little more of the product of one's labor than is the case in New York, California, or most of the other large states.

Economic Freedom
The freedom to own and to use property, to operate a business, to work, are all too frequently overlooked in this era of the all-knowing nanny state tenderly seeking to save us from ourselves. Call it "economic freedom." Every bit as important to the early American political giants as religious freedom, or freedom of speech, economic freedom, was, as Abraham Lincoln said in the context of slavery, the idea every man had a natural right "…to eat the bread which he has earned by the sweat of his brow."

The economic freedom in Texas stands in stark contrast to the shrinking sphere of the freedom of action Americans see in other states. In California, not only does the average taxpayer work an extra nine days to pay their state taxes as compared to Texas[22], but the typical business owner in the Golden State is also burdened with a confusing and often crushing array of regulations, estimated by a state government commissioned study completed in 2009 to cost $493 *billion* per year—almost five *times* the state's general fund budget and about a third of California's economic output.[23]

While taxes are easy to measure, and government spending only somewhat less so, regulations are a hidden form of taxation—put into place by lawmakers who draft bills that empower unelected government experts to draw up rules that compel people to act or not to act in a certain way. Some rules are generally regarded as needed, for instance, laws or regulations that improve air and water quality in a common sense, economically efficient manner. Other regulations, for instance, arcane restrictions on the use of private property or restrictive labor rules, are harder to justify. The financial impact on California business amounts to a *de facto* tax of $134,122.48 per

---

[22] The Tax Foundation, a national non-profit founded in 1935, annually calculates each state's "Tax Freedom Day" measuring how many days it takes for average taxpayers to meet all their federal, state and local obligations before working for themselves.

[23] Concerned about the growing negative impact of regulations in California's economy, the legislature passed AB 2330 in 2006 which authorized a comprehensive study on the regulatory burden to California businesses. The "Cost of State Regulations on California Small Business Study" was issued in September, 2009 by Varshney and Associates, Sanjay B. Varshney, Ph.D., CFA and Dennis H. Tootelian, Ph.D. authors, California State University, Sacramento
http://www.sba.ca.gov/Cost%20of%20Regulation%20Study%20-%20Final.pdf.

small business.[24] And, since small businesses are 99.2 percent of all employer businesses in California and all non-employer businesses by definition, this mess of red tape has depressed employment in California by 3.8 *million* jobs—lost jobs that would likely balance California's chronic multibillion dollar budget deficits.

No wonder productive people are fleeing California to the welcoming embrace of Texas and other friendlier climes. The search for economic freedom, as the search for religious freedom that compelled the Pilgrims to make the difficult journey to the New World, creates thousands of new "settlers" every year in America, many who pack up and leave for Texas.

In spite of its tremendous economic importance, economic freedom isn't discussed much by our elected leaders or the media. The courts give an even shorter shrift to it as jurists frequently rule in favor of unelected regulators and against an individual's ability to work or to quietly enjoy their property.

This shouldn't be so because economic freedom is the most fundamental of all of our freedoms. The freedom to speak, to assemble, to petition our elected officials—these pale if our ability to work and keep our money and our property is in doubt.

Today it seems the government itself operates to take away our freedom to work and support ourselves through bureaucratic decisions and court cases—for instance, the attempt by the Federal government to block The Boeing Company from building a new assembly line in South Carolina; or the Federal biologists who "discover" that a common lizard might be endangered by oil well drilling in Texas, then move to shut down new oil production. Then, when government meddling predictably harms the economy, causing jobs to disappear, government comes charging in with a multitude of schemes fueled by borrowed money: stimulus, programs, welfare.

Is it too much to ask to simply have our freedom—and our jobs back?

Make no mistake, the two are tightly linked. A study by the Federal Reserve Bank of St. Louis shows the connection between economic freedom and jobs, saying, "We find that states with greater economic freedom—defined as the protection of private property and private markets operating with minimal government interference—experienced greater rates of employment growth." If only this statement of common sense were more appreciated in the halls of Congress and in the White House.

The Fraser Institute of Canada examined economic freedom in U.S. states and Canadian provinces in 2011. The peer reviewed study used "10 components chosen fall into three areas: Size of Government, Takings and Discriminatory Taxation, and Labor Market Freedom." They ranked Texas as the second-most-free state behind Delaware—third, if Canadian provinces are included.[25] America's other large states lag far behind. They write:

---

[24] Ibid. Estimated 2007 cost.
[25] "Economic Freedom of North America, 2011," by Nathan J. Ashby, Avilia Bueno, and Fred McMahon, with

Average economic freedom in the US states peaked in 2008. Unfortunately, in 2009 the average dropped to levels last seen in the year 2000. The 10 states at the bottom of the all-government index were West Virginia, New Mexico, Mississippi, Hawaii, Alaska, Montana, Maine, Vermont, Rhode Island, and Kentucky. Their average per capita GDP in 2009 was $41,459 (in constant 2009 dollars) compared to an average of $45,902 for the other 40 states. The top 10 states were Delaware, Texas, Nevada, Colorado, Georgia, South Dakota, Wyoming, Utah, North Carolina, and Nebraska. Their average per-capita GDP in 2009 was $49,818 compared to $43,812 for the lowest 40 states.

Meanwhile, *Forbes* magazine listed the top ten "Boom Towns" out of America's 52 metropolitan areas with a population of at least a million.[26] Using criteria such as job growth, family formation, growth in the numbers of people with college degrees moving to an area, and the attractiveness of the region to newcomers in terms of housing, earning money, and starting a business, *Forbes* ranked the four largest metropolitan areas in Texas in the top ten with Austin #1, San Antonio #4, Houston #5, and Dallas #7.

Of the eight largest states in the U.S. (more on them in the next chapter), only Florida had a region in the top ten with Orlando. Los Angeles tied with Chicago near the cellar at #47, because, as *Forbes* observes, its "once huge and vibrant industrial sector has shrunk rapidly, in large part the consequence of ever-tightening regulatory burdens. Its once magnetic appeal to educated migrants faded and families are fleeing from persistently high housing prices, poor educational choices and weak employment opportunities. Los Angeles lost over 180,000 children 5 to 17, the largest such drop in the nation."

Or, as *Forbes* might have put it: it's about the economic freedom—Austin, San Antonio, Houston and Dallas have it, Los Angeles and Chicago don't.

Deborah Martinez, Fraser Institute, http://www.fraserinstitute.org/uploadedFiles/fraser-ca/Content/research-news/research/publications/economic-freedom-of-north-america-2011.pdf accessed on June 14, 2012.
[26] "The Next Big Boom Towns In The U.S.," by Joel Kotkin, *Forbes* magazine, July 6, 2011, http://www.forbes.com/sites/joelkotkin/2011/07/06/the-next-big-boom-towns-in-the-u-s/.

CHAPTER TWO—COMPARING THE EIGHT BIG STATES

In gauging whether or not public policies in Texas have made a difference in the economic growth of Texas and the well-being of the people who call it home, a good place to start would be to compare Texas to the other big states.

America's eight largest states comprise 47 percent of the nation's population. They have enough in common to make a discussion of the areas where they differ interesting and meaningful.

How Texas stacks up in the ongoing interstate competition for jobs and economic growth with California, New York, Florida, Illinois, Pennsylvania, Ohio and Michigan not only presents ideas on how the states may do better economically, but may also suggest ways for America to improve its competitive posture with Asia and Europe.

The data we present in this chapter shows that Texas is consistently at or near the top of its eight large state peers in job growth, new business creation, minority business opportunities, economic well-being, educational outcome, and other social indicators. The fact is, the official unemployment rate in states such as California, Michigan, New York, and Ohio would be even higher were not so many Americans seeking a job and a better life in Texas.

In Search of Prosperity

Individuals vote with their feet. Daily, Americans decide to move to seek opportunities for their families. Our comparison, then, begins with population growth and domestic migration. Figure 3 shows Texas leading the way in population growth among the eight largest states in the past ten years.[27]

Some critics have dismissed Texas' economic strength by claiming that the Texas economy grew because the number of Texans grew more quickly than did the population of other states.[28] But

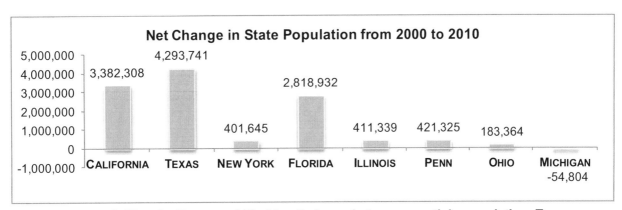

Figure 3—While California, Texas and Florida all showed strong growth in population, Texas grew at more than double the rate of California, 20.6% to 10.0%.

---

[27] U.S. Census Bureau, 2010 Census.
[28] "The Texas Unmiracle," by Paul Krugman, *New York Times,* August 14, 2011.

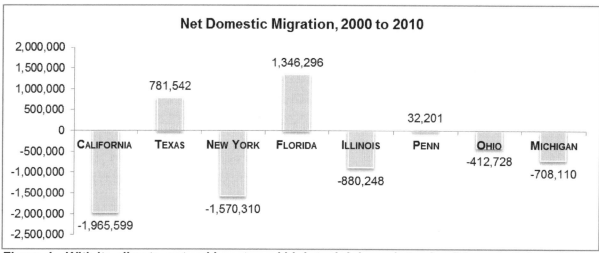

Figure 4—With its climate, natural beauty and high-tech job market, why did a net of almost 2 million Americans move out of California in the past 10 years?

this criticism misses the main issue: why are people moving to Texas in the first place? It's akin to saying a baseball player is successful because he hits a lot of home runs—isn't that the point?

Figure 4 tracks domestic migration, people who move from one state to another. This figure is especially illuminating as it shows a massive outflow of 2 million Americans out of California and 1.6 million out of New York with more than 2 million moving to Florida and Texas.[29] As one might expect, absent catastrophes such as famine or war, prior to retirement (the reason many move to Florida), people move to get a better job or to find work.

Figure 5 shows that the number of people working in Texas (nonfarm employment) increased by 1,093,600 from 2000 to 2011, 1,030,400 more than what was seen in the second-best state, New York which only netted 63,200 jobs in the past 11 years. As a percentage of its nonfarm workforce, Texas saw an 11 percent increase, while the number of people working in New York

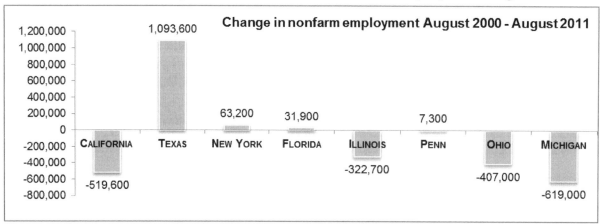

Figure 5—Not even close: when looking at the net change in jobs over the past 11 years, Texas leads all the 8 big states with 1,093,400 jobs created. Michigan lost 619,000 jobs.

[29] U.S. Census Bureau, RLS Demographics.

was 1 percent higher in 2011 than in 2000. Michigan shed 14 percent of its workforce while Ohio saw a 7 percent decline, Illinois, 5 percent, and California, 4 percent.[30] Given the large number of retirees who move to Florida, it isn't a surprise that the Sunshine State saw population gains and strong net domestic migration, but weak job growth.

Further, these strong job creation numbers are expected to continue for Texas. According to IHS Global Insight, an international economic forecasting firm, Texas and Florida will lead the eight largest states in job growth with 2.1 per year increases in payroll through 2017. California's employment picture is expected to grow by only 1.5 percent per year, New York and Illinois, 1.3 percent, Pennsylvania and Ohio, 1.2 percent, and Michigan, 1.1 percent, about half the rate of job growth expected in Texas and Florida.[31]

Of course, all those jobs didn't just create themselves. Small businesses represent 99.7 percent of all firms with employees, employing slightly more than half of all non-government employees in America. And, since most small business owners pay a personal income tax on their business profits rather than a corporate income tax, how a state taxes personal income, or doesn't, as is the case in Texas and Florida, matters greatly to these entrepreneurs. From 2000 to 2008, compared to their large counterparts, only Florida and Texas saw a net increase in business creation, while California, home to the nation's highest and most progressive income tax during the years measured, lost 207,986 businesses, the most of the eight big states.[32]

The nature of the businesses operating in state tell a lot about the state itself. According to the U.S. Small Business Administration, the number of single employee businesses in Texas rose from 1.27 million in 2000 to 1.84 million in 2008, an increase of 44 percent, while in Florida, the number of single employee businesses rose from 1.07 million to 1.60 million in the same time, an increase of 50 percent.[33] Most of these businesses are not incorporated, but they do pay personal income taxes in states that levy it, such as California, with one of the highest state income taxes in the nation. The number of sole employee businesses in California rose from 2.10 million in 2000 to 2.69 million in 2008, an increase of 31 percent.

Further, for those concerned about equality of outcome as much as liberty, the number of businesses owned fully by women or owned equally by women and men was 47.7 percent in California, the highest among the big eight states, with Texas a very close second, at 47.2 percent. New York was the most patriarchal of the large states, with only 39.9 percent of its

---

[30] U.S. Bureau of Labor Statistics, http://data.bls.gov/cgi-bin/surveymost?sm.
[31] "Which States Are Poised for Jobs Growth?" by Phil Izzo, *Wall Street Journal*, October 20, 2011.
[32] "Table 742. Employer Firm Births and Deaths and Business Bankruptcies by State," U.S. Employment and Training Administration, unpublished data and Administrative Office of the U.S. Courts, "Bankruptcy Statistics."
[33] Florida's singularly impressive corporate creation record shown in Figure 4 parallels the pattern seen in Nevada over the same period of time where a net of 19,033 firms were created. This large net number of incorporations but weak job growth compared to Texas may signal the phenomena of residents of New York, in Florida's case, and residents of California, in Nevada's case, incorporating in an income tax-free state to avoid high state income taxes. Living out of state for 183 days a year and owning a home of equal or greater value out of state generally qualifies a taxpayer to claim a different state as his domicile for state tax purposes.

businesses owned by women or equally owned by women and men.[34] Figure 6 summarizes these results across the large states.

Figure 6 also shows that Texas compares well to its peer states in the rates of Hispanic and African-American business ownership. Comparing the percentage of minority-owned businesses to the population as a whole gives a good indication of the access to capital needed by minorities to succeed in business. This measure should be as important or more so to minority-rights advocates as the measure of poverty or of government assistance to the poor because business ownership, not welfare payments, is the path to upward mobility and prosperity. Texas ties with California for second behind Michigan in the rate of African-American business ownership as a

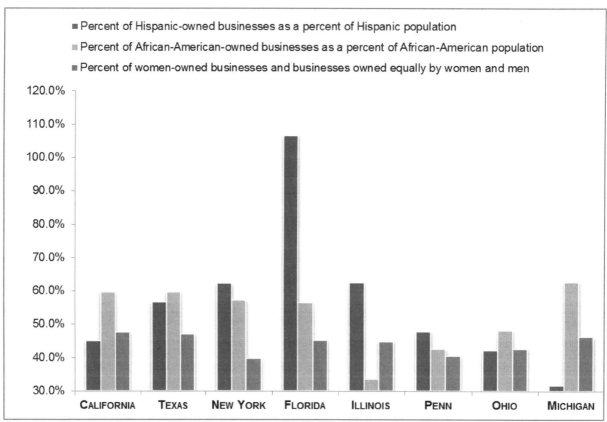

Figure 6—Measured by women's and minority business ownership rates, Texas places second twice and fourth in one category among the 8 big states tying the Lone Star State with California as a state with strong minority business ownership opportunities.

[34] An irony perhaps lost on *New York Times* columnist, author, and Texas critic Gail Collins, who, in "How Texas Goes…: How the Lone Star State Hijacked the American Agenda," makes numerous references to how terrible things are for women in Texas. Collins also commits two errors of fact on Texas founding father Sam Houston. She incorrectly writes that he said, "Texas has yet to learn submission to any oppression, come from whatever source it may" in regard to separating from "…a country to which Texas was then attached" (p.3) which would have been hard as Houston said that in 1850 on the floor of the U.S. Senate and Houston was pro-Union and anti-secession. She compounds the error by writing that Houston committed political suicide as a senator by opposing secession when (p. 23), in fact, Houston was elected Governor of Texas after working to stop secession as a senator.

percentage to the state population of African-Americans and ranking fourth of the large states in the rate of Hispanic business ownership as a portion of the state's population.[35,36]

Figure 7 marks the total percentage change in the economic output (gross domestic product) of the large states, showing, once again, Texas doing far better than the other states.

Some have claimed that Texas' economic growth was due to its population growth, as if people move to Texas to work for other people who have moved to Texas. But, if Texas' economy was really just driven by more people living in the state, it would likely show economic growth, but lag behind in the measure of economic output per resident. Figure 8 tests that proposition, showing the economic growth per capita of the eight large states. In this measure, Texas comes in third, with a respectable 37 percent increase in per capita output, behind New York at 47 percent and Pennsylvania at 39 percent. However, given that at least $135 billion of Federal assets in the from the Troubled Asset Relief Program (TARP) went to six New York-based financial institutions in 2008 and 2009, equal to some 12 percent of the New York state economy, one wonders what New York's economic output would have been in 2010 had it not been for massive Federal intervention in the financial markets?

When estimating the relative strength of nations, the U.S. Central Intelligence Agency uses a metric called "Purchasing Power Parity." This measure of a nation's economy takes into account the value of that nation's currency as well as the cost of living within a nation, rather than simply

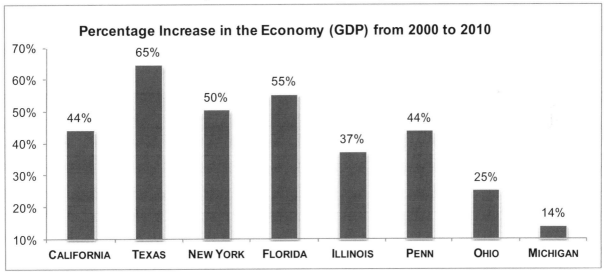

Figure 7—The large states with the strongest economic growth, Texas and Florida, have something in common: no state income tax.

---

[35] Population information from the U.S. Census Bureau, Statistical Abstract of the United States, July 2008; business ownership information from the state Small Business Profiles, U.S. Small Business Administration, Office of Advocacy, February, 2011.

[36] About one-third of Florida's Hispanic population was driven by the Cuban diaspora caused by the communist takeover of the island nation in 1959 and subsequent mass migration of much of the island's business and professional classes to Florida.

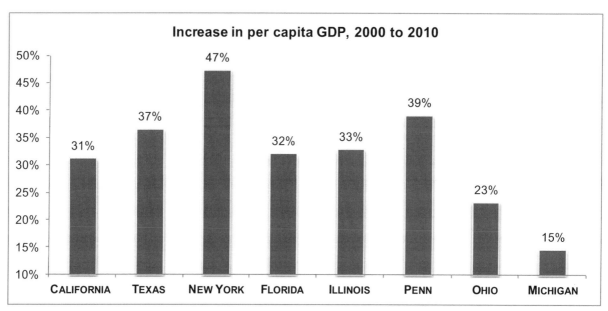

Figure 8—In terms of the improvement of economic output per person, one gauge of the quality of jobs being created, Texas ranked third among the big states at 37 percent.

its economic output as measured in dollars. Similarly, Figure 9 looks at the large states' per capita economic output numbers, as adjusted for the cost of living in each state, showing that the residents of Texas are better off than the people living in any of the other seven states.

So far we've reviewed Federal government data that shows Texas growing the most of the eight big states. Texas received the second-largest number of Americans domestically migrating, generating 1.1 million jobs in 11 years while the other seven large states lost a total of 1.8 million jobs. Texas saw a net increase in businesses while six of the other seven states lost

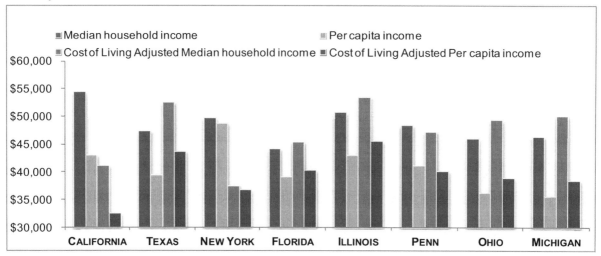

Figure 9—Just looking at median household income and per capita income shows California and Illinois to be the richest states, but, adjust for cost of living and Illinois moves into sole possession of first, followed by Texas, not California—and that's before state and local taxes take a bite out of take home pay.

entrepreneurs while women and minorities owned those businesses at rates better than most of its peers. Lastly, Texas turned in robust economic and personal income growth, with the best GDP increase, the third-highest rise in per capita GDP, and the second-best cost of living adjusted per capita income.

Texas' robust economic growth begins to make sense when you consider that, in 2011, *Site Selection Magazine*, a journal of "corporate real estate strategy & area economic development" ranked Texas #1 in America after nine years at #2, writing:

> "...*Giving businesses some certainty with which to risk investment capital and expand their enterprises has been central to the state's economic success.*
>
> "*Companies are flocking to the Lone Star State—Atlas Van Lines' annual study of corporate relocations in 2010 logged more than 7,200 relocations inbound to Texas, the sixth highest, and 5,300 outbound relocations. Overall, Texas claimed 58 percent of the inbound relocations. More to the point, 40 percent of the new U.S. jobs created since June 2009 were created in Texas, giving Gov. Rick Perry an enviable credential with which to make a run for the Republican presidential nomination.*"[37]

What's Fueling Texas?
So, it was all about the oil, right?

Well, that claim is easy to test. The U.S. Bureau of Economic Analysis (BEA) tracks the performance of the U.S. economy at a detailed level down to the states. Using their data, we can check the claim that all of Texas' success is due to the fact that it sits on enormous pools of oil and natural gas (later on we'll detail how California has America's third-largest proven reserves of oil, but state environmental laws make extraction of that oil a slow and more expensive process).

The BEA data shows that, of the eight large states, only California, Texas, Illinois and Ohio produced and refined enough petroleum and natural gas to meet or exceed one percent of their economic output in 2009. Three states, California, Texas, and Ohio saw an appreciable increase in the value of oil and gas extraction and refining as a percent of their economy from 2001 to 2009: with GDP share of California's oil industry rising one percent, to 2.3 percent of its GDP; Texas' increasing 1.3 percent to 8.7 percent; and Ohio's almost doubling to 1.1 percent.

A note about economics would be in order here. When the government statisticians track the value of things in an economy, stuff like oil and computers, the value can go up because more is made, it gets more expensive, or some combination thereof. So, when oil prices rise, all things being equal, you would expect states with lots of oil to do well. That said, the GDP data would clearly show a massive increase in the share of a state's economy being generated by oil. Texas did see a bump in the relative contribution of oil to its economy in 2007 and 2008, but, Texas'

---

[37] "A Better Mousetrap," *Site Selection Magazine*, November, 2011, http://www.siteselection.com/issues/2011/nov/cover.cfm.

job generating machine had been in full gear well before that and remains strong today, even as the price of oil retreated in 2009.

So, while the relative value of the petroleum industry to Texas is almost four times greater than it is in California, the important thing to remember is that we are tracking growth in the respective states. If oil was strong in Texas 40 years ago and if it's strong today, Texas' economic performance wouldn't have changed much.

Analysts with the Dallas branch of the Federal Reserve confirm the declining importance of oil to the Texas economy, finding that, in the period 1997 to 2010, a 10 percent rise in the price of oil would increase the state's economic output by 0.5 percent, boosting employment by only 0.36% (the oil industry is capital-intensive, meaning it needs more machinery relative to workers). Conversely, in the period 1970 to 1987, a 10 percent hike in the price of oil would have boosted Texas economy by 1.9 percent and employment by 1 percent.[38]

Further, Karr Ingram, a Texas Petroleum Institute economist, only claims credit for 13 percent of the Lone Star State's net jobs growth from June 2010 to July 2011.[39]

Figure 10 reviews manufacturing activity in each state as a percentage of its economy. The government counts refining of oil and gas as manufacturing, so, that activity has been backed out of this chart, rendering manufacturing oil-free.

What's truly astounding about this figure and the prior discussion about oil is that California saw about as large an increase in oil-based economic output (most of it due to refining the Golden State's specially formulated and costly air pollution fighting gasoline) as did Texas while every

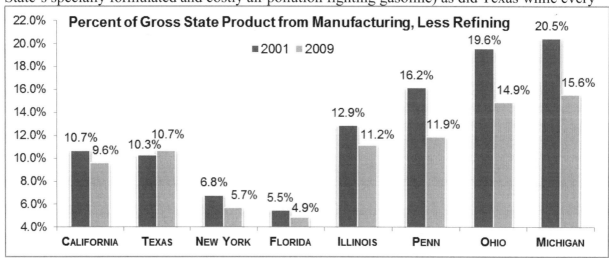

Figure 10—Only Texas posted a gain in the relative importance of non-oil manufacturing from 2001 to 2009—perhaps low taxes, a light and predictable regulatory burden, and a good lawsuit climate have a hand in this.

---

[38] "Oil and Gas Rises Again in a Diversified Texas," Dallas Federal Reserve Bank, by Mine K. Yücel and Jackson Thies, 1st Quarter, 2011, http://dallasfed.org/research/swe/2011/swe1101g.cfm.
[39] "Interrogating the 'Texas Miracle,'" by E.G. Austin, *The Economist*, August 16, 2011.

state, except for Texas, saw a decline in manufacturing output as a percentage of the state's economy. Interestingly, while Texas has about double the proven oil reserves of California, the value of California's refined petroleum has exceeded that in Texas for four of the last five years.

So, what's happening in Texas isn't just about the oil.

In fact, Texas has a diversified, modern economy with a larger manufacturing base than any state except America's most-populous, California. Further, in only one year out of nine from 2001 to 2009, did oil extraction and refining exceed manufacturing as a percentage of the Texas economy: 2008—the same year that oil and refining accounted for almost four percent of the California economy, almost half of manufacturing without oil.

Inflated Unemployment
A recent criticism of Texas is that the unemployment rate there isn't much lower than the national average. True. Texas had an official unemployment rate of 6.9 percent in May 2012, 1.3 percent lower than the U.S. average of 8.2 percent.

But, Texas has created far more jobs than the other states, in fact, some 40 percent of the jobs created in America since the Great Recession bottomed out in 2009 were to be found in Texas.

So, why isn't the unemployment rate in Texas lower? Simple. When an unemployed auto worker from Detroit who is about to exhaust his unemployment benefits looks for a better job climate and moves to Texas, he's now counted as unemployed in Texas, not Michigan. The fact is, that those three-quarters of a million Americans who moved to Texas since 2000 not only boosted the Texas workforce, they also served to reduce the unemployment rate of slow to negative employment growth states such as New York and Massachusetts.

As Figure 5 showed previously, Texas led the large states in overall job growth, with almost 1.1 million jobs added from August 2000 to August 2011. Figure 11 tracks the percentage increase or decrease in nonfarm workers in the eight largest states: four states showed a net gain in employment: Texas, with a 13.2 percent increase, New York with 2.5 percent, Florida with 2.3 percent and Pennsylvania, with a 0.5 percent increase. Michigan lost 12.7 percent of its workforce from 2001 to May 2012. The net change in employment number is a far more useful measure of economic strength than is the official unemployment number for two reasons: the those who are unemployed for too long in one state often move to seek work in another, thus reducing their former home state's unemployment rate; and, long-term unemployed workers who get discouraged aren't counted in the official unemployment statistics.

Figure 12 looks at each of the large state's official unemployment rates from 2001 to May 2012. Official unemployment statistics only count those people who are receiving government unemployment checks and thus, are formally considered to be still seeking employment. In 2001, the rates were within a tight, one percent band, ranging from a low of 4.4 percent in Ohio to a high of 5.4 percent in California and Illinois. But, beginning in 2003, the trends begin to diverge

27

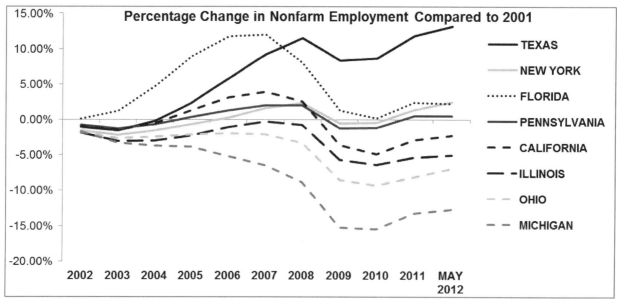

Figure 11—From 2001 to May 2012, Texas gained 1.26 million jobs while the other 7 big states lost a combined 1.19 million jobs.

significantly, with Michigan trending far higher, and Florida far lower, than the other states until the economy began to slow in 2006.

Yet another charge leveled against Texas is that it is a low-wage state with millions mired in poverty. It's true that wages in Texas are generally lower than average—but what critics fail to

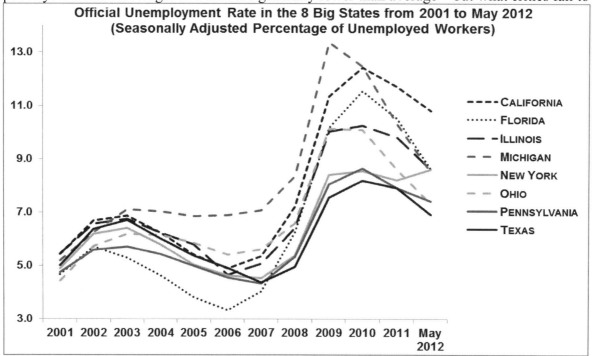

Figure 12—While receiving 781,542 Americans from other states, Texas maintained an unemployment rate at or below the other 7 large states since 2008; the unemployment rate of states that have been losing population would be far higher had those without jobs not moved.

mention is that Texas has the second-least expensive cost of living in America, after its neighbor to the north, Oklahoma. If housing, food, and transportation—the basic necessities of life—cost less, then it stands to reason that one would need less to earn a living.

Net worth is an important measure of the financial health and well-being of a population. Again, we see criticism against Texas in the claim that the net worth of Texas families lag behind the national average. This claim has an element of truth to it, but, without context, it too fails to convey much meaning. According to one claim by a low-income advocacy non-profit, Texas household average net worth ranked 48th in the nation at $34,500 in 2007.[40]

Again, there's an issue with the data: according to the Federal Reserve, home equity accounted for 16.2 percent of net worth at the end of the second quarter, 2010. Since housing costs in Texas were only 82 percent of the national average, this means that it costs less for Texans to own their homes while at the same time tying up less equity in purchasing a house.

This difference in home equity accounts for almost three percent of the total that, if normalized, would boost the net worth of the average Texas family a full $1,000 (perhaps not unsurprisingly, California ranks 4th in net worth, but 48th in homeownership, while Hawaii, with the nation's highest housing costs, ranks 1st—for those fortunate enough to own a home in that island state, having the 49th lowest rate of homeownership).

Further, the national housing market collapsed after this particular non-profit's study was completed, depressing house prices significantly in places such as California. As measured by the National Association of Homebuilders, the median sales price of an existing home declined 23 percent nationally from its peak of $217,900 in 2007 to $168,400 in August 2011.[41] In same period, the median sales price of an existing home in Texas *increased* five percent from $146,450 to $153,200.[42] California housing prices for existing homes hit a peak of $594,530 in 2007, declined 59 percent to $245,230 in February 2009, and have since rebounded to $297,060, a decline of 50 percent from 2007's highs. Thus, most Texas homeowners have seen an increase in the value of their homes since 2007 while homeowners nationally or especially in California have seen the value of their home decline.

The Federal Reserve verified the impact housing prices have on family net worth, further devaluing this line of attack on Texas, when it issued a report in June 2012 which observed that the median net worth of an American family dropped 38.8 percent from 2007 to 2010 due mainly to "a broad collapse in house prices" especially in the West where "Housing was of greater importance than financial assets for the wealth position of most families."[43] The study by the left-leaning Corporation for Enterprise Development cited two states in the West, California and Hawaii, for their high family net worth in 2007, the very height of the housing price bubble.

---

[40] Corporation for Enterprise Development (CFED) see: http://cfed.org/assets/pdfs/2007_DRC.pdf.
[41] http://www.nahb.org/fileUpload_details.aspx?contentID=55764.
[42] http://www.texasahead.org/economy/tracking/.
[43] "Weak house prices drag family wealth: Fed," *Reuters*, June 11, 2012, http://www.reuters.com/article/2012/06/12/us-usa-economy-networth-idUSBRE85A1A220120612

Puncturing the Texas Poverty Myth

Another measure of personal income is the poverty rate in a state. If only a small number of wealthy are doing well, then the personal income average can rise, even if the majority of people see no benefit. Advocates for the poor, many of whom are harshly critical of Texas for not taxing and spending more, devalue the huge jobs gains seen in the Lone Star State, dismissing these jobs as low-paying. As proof, they frequently cite Federal government data showing Texas has the nation's 6th highest high poverty rate, with some 18.4 percent of Texans considered impoverished in 2010.

There's one big problem with the Census Bureau data though: it counts same income threshold across the nation. This is a big oversight, however, because according to data from the Council for Community and Economic Research, the cost of living varies widely within America, with Oklahoma being America's least expensive state in which to live and Hawaii being the most costly—meaning that a dollar goes a lot further in Oklahoma than it does in Hawaii.

Cost of living matters; especially to people who, for whatever reason—inexperience, lack of education, or hard luck—are earning low wages.

Critics of Texas also often cite the fact that 9.5 percent of its hourly wage workers earn the Federal minimum wage of $7.25 an hour. California has its own, higher, state minimum wage, set at $8.00 an hour. In other big states, New York and Pennsylvania follow Federal law at $7.25, Florida sets theirs at $7.31, Illinois at $8.25, Ohio at 7.40 ($7.25 for small businesses), and Michigan pegs theirs at $7.40.

Based on this superficial understanding, people writing about the working poor often claim that they are better off in Illinois and California, than in New York, Pennsylvania or Texas.

But income is only half of the equation—money is spent to live, and when the cost of food, housing, utilities, transportation, health care and other services are taken into account, we find that Texas is the second least expensive state after Oklahoma.[44] The eight largest states show a wide range in their cost of living compared to the national average with California at 132 percent of the national average; Texas at 90 percent; New York, 133 percent; Florida, 97 percent; Illinois, 95 percent; Pennsylvania, 102 percent; Ohio, 93 percent; and Michigan, 92 percent.

---

[44] 2nd Quarter, 2011 data from The Council for Community and Economic Research, http://www.c2er.org/. The Council for Community and Economic Research explains on their website that: Cost of Living Can Significantly Affect "Real" Median Household Income—Among 170 large counties, Fairfax and Loudoun Counties in Washington's Northern Virginia suburbs have the highest median household income areas in 2006, according to the US Census Bureau. However, when factoring in the cost of living, Williamson County, Tennessee, in greater Nashville and Forsyth County, Georgia in the Atlanta metro area rank as the two counties with the highest "real" median household income among the counties studied, based on an analysis of the most recent Cost of Living Index data. Policy makers who are using the median household income data should pay more attention to the effects of cost of living adjustment. In areas with higher cost of living, the current median household income report overstates the buying power of household incomes. At the same time, households in areas with a lower cost of living frequently do better than their ranking might suggest. …the ranking of the nation's wealthiest counties changes considerably when adjusted for the Cost of Living Index. http://www.coli.org/COLIAdjustedMHI.asp.

In fact, when adjusted for the cost of living, the minimum wage in Texas is equivalent to earning a wage of $8.04 per hour in California. California's higher minimum wage on paper effectively pencils out to $6.06 per hour in real earnings power. New York is even lower, at $5.47 per hour, and yet, we hear little of poverty in New York as compared to Texas. New York's high cost of living is likely one of the chief contributing factors as to why a net of 1.6 million people moved out of the state from 2000 to 2010. The minimum wage in Illinois adjusted for buying power is $8.71, while in Florida it's $7.52, in Pennsylvania, $7.09, Ohio, $7.94 and Michigan, $8.00. Figure 13 shows that the only state out of the largest eight with a higher effective minimum wage than Texas is Illinois.

Political discussions about the minimum wage are often tied to the poverty rate. Raising the minimum wage, the argument goes, will lift the working poor out of poverty by giving them a "living wage." Absent from these arguments is the fact that minimum wage jobs are often entry-level jobs, giving otherwise inexperienced people their first chance at learning the habits required for keep a job and advance up the ladder of success.

Further, the consensus opinion among economists is that increasing the minimum wage causes higher unemployment among the very people who can most ill-afford to be unemployed.

The Federal government calculates Texas' poverty rate at 18.4 percent with an unemployment rate of 8.4 percent while California's poverty rate is estimated at 16.3 percent, higher than the national average of 15.1 percent, with an unemployment rate of 12 percent. New York's poverty rate is 16 percent, Florida's 16 percent, Illinois' 14.1 percent, Pennsylvania's 12.2 percent, Ohio's 15.3 percent, and Michigan's 15.5.[45]

But, as the Census dryly states, "The poverty thresholds are the same for all parts of the country—they are not adjusted for regional, state or local variations in the cost of living."[46]

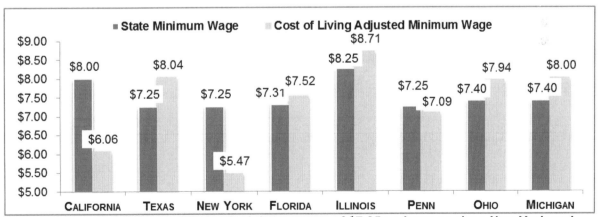

Figure 13—Texas follows the Federal minimum wage of $7.25 an hour, as does New York and Pennsylvania, but, when adjusted for the cost of living, only Illinois provides a higher effective minimum wage as measured by buying power than does Texas.

[45] U.S. Census Bureau, "Income, Poverty, and Health Insurance Coverage in the United States: 2010."
[46] U.S. Census Bureau, State & County QuickFacts, definition of Household Income and Persons Below Poverty, http://quickfacts.census.gov/qfd/meta/long_IPE120209.htm.

Some economists have estimated that taking California's high cost of living into account would result in real poverty rate of 26 percent.[47] On the other side of the ledger, if Texas' lower cost of living were taken into account, its poverty rate would be much lower than stated by the Federal government. In all likelihood, the real poverty rate in Texas could be as much as 10 percent lower than it is in California.

Looking at it another way, if about 6 million Californians were below the federal poverty line of $22,113 for a family of four in 2010, while 4.6 million Texans met the same threshold, what would the numbers be revised to adjust for the actual buying power in each state? Figure 14 illustrates how misleading the one-size-fits all Federal poverty rate statistics are by comparing how much a family of four would have to earn to actually live at the poverty line in each state.

The far higher cost of living takes its toll on working families in California and New York, while Texas is the most cost-effective state among America's largest.

The U.S. Census, in a 2010 report[48], breaks down U.S. poverty data by age, race and income level, showing that the highest poverty rate occurs when Americans are at college age, 18-24, while showing that Blacks and Hispanics are generally twice as likely to be in poverty as Asians or Whites. This data shows that a state's poverty rate is highly dependent on demographic factors with states having a younger average age and more minorities likely to show a higher poverty rate than states with fewer minorities or an older population.

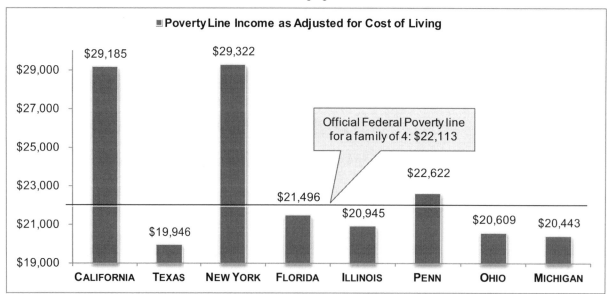

Figure 14—The Federal government calculates the poverty threshold at $22,113 for a family of four, regardless of a state's cost of living. Taking cost of living into account, the wages of a poor family in Texas go much further than in California or New York.

---

[47] "California is becoming 'post-industrial hell,' economist says," by Lance Williams, *California Watch*, October 12, 2011, http://californiawatch.org/dailyreport/california-becoming-post-industrial-hell-economist-says-13042.
[48] U.S. Census Bureau , "Income, Poverty, and Health Insurance Coverage in the United States: 2009," September 2010, Table 6, page 18, http://www.census.gov/prod/2010pubs/p60-238.pdf.

Beyond that, however, a true measure of a state's poverty level would also account for the cost of living in the state.

A separate Census study, this one using 2010 American Community Survey data, estimated the number of people in each state with income in various brackets: under 50 percent of the poverty level, 50 to 74 percent, 75 to 99 percent, 100 to 124 percent, and 125 to 149 percent.[49]

With a more detailed understanding of how many people are earning a certain percentage of poverty threshold incomes—the same around the nation—then adjusting those income levels to take into account the real earning power of their income, state-to-state, we can see a more accurate picture of poverty. Figure 15 shows that when adjusting for cost of living, California's official poverty rate of 16.3 percent spikes to 23.3 percent; Texas, criticized as having the nation's sixth-highest poverty rate at 18.4 percent, declines to 16.1 percent; New York's 16.0 percent rate rises to 22.0 percent; Florida's 16.0 percent rate goes to 15.5 percent; Illinois' 14.1 percent rate dips to 13.3 percent; Pennsylvania's 12.2 percent rate edges up to 12.6 percent, Ohio's rate declines from 15.3 percent to 14.2 percent, and Michigan's rate goes from 15.5 percent to 14.2 percent.

The Census Bureau has been aware of the shortcomings of its own poverty measures for some time, with the U.S. Congress appropriating money for a study into the issue in 1990. In November 2011, the Census published a study which used an alternative method of calculating poverty that took many cost of living elements into account, such as the cost of getting to work. Factors that impact disposable income such as payroll taxes as well as welfare programs were also included in the Census effort. The Census findings parallel our own calculations, with the official poverty rate in the South declining from 17.0 percent to 16.3 percent, while the poverty

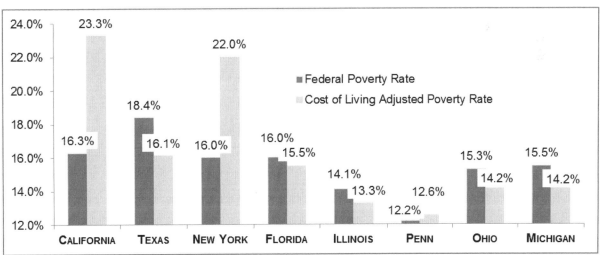

Figure 15—When official poverty data takes into account cost of living, which varies widely from state-to-state, Texas ends up with lower true poverty rates than both California and New York because Texas enjoys the second least-expensive cost of living in America after Oklahoma.

---

[49] "Ratio of Income to Poverty Level in the Past 12 Months," Report series B17002, Universe: Population for whom poverty status is determined, 2010 American Community Survey 1-Year Estimates.

rate in the West jumps from 15.4 percent to the nation's highest at 19.4 percent when cost of living factors were included.[50]

In late 2012, Census revised its state level one-size-fits-all poverty calculations, releasing a new poverty rate estimate that included cost of living. California's poverty rate was set at 23.5 percent while Texas came in at 16.5 percent—within a fraction of the calculations made above.[51]

In addition, as previously mentioned, one of the highest predictors of poverty is age, with younger people more likely to be temporarily poor than older people. Given this information, Texas, with a median age of 32.9, the second-youngest population in America after Utah, compares very well with Florida, median age 39.3, and Illinois, median age 35.4.

Lastly, critics often assert that Texans are mired in poverty, while California, in spite of its high unemployment rate, is a better place to be, especially for those at the lower end of the income spectrum. But, if that is the case, why, as Figure 16 shows, does California have the nation's highest rates of adults on welfare?[52] California's rates of people receiving Temporary Assistance to Needy Families (TANF) are even higher than entirely urban Washington, D.C., which has the nation's second-highest welfare caseload among adults as a percentage of the population. In fact, the average California adult is more than two-and-one-half times more likely to be on welfare than the national average. In Illinois, adults are one-ninth as likely to be on welfare as the national average while Texas shows the second-best numbers among the large states. A Texas adult is less than one-fifth as likely to be on welfare as the national average. Compared to California adults, adult Texans are almost 14 *times* less likely to be receiving welfare.[53]

Figure 17 looks at one more aspect of welfare spending, an analysis of households which receive any measure of cash public assistance.[54] A broader measure than that shown in Figure 16, it

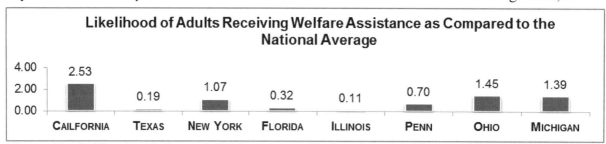

Figure 16—California adults are 2-1/2 times more likely to be on welfare than average Americans.

[50] "Supplemental Poverty Measure: 2010, Nov. 7, 2011," U.S. Census Bureau.

[51] "The Research Supplemental Poverty Measure: 2011," by Kathleen Short, U.S. Census Bureau, November 2012, Table 4, Percentage of People in Poverty by State Using 3-Year Averages Over 2009, 2010, and 2011, http://www.census.gov/prod/2012pubs/p60-244.pdf.

[52] "How California Creates Greater Income Inequality for Itself," by Steven J. Balassi, *Journal of Business and Public Affairs*, Volume 2, Issue 1, 2008, on page 17 explains: "California tried to modify the federal welfare program in 1997. The state's caseload did drop but not as much as the rest of the nation. One major reason was that California was paying out more in welfare benefits and paid them out after the time limits had expired."

[53] National TANF Datafile as of 12/29/2010 for FY 2008-09, Table 18.

[54] "Public Assistance Receipt in the Past 12 Months for Households: 2008 and 2009," American Community Survey, U.S. Census Bureau, Oct. 2010, http://www.census.gov/prod/2010pubs/acsbr09-13.pdf.

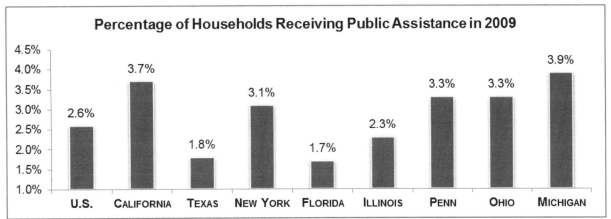

Figure 17—Looking at all cash assistance to the poor, Michigan and California lead the list.

includes cash general assistance and TANF but does not include food stamps and medical services. Of the large states, Michigan and California have the highest rates of households getting cash assistance, Florida and Texas, the lowest. Comparing these rates to the 50 states and the District of Columbia, we see that Michigan has the 5th-highest rate of cash assistance, California, 6th, Pennsylvania and Ohio tied for 10th, New York, 14th, Illinois, 32nd, Texas 43rd, and Florida, 45th. One reason for California's high welfare caseload is that the state continually sought and received Federal waivers from the requirement in 1996's historic welfare reform act that able-bodied adults have a five-year time limit on lifetime welfare benefits. As a result, welfare recipients have less incentive to cease taking taxpayer assistance. Further, California even strains the definition of "work"—considering people who enroll in community college classes for skill training, but don't actually *attend* any classes, as "working."

Figure 18 compares the big states' rate of removing people from the welfare rolls when they hit the five-year lifetime limit on benefits.[55]

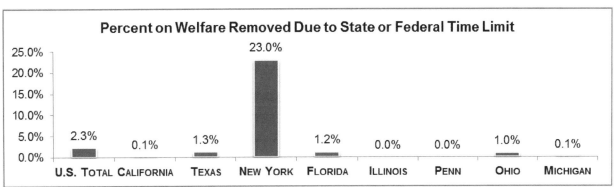

Figure 18—Nationally, about 2.3 percent of welfare recipients each year are removed from the rolls because they hit the 5 year limit for able-bodied adults to draw welfare, Texas came the closest to the national average of the large states.

---

[55] National TANF Datafile as of 12/29/2010 for FY 2008-09, Table 46.

State and Local Government Spending

In comparing the big states to each other and previously in this book, we've started to lay out the case that Texas is doing better than its peers because it taxes less, spends less, regulates less and has fewer frivolous lawsuits than other states.

One way to measure the size of government and government spending is to look at the percentage of the state's economy that goes to state and local government. The U.S. Bureau of Economic Analysis (BEA) calculates the percentage of a state's economy that is spent on state and local government. By this measure, Michigan spent the most of the eight big states over the past ten years while Illinois spends the least. But, this data does not convey the entire story. Looking at the definition of government spending used by the government analysts, we see that the majority of spending isn't accounted for at all, with public education, healthcare, welfare, and infrastructure spending listed elsewhere. Thus, the BEA data only shows administrative costs and outlays for the courts, prison system, police and fire. Of this, the criminal justice system consumes about one-fifth of the total.[56]

Still, by measure of the rate of growth in general government, Texas, Florida, and Pennsylvania each saw a small increase, 0.1 percent, in the share of their economy going to administrative government functions from 1997 to 2010, while Michigan experienced a 1.1 percent increase in the size of general government relative to the economy as a whole.

As a share of the economy, general government was 12 percent larger in Michigan in 2010 than it was in 1997, while general government consumes 1 percent more in Texas.

But the BEA economy data only accounts for a thin slice of government spending—it isn't comprehensive. A more accurate and comprehensive measure of state and local government spending can be found through the Tax Foundation, a national non-profit think tank that has been studying state and Federal taxes and spending since 1937.

Figure 19 uses Tax Foundation data to illustrate the most basic measure of how the eight large states prioritize their spending: government employees.[57] Texas employs the least per capita number of general government workers among the eight large states, 196 per 100,000, 22 percent less than the national average of 253. At the other end of the spectrum, Illinois favors a bloated government payroll, with 341 employees per 100,000, 35 percent above the national average and a full 145 per 100,000 more than Texas!

Other than simply raising taxes to cover spending shortfalls, it stands to reason that if a state has more general government employees it can afford to hire fewer educators. Texas has the second-

---

[56] According to "California's Criminal Justice System: A Primer," by the California Legislative Analyst's Office, January 31, 2007, at the state and local level, California spent a little more than $25 billion to operate its criminal justice system in the 2003-04 budget year, about 21 percent of the inflation-adjusted GDP estimated by the Bureau of Economic Analysis to have been spent on State and Local Government administration in California.
[57] Tax Foundation calculations based on 2007 Census of Government Employment total pay and total employment by function data, and the Bureau of Economic Analysis.

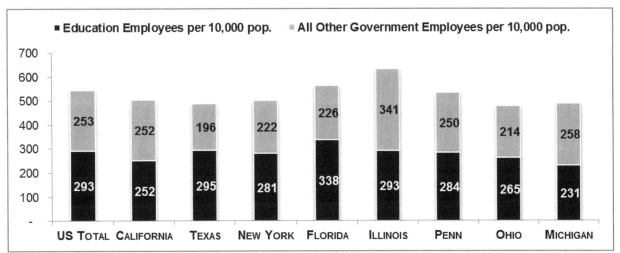

Figure 19—Texas has the fewest number of non-education government employees per capita of the large 8 states, while employing the second-greatest number of educators, after Florida.

highest number of government education employees, 295 per 100,000, after Florida, which has 338—the only two large states with an above-average numbers of teachers. Conversely, California, with just an average number of general government workers, has the highest-paid teachers among the large states (and is often ranked as having the highest paid teachers in the nation), thus, it isn't surprising that California employs the second-fewest teachers, with economically-battered Michigan in last.

Less Taxes, Less Debt in Texas

Since the U.S. Constitution prohibits states from printing money, they have a limited ability to finance deficit spending. As a result, looking at the revenue states generate is a good measure as to how much government, including debt payment, their residents are funding. Figure 20 measures state tax collections per capita in 2009. It shows that Texas collects the least from its

Figure 20—A family of 4 would, on average, owe $6,688 more in taxes in New York than in Texas.

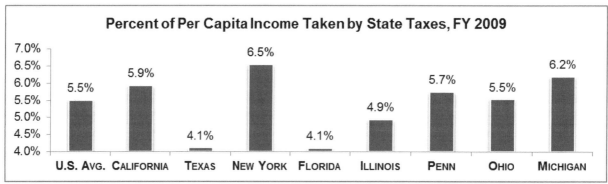

Figure 21—Adjusted for income, New Yorkers, with per capita income of $51,055, pay a far greater portion in taxes to state government than do Texans, with per capita income of $40,498. With the cost of basic necessities being 43 percent less in Texas than in New York, is it any wonder a net of 1.6 million New Yorkers left the Empire State in the last decade?

citizens, while New York collects the most. In fact, Texas ranks 46th among the 50 states in per capita tax collections.[58]

Some might argue that Texas collects less in taxes because Texans earn less than Californians. It's true that, despite having a higher cost-of-living adjusted poverty rate than Texas, Californians do have higher per capita income than Texans. Figure 21 factors that into account, looking at the percentage of per capita income that flows to state government.[59] Again, not surprisingly, since Florida and Texas don't levy individual income taxes, those two states come out best for taxpayers while New York and Michigan fare the worst.

Figure 22 encompasses even more taxing data, this time using data from a variety of government and independent groups compiled by the Tax Foundation to provide an estimate of the total state

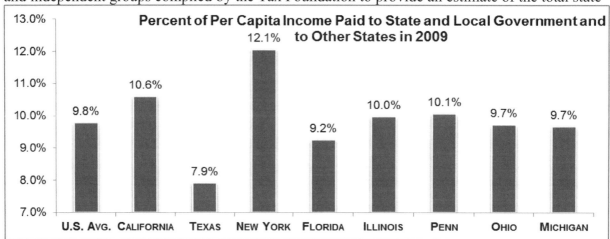

Figure 22—Even adjusted for income, New Yorkers, with per capita income of $51,055, still pay a far greater portion of their income for government.

---

[58] The Tax Foundation, "State Tax Collections Per Capita, Fiscal Year 2009," February 25, 2011, as derived from U.S. Census data and Tax Foundation analysis, http://www.taxfoundation.org/taxdata/show/289.html.
[59] Ibid., and The Tax Foundation, "Income Per Capita by State, Fiscal Year 2009," February 25, 2011, as derived from U.S. Census data and Tax Foundation analysis, http://www.taxfoundation.org/taxdata/show/290.html.

and local level tax burden as well as taxes paid to other states as a percentage of per capita income—the most basic measure of the taxpayers' ability to pay. Again, Texas fares the best. In Figure 21, Texans had a 2.4 percent advantage over New Yorkers, or, put another way, New Yorkers paid 58 percent more to the state as a percentage of what they earned than do Texans. When considering the wider net cast by local taxes and imputing taxes paid by residents of one state to another state, New Yorkers pay "just" 53 percent more of their income in state and local taxes than do Texans.

A thought about taxes, government services, and income: if government is to do for those the things they cannot do for themselves then shouldn't a wealthier society require less government? Why should a wealthy state like New York require more of its wealthier citizens' income than a state with less income, such as Texas? Perhaps all those Americans who fled high-tax New York and high-tax California, moving to low-tax Texas and low-tax Florida, were on to something.

The Tax Foundation and the Census Bureau provide estimates of state debt.[60] States can issue bonds to build schools, roads, dams or bridges, or, as in the case of California, $15 billion to refinance deficit spending (2004), $3 billion to fund stem cell research (2004), or $10 billion for a government-run high speed train (2008) and Illinois' issuing of $3.7 billion in bonds to bridge its unfunded government employees pension liability (2011).[61] Regardless of why the state bonds are issued, taxpayers have to repay the bonds with interest, incurring about double the cost of the bond issue over 20 to 30 years' time. Figure 23 shows the per capita state debt of the big states.

As a practical kitchen-table bottom line, the difference to a taxpayer between New York's debt of $5,048 and Texas' debt of $1,240, is about $420 per year of interest and principal—or, almost $1,700 per year in higher taxes or less services for a taxpaying family of four to service the debt.

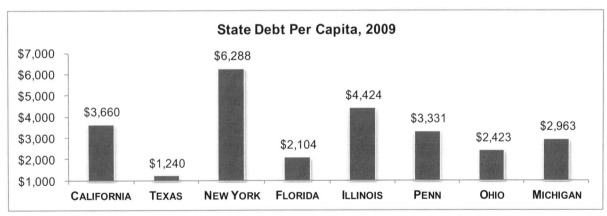

Figure 23—Texas has the least state debt of the big states, and has the 49th-lowest debt per person in the nation.

[60] The Tax Foundation, "Map: State Debt Per Capita, Fiscal Year 2009," June 2, 2011, http://www.taxfoundation.org/taxdata/show/27322.html.
[61] Illinois' issuance of $3.7 billion in pension obligation bonds added about $287 of per capita debt to Illinois residents – $1,146 of debt that a family of four will have to repay through a combination of higher taxes or less government services.

The review of state debt wouldn't be complete without looking at the whole debt burden in a state, to include local borrowing. School districts, cities, and special assessment districts can issue bonds to borrow money for a host of reasons: to build schools, roads, or water projects. Usually, a state with a lot of growth, such as Texas, can finance these projects one of four ways: with ongoing taxes, with state borrowing, with local borrowing, or by allowing the private sector to build the facility, then charge a fee to use it, as with toll roads. Figure 24 displays this larger, more inclusive measure of debt, showing Ohio as having the least debt per capita while New York has the most.[62]

As mentioned before, debt repayments crowd out current spending, and defaults, missing debt payments, increase the cost of borrowing. California must now dedicate 8.7 percent of its budget towards debt servicing. A California city of 120,000, Vallejo, declared bankruptcy in 2008, and is proposing to give creditors five cents on the dollar, the first time a city or county has used Federal bankruptcy laws to stiff creditors out of their money.[63] Meanwhile, Harrisburg, the capital of Pennsylvania, announced its bankruptcy in October 2011.[64] In addition, there is expectation that three cities will soon declare bankruptcy in Michigan, with several other expected in Pennsylvania, Illinois and California.

As one might expect, if a one state taxes more than another, then all things being equal, people, small business owners, and large corporations alike may decide that the fiscal grass is greener elsewhere, moving their earnings—and jobs—from one state to another.

We already noted how, in the past decade, California saw net domestic outmigration of almost two million Americans while together, Florida and Texas saw an influx of some two million.

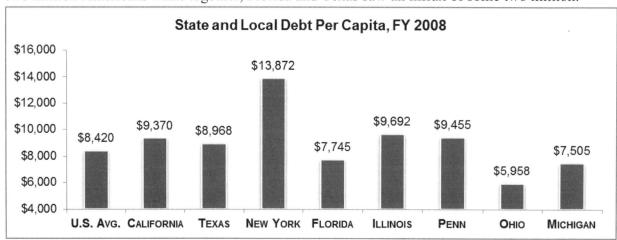

Figure 24—Measuring debt at all levels: New York is still tops, while Ohio shows the least debt.

---

[62] The Tax Foundation, "State and Local Debt Per Capita, Fiscal Year 2008," February 25, 2011, as derived from U.S. Census data and Tax Foundation analysis, http://www.taxfoundation.org/taxdata/show/23409.html
[63] "Vallejo Bankruptcy Plan Would Pay Creditors as Little as 5%," *Bloomberg Business Week*, January 19, 2011.
[64] The trigger of the Harrisburg bankruptcy is more complex than simple financial mismanagement and pension overspending. Harrisburg's problems are due to a city-owned garbage incinerator, built in 1972, that required $125 million in upgrades to stop Federal Clean Air Act violations.

The Tax Foundation offers one compelling rationale: the state business tax climate. Measuring state and local taxes, their complexity and compliance costs, as well as how uniformly tax laws treat different types of economic activity, the foundation rates each state's climate as they compete for jobs with each other, and, increasingly, compete overseas as well. Comparing the large states' business tax climate ranking among the 50 states shows Florida as having the 5th-best business tax climate.[65] Texas is 13th, Michigan, having improved in recent years, is 17th, Illinois and Pennsylvania rank in the mid-range at 23rd and 26th, respectively, while Ohio comes in at 46th, and the competition for the cellar features California at 49th and New York at 50th.

Education

Given Texas' low state spending and given that K-12 public school expenditures are the largest portion of a state budget one might think that Texas was seriously short-changing the education of its children. You may be excused for thinking that, but comparative test scores indicate otherwise.

A common line of criticism against the Texas educational record, usually leveled by government teachers unions, is that Texas lags the nation in spending and thus, in classroom results, with lower test scores than the national average. As Figures 1 and 20 showed previously, Florida, then Texas, employs the largest ratio of public school workers, while California employs the fewest per capita.

Let's examine the grades among the eight states in our class.

The only consistent, national testing is done under the auspices of National Assessment of Educational Progress (NAEP). Every two years America's school children are tested in the 4th and 8th grades with three subjects typically tested: math, reading, and science. In the 2009 results for both grades in the three subjects, the results might appear, at first glance, to be inconclusive. With two grades and three topics, there are six measures that can be made. Texas did better than the national average on three of the six measures, while coming in below the national average on the other three categories.

But, as with income, unemployment, and poverty, race and ethnicity play a meaningful statistical role in standardized educational testing data, with Asians and non-Hispanic Whites on average, scoring better than Hispanics and Blacks. Reviewing the results for the 2009 testing data among the eight big states with race and ethnicity considered—all students, White students, Hispanic students, and African-American students—showed Texas as having the strongest scores in 11 of 24 categories while California was last in 15 of 24 categories. Further, Texas showed no areas of weakness compared to the national average.

In another key area of academic achievement, national testing also measures test score differences by race and ethnicity. If a state has a low achievement gap, it is one indicator showing that the state's education system is investing effort in teaching all the children in their

---

[65] The Tax Foundation, "Map: State Business Tax Climate Index, 2011," October 26, 2010, http://www.taxfoundation.org/taxdata/show/25267.html.

state, regardless of income level or background. In this measure, the 2009 test results show Texas doing better than the other large states except Florida where Hispanic children have historically done very well compared to the national average.[66] The NAEP results for 2011 in math and reading show that minority 8th grade students in Texas improved in both topics while 4th grade minority students showed improvement in math with a slight decline in tested reading skills.

Elected members of the Texas State Board of Education think Texas may show an even wider positive achievement gap with other states in the future as Texas opted out of the Obama Administration's attempt to impose Federal standards on local schools through the Common Core Standards. Instead, Texas decided to write and adopt its own public school curriculum standards, with the standards for English, language arts, reading, science, and social studies completed and approved while the new math standards are in work. Texas State Board of Education members are especially focused on math as a gateway skill to many high technology jobs, intending to craft the best math curriculum in the nation with K-5 students learning basic math without calculators.

There may be other factors in play but, at the very least, it appears that critics are off-base in their contention that, "California gives a better education system," than Texas.[67]

The 2011 NAEP tests were administered and reported for math, science and reading in the 8th grade but the 4th grade testing omitted one topic. Figure 25 displays these most recent results by topic and race and ethnicity for the U.S. and the eight biggest states. The best results are marked with double up arrows and with second-place results marked with a single up arrow. Last place results are highlighted with double down arrows while the penultimately last results are shown with a sole down arrow. Note that Texas is first in six of nine categories and second in another, scoring at the national average for 8th grade reading for White students and two points above the national average for 8th grade Hispanic students. This stands in stark contrast to the myriad critics who keep repeating, falsely, that Texas' educational system is horrific and failing.[68]

---

[66] About 36% of Florida Hispanics trace their heritage to Cuba and, as such, their parents and grandparents are statistically more likely to be professionals or business owners than are other Latin American immigrants. This results in a higher degree of "human capital" among the Cuban immigrant community than is often the case with other Hispanic immigrant communities.

[67] "The jobs that have been created in Texas are largely in minimum wage or below minimum wage. Can you support a family? Can you lift them out of poverty? No. Texas does not provide a model. California gives a better education system and [venture capital] business. What really is at issue right now is the American dream, and the American dream is based off of good jobs." – Robert Sheer; editor, *Truthdig*.

[68] In "Lone Star Tarnished: a Critical Look at Texas Politics and Public Policy"(2012), Cal Jillson, a professor of political science at Southern Methodist University in Dallas makes several assertions about education in Texas, citing the topic 227 times, writing, "...that while Texas has done very well on population and job growth, its ranking among the states on income, education, social services, criminal justice and the environment have been stagnant or falling for decades" and "In 2009, Texas ranked 47th in state aid per pupil and 44th in state and local expenditures per pupil. And the educational results are bleak. Texas ranked 43rd in public high school graduation rates and 49th in the percent of population graduated from high school." Prof. Jillson makes the claim but doesn't connect the dots to demographics, for instance, high school attainment is directly tied to the number of illegal immigrants in a state— California usually ranks up there with Texas on that measure. The professor also ignores cost of living data and, since Texas is the second-least expensive state in the nation, its per pupil expenditures are effectively just above the national average (see Figure 1).

	Reading White	Reading Hispanic	Reading Black	Math White	Math Hispanic	Math Black	Science White	Science Hispanic	Science Black
U.S.	274	252	249	293	270	262	163	137	129
California	↓↓268	↓↓245	↓↓243	290	↓↓260	↓254	↓↓159	↓128	↓124
Texas	274	254	↑↑252	↑↑304	↑↑283	↑↑277	↑↑167	↑146	↑↑137
New York	↑↑276	251	↑251	291	↓263	↑264	163	129	130
Florida	270	↑259	248	↓287	↑274	258	↓161	144	127
Illinois	274	257	249	294	272	260	↓161	135	↓↓120
Pennsylvania	↑275	↓250	↓244	294	269	257	163	↓↓118	↓↓120
Ohio	274	252	247	↑295	273	263	↑165	↑↑151	↑132
Michigan	↓269	↑↑260	↓244	↓↓286	↑274	↓↓250	↑165	↑146	↓124

Figure 25—Texas' 8ᵗʰ grade national standardized testing results lead its big state peers.

Students in California, a model for so many on the left, placed last in five of nine categories and second-to-last in the three more—a continuation of the state's dismal results from the 2009 battery of national standardized tests for both 4ᵗʰ and 8ᵗʰ grade.

Crime

Lastly, before we engage in a more detailed discussion of the two largest states and how their fiscal policies diverged in 2003, setting the stage for the outflow of business from California, and its influx to Texas, let's compare crime statistics. The U.S. Federal Bureau of Investigation (FBI) compiles yearly statistics on violent crime rates in America. Figure 26 shows that Florida has the highest per capita crime rate among the large states, with Ohio having the fewest crimes.[69]

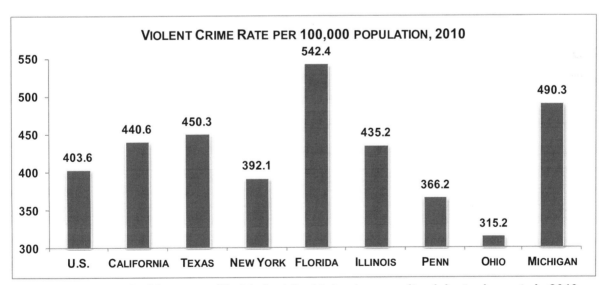

Figure 26—Among the big states, Florida had the highest per capita violent crime rate in 2010.

[69] Federal Bureau of Investigation, "Crime in the United States, by State, 2010, Table 5," http://www.fbi.gov/about-us/cjis/ucr/crime-in-the-u.s/2010/crime-in-the-u.s.-2010/tables/10tbl05.xls.

However, as with statistics on income and education, crime rates are highly influenced by demographic factors. For instance, men ages 20 to 24 are more likely to commit violent crime while males ages 15 to 19 are far more likely to commit property crimes.[70] Adjusting for the age cohorts in each state, one would expect to see the fairly young populations of California and Texas have higher violent rates while the older population of Florida should have fewer crimes. Adjusting for age, Texas still has the third-highest violent crime rate, but, instead of being three percent higher than number four, Illinois, it's two-percent higher. Unfortunately, a large statistical indicator of crime rates remains race, with Black Americans about three times more likely to be arrested for a violent crime and 2.3 times more likely to be arrested for property crime. With this statistic in mind, California's race-adjusted violent crime is far higher than it should be.

In June 2012, the FBI released its 2011 crime statistics for the 280 largest cities in America. Figure 1 showed how, among the eight biggest states, Texas had no cities in the top-25-worst cities for violent crime while California had two (Oakland and Stockton, a city facing bankruptcy), Florida had two (Miami and Orlando), Illinois had two (Rockford and Springfield—Chicago was listed as 35th, but they did not report their rape statistics and so, would likely place higher), and Michigan had two (Flint and Detroit, first and second-worst cities, respectively) while New York, Pennsylvania and Ohio had one each (Buffalo, Philadelphia and Cleveland). The highest ranking Texas municipality for violent crime was Houston, the fourth-largest city in America, which ranked 38th nationally in 2011.

We've now compared Texas to its large states peers, California, Florida, New York, Illinois, Ohio, Michigan and Pennsylvania in the areas of population growth and interstate migration, economic growth, jobs, business creation, personal income, manufacturing strength, unemployment, poverty, state taxes, state and local debt, the composition of state employees, educational effectiveness, and violent crime rates.

We've seen that, in measure after measure, Texas' critics are wrong—Texas is growing and its residents are doing well—in spite of (or, we'd say, because of) the low-tax and low-spending ways of its government.

California and Texas: Mano-a-Mano

Of the eight largest states, the state most like Texas is America's largest, California. California is home to 37 million people, Texas, 25 million. Both states have a long coastline with busy ports. Both states border Mexico and have large immigrant populations, including sizable populations of illegal immigrants. Both states have experienced booming population growth over the past 60 years, although, in the last decade, California's growth rate cooled to a rate slightly above the national average, 10 percent, while Texas grew at double the national pace, 21 percent. Both states have large, diversified economies. And, Texas has the largest proven oil reserves among the states, but California ranks third in the nation, behind Alaska, with reserves about half as large as Texas.

---

[70] Federal Bureau of Investigation, "Crime in the United States, Arrests, by Age, 2010, Table 38," http://www.fbi.gov/about-us/cjis/ucr/crime-in-the-u.s/2010/crime-in-the-u.s.-2010/tables/10tbl38.xls.

With so much in common, one would think that both states would be doing similarly well. But, it's not that simple. As Tom McClintock, a U.S. Representative from California, who previously served in the state legislature for 22 years, remarked on October 2011:[71]

> *"Of course, in spite of all of its problems, California is still one of the best places in the country to build a successful small business. All you have to do is start with a successful large business...*

> *"When my parents came to California in the 1960's looking for a better future, they found it here. The state government consumed about half of what it does today after adjusting for both inflation and population. HALF. We had the finest highway system in the world and the finest public school system in the country. California offered a FREE university education to every Californian who wanted one. We produced water and electricity so cheaply that some communities didn't bother to meter the stuff. Our unemployment rate consistently ran well below the national rate and our diversified economy was nearly recession-proof.*

> *"One thing—and one thing only—changed in those years: public policy. The political Left gradually gained dominance over California's government and has imposed a disastrous agenda of radical and retrograde policies that have destroyed the quality of life that Californians once took for granted.*

> *"The Census bureau has reported for the better part of the decade that California is undergoing the biggest population exodus in its history, with many fleeing to such garden spots as Nevada, Arizona and Texas. Think about that. California is blessed with the most equitable climate in the entire Western Hemisphere; it has the most bountiful resources anywhere in the continental United States; it is poised on the Pacific Rim in a position to dominate world trade for the next century, and yet people are finding a better place to live and work and raise their families in the middle of the Nevada Nuclear Test Range.*

> *"I submit to you that no conceivable act of God could wreak such devastation. Only acts of government can do that. And they have."*

So, are the large and growing differences in the economic trajectories of the nation's two largest states solely due to government policies? Policies, that, if swapped, Texas for California and California for Texas, would cause a noticeable change in the trajectory of economic activity?

The short answer is yes.

Further, to the degree which policymakers in Washington, D.C. seek to expand the power of government, increase taxes, heighten the regulatory burden, and place more multi-billion dollar mandates on the states—in short, make Federal policy more like California state policy—then

---

[71] Excerpted from a speech delivered to the Council for National Policy in October, 2011.

understanding the public policy differences between Texas and California isn't just of regional concern, but is of extreme national importance.

In 1978, in response to rapidly rising property taxes due to the high inflation rate at the time, California voters passed Proposition 13, a ballot measure that placed limits on property taxes. In one year, the state and local tax burden plunged from 11.9 percent to 10 percent of personal income.[72] The era of big government was over—temporarily.

Then, President Ronald Reagan's tax cuts helped stimulate a U.S. economic recovery from the energy crisis stoked stagflation of the 70s. With a large defense industry, California was well-positioned to benefit from Reagan's Cold War build up as well.

For 16 years, from 1983 to January, 1999, California was led by two Republican governors while the legislature was solidly in Democratic hands, with the exception of the State Assembly for two years: 1995 and 1996. During that time California government grew steadily, but not excessively so, while tax rates remained fairly constant.

But, in 1989, California manufacturing began slowing as the Reagan-era defense build-up ran its course. Manufacturing peaked in 1991, the year the Cold War formally ended with the fall of the Soviet Union. While the rest of the nation fell into a mild recession, California was hit hard.

That year, Gov. Pete Wilson signed off on a $7 billion state tax increase—at the time, the biggest state tax increase in California and U.S. history. Wilson was to later say the tax increase was, "… the biggest mistake of my governorship." The following year devastating riots hit Los Angeles.* California couldn't seem to catch a break. In 1992, California taxes as a percentage of income hit their highest mark since 1978.

But, even as the defense industry was winding down, a new and remarkable industrial transformation began to take hold: the personal computer came into mass use. Throughout California new high tech businesses sprung up; many were spin-offs from legacy defense contractors. The rate of California manufacturing, which had stalled in 1991, had recovered three years later and shot up at a faster pace than was seen at the peak of the defense boom.

During the eight years of Republican Pete Wilson's time in office, from 1991 to 1998, state government grew at 4.8 percent per year.

California leaders were blessed with a windfall of tax money—and they promptly spent it all, retroactively hiking pensions by billions of dollars for government employees, enacting expensive new programs, while temporarily cutting taxes. Spending went up from $71.9 billion

---

[72] The Tax Foundation, California's State and Local Tax Burden: 1977 to 2009, February 23, 2011, http://www.taxfoundation.org/taxdata/show/443.html.
* The author was a California Army National Guard captain and led foot patrols in the hardest-hit L.A. neighborhoods.

in the 1998-99 budget year to $99.4 billion in the 2000-01 budget year, a whopping 38 percent increase in only two years.

But, the wave of high tech manufacturing hit a wall in 2000 when the Dot.com bubble burst and Y2K proved a bust. The value of California's manufactured goods as adjusted for inflation wouldn't reach 2000 levels until 2005 while durable goods, more than half of the value of manufacturing, wouldn't fully recover until 2010.

In the midst of this slowdown, California leaders raised taxes and papered over a $38 billion deficit with accounting gimmicks and borrowing. State spending was reduced from $103.3 billion in the 2001-02 budget year to $98.9 billion in 2002-03, a four percent cut, but still 22 percent higher than it was three years earlier. State government ended up growing at the rate of about 7.1 percent per year for the five years of Democrat Gray Davis time in office from 1999 to 2003.

Voter disgust over fiscal mismanagement in Sacramento, and an earlier, botched half-deregulation of the electricity market, led to the second successful recall of a state governor in U.S. history in 2003 with the election of Austrian-born action film actor Arnold Schwarzenegger.

A dilettante with no political experience, Schwarzenegger promised to cut taxes and "tear-up the state credit cards." He did manage to reduce the previously hiked and very unpopular car tax. But, his first major initiative in early 2004 was placing on the ballot a measure to borrow $15 billion to pay back higher-interest short-term loans, saving a few billion as a buffer for later deficits. By 2008 the remainder of the credit line was used and by 2009, Schwarzenegger helped broker the largest state tax increase in U.S. history, a two-year, $24 billion hike in income, sales, and vehicle taxes. That same year, California appropriated 11 percent of the personal income of its residents, the highest amount since 1978.

State spending in 2007 was 33 percent higher than it was in 2003, an increase of 8.1 percent per year during the first four years of Schwarzenegger's two terms. Further, California paid about three percent of its general fund budget to service its debt in 2003. By 2008, that rose to seven percent. In 2011, California State Treasurer Bill Lockyer, a Democrat, warned that debt service would consume 7.8 percent of the state budget, its highest level in 34 years.

By stark contrast, Texas, through Democratic and Republican governors, and periods of Democratic and Republican control of the legislature, has shown remarkable consistency in keeping the overall tax burdens in Texas among the lightest of the 50 states.

Texas taxation and spending trends did show a degree of sensitivity to oil prices three decades ago, seeing the relative tax burden decline when oil prices spiked. But today's Texas economy is highly diversified with manufacturing a larger share of Texas output than oil, and growing as a share of the economy. By contrast, compared to today, oil and gas extraction and refining were proportionately 52 percent more important to the Texas economy in 1963; the earliest year Bureau of Economic Analysis data is available.

In the run-up to the Dot.com bubble, not once did Texas lawmakers indulge in double-digit budgetary growth, restraining state spending to just under six percent per year from 1996 to 2000 compared to California's torrid, 13 percent per year spending growth. And this, in spite of the fact that the rate of population growth in Texas was almost double that of California in the 1990s.

Thus, when budgetary pressures hit both states in 2001, California had far less room to maneuver. By 2003, when both California and Texas state lawmakers were dealing with tremendous fiscal challenges, each state's reaction to the situation was far different.

California raised taxes, recalled a governor, then lowered taxes and borrowed $15 billion, leaving spending in 2004 38 percent higher than it was five years before.

Texas lawmakers faced a $9.9 billion shortfall, some eight percent of the two-year general fund budget of about $124 billion. (Texas operates with a two-year budget cycle and a part-time legislature that meets every other year while California's full-time legislature writes a budget every year.) But, rather than borrow and set the stage for large tax increases a few years later, the Texans cut state spending by $3.2 billion in their 2004-2005 two year budget cycle. Adjusted for constant dollars, state spending dipped from 2003 to 2004. Texas' state spending in 2004 was 33 percent higher than it was five years before, showing far less erratic peaks and valleys than in California.[73]

Again, in 2008, Texas lawmakers faced austerity. But unlike in California, which enacted a huge tax increase, Texas trimmed state spending from $85.7 billion to $82.1 billion in 2009.

Finally, in 2011, history again repeated itself: facing a $27 billion, two-year deficit, Texas lawmakers managed to produce a balanced budget through cuts and restructuring with approved spending some $15 billion lower than the previously approved budget; California, on the other hand, approved a budget that assumed $4 billion in higher-phantom revenue and was only $5.5 billion lower than the prior year's spending.

Lastly, a word on regulatory compliance costs in California. While taxes are easy to measure, and government spending only somewhat less so, regulations are a hidden form of taxation—put into place by lawmakers who draft bills that empower unelected government experts to draw up rules that compel people to act or not to act in a certain way. Some rules are generally regarded as needed, for instance, laws or regulations that improve air and water quality in a common sense, economically efficient manner. Other regulations, for instance, arcane restrictions on the use of private property or restrictive labor rules, are harder to justify. The financial impact on California business amounts to a *de facto* tax of $134,122.48 per small business.[74] And, since

---

[73] The main reason for California's volatility in revenue and spending is that it has a steep and highly progressive income tax structure designed to "soak the rich" – if you consider making over $65,376 per year "rich." This reliance on the income tax leads to huge swings in revenue as capital gains and bonuses in one year give way to losses and no bonuses the next. Texas relies on property taxes and sales taxes, far more stable sources of income.

small businesses are 99.2 percent of all employer businesses in California and all non-employer businesses by definition, this mess of red tape has depressed employment in California by 3.8 *million* jobs—lost jobs that would likely balance California's chronic multibillion dollar budget deficits.

These regulations can have a clear and devastating impact on jobs. In October, 2011, Los Angeles-based oil producer, Occidental Petroleum, the biggest onshore oil producer in the U.S., announced that its oil output would likely decline for the first time since 2005 because of a delay in drilling permits in California. California's bureaucracy that approves oil permits had only granted14 of 199 applications in 2011 vs. 27 of 100 in 2010 and 37 of 52 in 2009—and this in a state with 12.1 percent unemployment. Some economists estimate that drilling permit delays have held up $1 billion in investment and more than 6,000 jobs.[75]

Of course, California can always point to its "green jobs" successes such as Solyndra…

Thus, amidst America's most difficult economy since the Great Depression, Texas continues its competitive advantage over California. The differences between the two largest states in terms of tax and regulatory policy, the legal climate, and respect for property rights appear to have deepened, even as California's economy slips further behind. And, despite sending a delegation of lawmakers to Texas in 2011 led by California's lieutenant governor to learn the secrets of Texas' success, it doesn't look like California will change its ways soon especially when stopping to consider the makeup of the respective state legislative bodies.

In California, 18 percent of the Democrats who control both houses of its full-time legislature worked in business, farming or medicine before being elected. The remainder drew paychecks from government, worked as community organizers, or were attorneys.

In Texas, with its part-time legislature, 75 percent of the Republicans who control both houses earn a living in business, farming, or medicine, with 19 percent being attorneys in private practice, almost all of whom work as transactional attorneys in business, rather than trial attorneys. Texas Democrats are more than twice as likely as their California counterparts to claim private-sector experience outside the field of law.

It may simply reflect the differing values of the two biggest states, but that one state's laws are drafted by makers and the other state's laws by takers, leads in a direct line to vastly different public policy priorities.

Confirming the fact that taxes and regulations factor into decisions by business leaders on where to invest and thus, create jobs, the Governor of Florida, Texas' main big competitor insofar as

---

[74] "Cost of State Regulations on California Small Business Study," by Sanjay B. Varshney, Ph.D., CFA and Dennis H. Tootelian, Ph.D., September, 2009, http://www.sba.ca.gov/Cost%20of%20Regulation%20Study%20-%20Final.pdf.
[75] "Occidental's Oil Output May Decline on Delayed California Drilling Permits," *Bloomberg*, October 19, 2011.

government tax policies that foster a good economic climate, wrote a letter to the Governor of Texas in May, 2011, saying, in part,

> *...congratulations to you and the rest of the Lone Star State on being named the top state for job growth and business development by Chief Executive Magazine. You understand, as I do, that government doesn't create jobs; it creates an environment where businesses can expand and grow.*
>
> *Not only have you achieved this top ranking this year, you have achieved it seven years in a row. Like everything else Texas does, you have done it in a BIG way...*
>
> *Be aware that same survey of CEOs ranked Florida's business friendly environment third in the nation, up from sixth last year. While we are grateful to move up three places, Florida will not settle for third place.*
>
> *In our 21st century economy, business owners can do business anywhere. Every entrepreneur is searching for the best place to get the greatest return on their investment, the best workforce, and the most convenient location. In addition, if possible, they'd like that place to also be a great place to live...*
>
> *Florida is eliminating job killing regulation, reducing the size and cost of government, and making sure we have the best educated workforce. We have no personal income tax and are phasing out the business tax, starting with eliminating it entirely for half the business that paid it. Florida is definitely on the road to be number one. Thank you for giving us the motivation we needed.*
>
> *Sincerely,*
>
> *Rick Scott*

The governor of Florida understands well the advantages of the Texas way of doing things. The following chapters delve into the Texas model—and how it is increasingly under threat from the Federal government.

CHAPTER THREE—TAX A LITTLE, GET A LOT

In the prior chapter, we made detailed comparisons between the eight largest states comprising almost half of the U.S. population. We showed that in measure after measure, Texas outperforms its competitors: in growth, in job creation, and educational results. That it does so while collecting less tax revenue is no coincidence. In fact, much of Texas' success is due to the fact that, as Florida's governor wrote in his letter to his Texas colleague: "…*government doesn't create jobs; it creates an environment where businesses can expand and grow.*"

This chapter takes a close look at the Texas tax system in the context of recent U.S. tax history. What does Texas tax and how much? What are the advantages and disadvantages of this system? And, how might it be made better?

A Brief Modern History of Taxes and Ronald Reagan

When he was the newly-elected governor of California in 1967, Ronald Reagan, only five years after switching his party affiliation from the Democrats to the Republicans, pushed through what was then the largest state tax increase in U.S. history. The top income tax rate went from 7 to 10 percent; sales tax collections went up 67 percent, from 3 percent to 5 percent; corporate taxes were hiked from 5.5 percent to 7 percent; and other taxes were boosted as well. California Democrats still lecture Republicans on how "enlightened" Reagan was for raising taxes then.

But, the Reagan we know today was a tax cutter. Intellectually far more curious than his many critics gave him credit for, Reagan revised his opinion on taxes when he interacted with a trio who made the case that high tax rates depress economic activity. Those three men were economist Dr. Arthur Laffer of "Laffer Curve" fame, Congressman Jack Kemp, and Jude Wanniski, a *Wall Street Journal* editorial writer.

Reagan embraced the concept that cutting taxes would stimulate economic activity, and put that concept to the test in his historic tax cuts of 1981. The top Federal income tax rate was reduced from 70 percent to 50 percent, essentially allowing the most productive taxpayers to keep a whopping 66 percent more of their income (a 70 percent rate means that one would keep 30 cents of every dollar earned vs. keeping 50 cents with a 50 percent rate—an increase in personal income of 66 percent). This unleashed an American economic boom that produced the greatest seven-year burst of economic activity seen in the U.S. up to that time, followed by the longest peace-time economic expansion in American history.

Why mention Reagan and U.S. tax policy at the beginning of a chapter about Texas and its tax policy? Because Texas has followed Reagan's tax-cutting tenets as a means to boost the state's economic performance—and it's worked for Texas as it worked for America when President Kennedy cut taxes in 1961 and when Reagan did so in 1981.[76]

---

[76] The 2001 tax cuts signed into law by President George W. Bush actually resulted in higher taxes for many wealthier taxpayers because of the "Alternative Minimum Tax." The negative impact of this oversight wasn't fixed until 2005, delaying the impact of the tax cuts for the U.S. economy until the verge of the financial crisis of 2008, a crisis largely caused by Federal housing and mortgage loan policies and regulations which caused the housing bubble.

The Laffer Curve, popularized by Dr. Arthur Laffer, is a simple concept based on the idea that a tax rate of zero percent would return nothing to the treasury while a tax rate of 100 percent would also return zero because all economic activity would cease if the government took 100 percent everyone's output. Thus, a rate of somewhere between zero and 100 would generate the greatest revenue for government—assuming that that's what lawmakers wanted.

One would think that Dr. Laffer's idea makes sense and should be uncontroversial, but it isn't. Many believers in big government and wealth redistribution see the tax code as something more than a way to generate revenue for government operations and programs—they also see it as a way to level society, taking from those who have more so as to give more to those who have less. Ironically, this attitude leads to high tax rates which in turn, if too high, can actually depress government tax revenue. This is such an elemental concept that, back in 1377 A.D., an Arab scholar by the name of Ibn Khaldun wrote about it:[77]

> *In the early stages of the state, taxes are light... but generate a large revenue... As time passes (government's) needs and exigencies grow... Hence they impose fresh taxes... and sharply raise the rate of old taxes to increase their yield... But the effects on business of this rise in taxation make themselves felt. For business men are soon discouraged by the comparison of their profits with the burden of their taxes... Consequently production falls off, and with it the yield of taxation.*

Thus, tax law writers can either design a tax code to maximize revenue, balancing the desire for taxes with the public good of economic growth and wealth creation, or they can design a tax code to soak the rich—pick one.

Or, as Dr. Laffer has previously noted:[78]

> *In more technical terms, in an economy the income effects of a transfer sum to zero. The people who receive the transfer do spend and employ more, that's true, but it is equally as true that the people who pay the transfer spend less and employ less. The net of all the income effects of government spending is therefore zero. The substitution effects, however, accumulate to discourage production everywhere. Just imagine what would happen to total Texas output if the government transferred 100% of GSP, so that everyone who worked and produced received nothing and all those who didn't work and didn't produce received everything. Output and employment would be zero.*

Unmoved by an academic treatment of tax rates? Here's a recent example to consider. In 2010, cash-strapped Illinois lawmakers increased income taxes by 67 percent for individuals while hiking the corporate income tax to 9.5 percent, the fourth-highest in America. This unwise action has increased pressure on business to leave the state as business receipts have increased by $300

---

[77] "Al-Muqqadima" (the Introduction [to history]), by Ibn Khaldun. (The author studied Ibn Khaldun at American University in Cairo, Egypt.)
[78] "Texas Fiscal Future," by Arthur Laffer, Ph.D., 2011.

million—but, with an ongoing $8 billion deficit. [79] However, to try to keep business in the state, the governor has doled out $230 million in corporate welfare, leaving a net to the state treasury of only $70 million. The CEO of a large financial services firm headquartered in Illinois testified to a state legislative committee that his shareholders wanted him to move out of Illinois due to tax hikes that hit his firm for $50 million alone ($50 million buys a lot of moving help). As Illinois most-productive citizens and most-profitable firms leave, who will be left to fund government?

Texas Taxes

States raise the vast majority of their revenue through three basic taxes: property, income and sales. The proportion they raise from each and the total amount they collect from their taxpayers varies greatly from state-to-state.

The Tax Foundation, whose data we cited earlier, says this about Texas taxes:[80]

Texas' State and Local Tax Burden Among Nation's Lowest
- Texas' state and local tax burden is currently estimated at 7.9% of income (45th nationally), below the national average of 9.8%. Compared to the 1977 data, Texas had a tax burden of 7.9% (48th nationally), remaining relatively constant. Currently Texas taxpayers pay $3,197 per capita in state and local taxes.

Texas' 2012 Business Tax Climate Ranks 9th
- Texas ranks 9th nationally in the Tax Foundation's State Business Tax Climate Index. The Index compares the states in five areas of taxation that impact business: corporate taxes; individual income taxes; sales taxes; unemployment insurance taxes; and taxes on property, including residential and commercial property. Neighboring states rank as follows: New Mexico (38th), Oklahoma (33rd), Arkansas (31st) and Louisiana (32nd).

Texas Levies No Personal Income Taxes
- Texas levies no individual income taxes, joining six other states with the same policy.

Texas Corporate Income Tax System
- Texas, in addition to collecting no personal income taxes, collects no corporate income taxes. However, the state recently instituted a gross receipts tax called the Texas Margins tax. It went into effect January 1, 2007. Texas joins Washington, Delaware, Michigan and Ohio as the only states that levy an economy-wide gross receipts tax.

Texas Sales and Excise Taxes
- Texas levies a 6.25% general sales or use tax on consumers, slightly above the national median of 6.0%. In 2009, Texas state and local governments collected $1,081 per person in general sales taxes and $543 per person in excise taxes, for a combined figure of $1,624, which ranked 12th highest nationally. Texas' gasoline tax stands at 20 cents per gallon, ranking 38th highest nationally. Texas' cigarette tax stands at $1.41 per pack of twenty and ranks 23rd highest nationally. The sales tax was adopted in 1961, the gasoline tax in 1923 and the cigarette tax in 1931.

Texas Property Taxes
- Texas local governments collected $1,475 per capita in property taxes during fiscal year 2009, which is the latest year the Census Bureau published state-by-state property tax collections. Texas is one of the 13 states that collect no state-level property taxes. Its per capita property tax collections in FY2009 rank 14th highest nationally.

---

[79] "Illinois Tax Firesale: A case study in high corporate rates and special favors," Opinion, *Wall Street Journal*, June 11, 2011.
[80] "The Facts on Texas's Tax Climate," Tax Foundation, http://www.taxfoundation.org/research/topic/60.html.

So, a non-partisan, national tax analysis foundation says that the overall state and local tax burden in Texas is 45th nationally and that this burden has been "relatively constant" for more than 30 years. But, while Texas has no income tax, it does have the 14th highest property taxes in the nation and its sales taxes are "slightly above the national median."

In other words, Texas taxes have been light and steady over the years. And, while Texas' low rate of taxation is important to business formation, the mix of taxes it collects is important too, since any tax collected operates to depress the particular activity being taxed (with the exception that estate taxes probably don't slow the rate of death, since living is its own reward). Sales taxes reduce consumption. Income taxes reduce the incentive to earn. Business taxes discourage entrepreneurship, and so on. But, taxes are a necessary evil, so some means of revenue must be found for government. The policy challenge for lawmakers is to make taxes as inconsequential as possible for society as a whole and the free market in particular.

In 2008, Texas collected 39 percent of its state and local revenue from property taxes, 31 percent from sales taxes, and 30 percent from other taxes, such as taxes on fuel, a franchise tax, and insurance (taxes on oil and natural gas production only amount to about 4 percent of taxes collected[81,82]) while collecting none from either personal or corporate income taxes.[83]

Thus, compared to other states, the relatively lighter Texas tax burden, with its emphasis on property taxes and sales taxes, with no income tax, would tend to discourage consumption (sales) and investment (property) while also discouraging land speculation (probably one factor in the low cost of Texas real estate) while encouraging productivity (income).

Ideally, a state's tax system should be simple to administer, adequate to fund needed government with a stable stream of revenue, and fairly applied or neutral in not picking winners and losers.

In this regard, income taxes fail on most accounts because income tends to fluctuate far more than property values or sales, thus causing sharp peaks and valleys of government revenue that exacerbate budget planning. Further, unlike property taxes and sales taxes, income taxes and corporate taxes tend to be subject to the most strenuous lobbying, leading, over time, to a highly-complex, loophole-filled tax code designed as much to reward the well-connected and direct economic activity as it is to raise money for the treasury. This manipulation of the markets by tax code so as to pick winners and losers results in higher marginal rates for the people and businesses who cannot afford recourse to high-priced and well-connected lobbyists.

---

[81] "Window on State Government," website maintained by the Comptroller of the State of Texas, data for fiscal year 2010, http://www.window.state.tx.us/taxbud/revenue.html.

[82] By comparison, Alaska, another state without an income tax, gets about 77 percent of its state revenue from "other" taxes, mostly taxes on oil production, an almost 20 times greater reliance on oil revenue to fuel state government than Texas.

[83] "Sources of State and Local Tax Revenue, Fiscal Year 2008," Tax Foundation, February 24, 2011, http://www.taxfoundation.org/taxdata/show/1739.html.

Tax transparency is important as well. By tax transparency, we mean that the average citizen should be able to see and understand the tax incurred and be able to make informed decisions about the level of government services desired in exchange for the taxes imposed. In this regard, the business tax has poor transparency, as businesses don't really pay taxes, but rather, simply pass the cost of taxes onto the consumer in the form of higher prices. Thus, insofar as transparency is concerned, a conventional sales tax that only charges the end-user is the most transparent—everyone participating in the economy sees the sales tax with every purchase.

Further, sales taxes are simply administered, with the seller needing only to add the tax onto the price of the product, then pass the tax collected onto the government. This simplicity eliminates the need for large organizations of government auditors, accountants, appraisers, and associated infrastructure such as appraisal districts and review boards, and income tax bureaus. Lastly, unlike with personal or corporate income taxes, businesses and taxpayers are incentivized to spend time figuring out perfectly legal, but often arcane ways to avoid paying tax—freeing up otherwise productive people to do something else with their time.

Sales taxes are also the least economically distorting class of taxes as they focus on consumption rather than investment or income. This eliminates preferential treatment of businesses over non-businesses—entities whose tax status is determined by the nature of their paperwork.

Lastly, a state with a greater reliance on sales vs. income taxes, encourages people and businesses to invest, promoting productivity gains which typically translate into income gains.

Perhaps that's why, in only one year (2007), the nine states without a personal income tax gained a net of 235,000 new residents from states that levied an income tax.[84] These internal "pioneers" brought their work ethic, talent, and capital to their new homes of choice, boosting the net adjusted income of the states they moved to by $12 billion in 2007.[85]

Further, over a ten year period ending 2006, the nine states without an income tax saw an average personal income growth of 79.2 percent while the nine states with this highest marginal income tax rates had personal income growth of 59.6 percent. Again proving how lower taxes on productivity and work reward productiveness and hard work.

Taxes: The Bottom Line Impact on Two Businesses
A practical example is in order here. Most small business owners pay personal income tax at the Federal, and, if their state has an income tax, at the state level as well. Imagine that there are two business owners, one lives in Dallas, Texas, the other, in San Diego, California. Married, they pay themselves $100,000 and have taxable income of $70,000. The business owner in San Diego has a house worth $650,000. In Texas, the house is larger and has more land, but is worth $450,000. So, what are the taxes they pay at the state level?

---

[84] "Cost of Government Day 2009," a report by Americans for Tax Reform.
[85] Source: U.S. Census Bureau and the Bureau of Economic Analysis.

The Texas resident pays no income tax, pays $7,024.08 in property taxes on their home valued at 25 percent above the median Dallas home price, and pays 8.25 percent sales tax on $13,000 worth of items purchased totaling $1,072.50 and, lastly, a gas tax on 800 gallons of fuel purchased yearly at $0.20 per gallon equaling $160.00 for a total state and local tax liability of $8,256.58, or a marginal rate of 8.26 percent on gross income or 11.8 percent on taxable income.

The California business owner pays an income tax of $2,491 on their taxable income of $70,000, $4,650 in property taxes on their San Diego home valued at 25 percent above the median sales price, pays a 7.75 percent sales tax rate (some areas are as high as 8.75 percent) on $13,000 in retail purchases for a total of $1,007.50, and gas taxes of $0.18 cents a gallon, plus a sales tax on the gas and the tax, plus a $0.015 per gallon "fee" for a total of $247.96 with a total state and local tax liability of $8,396.46, or a marginal rate of 8.4 percent on gross income or 12.0 percent on taxable income.

Each taxpayer can deduct from their Federal income taxes the property taxes they paid, and either state income taxes or sales taxes paid. This saves the Texas taxpayer some $2,024 and the California taxpayer $1,785, leaving the difference between the two taxpayers' tax liability a rather small $379 per year, or, less than 0.4 percent of their respective gross incomes.

But, watch what happens if our small business owners work harder, secure financing, and expand their businesses, boosting their gross income to $125,000 with taxable income of $95,000. Assuming they both buy the same amount of stuff and gasoline, the state tax liability for the Texas business owner remains the same as there's no income tax—essentially, no tax on increased productivity. But, the California business owner is about to get a rude surprise: their state income tax bill jumps over $2,000 from $2,491 to $4,492, an 80 percent increase in taxes for a 35.7 percent increase in taxable income!

Before taking into account Federal deductibility of state taxes, the marginal tax rate for the Texas business owner drops from 11.8 percent of taxable income to 9.2 percent—remember, their tax bill remained the same the state level—they just earned more that year, and likely employed more people, stimulating the economy. In contrast, the marginal tax rate on taxable income for the California business owner went from 12.0 percent to 11.6 percent (an all-inclusive figure that takes into account property, sales, and gas taxes) while they were paying $2,001 more on that $25,000 in new income.

Now, let's say that these business owners create a new service that really takes off with the public. They risk more capital and boost their gross income to $200,000 with a taxable income of $170,000. The Texas business owner, you guessed it, sees the same tax bill, dropping their marginal rate from the initial 11.8 percent to 4.6 percent while the California business owner sees their marginal rates on taxable income go from 12.0 percent to 10.3 percent. Importantly, on the increase in taxable income from $70,000 to $170,000, the Texan pays no additional state taxes while the Californian sees his income tax bill go from $2,491 to $11,655, a tax increase of 368 percent on an income increase of 143 percent. This means that the Texas business owner gets to keep $9,304 more of his income every year than the Californian—or, about $7,344 after deducting the additional state taxes on the Federal tax return (amounting to a subsidy from low-tax states such as Texas to high tax states like California). Seen another way, while the Texan's state tax bill remains the same, he will pay $1,960 more in Federal income taxes than the Californian since the Californian can deduct the higher state income taxes from his Federal return.

At what point does the California business owner begin to feel like the business owners in Ibn Khaldun's time?

> *But the effects on business of this rise in taxation make themselves felt. For business men are soon discouraged by the comparison of their profits with the burden of their taxes...*

Of course, some Americans of a more liberal persuasion might claim it *unfair* that Texas collects no state income tax while other states do, noting that, as Texans become more successful, they pay no additional state taxes. But is this really the case?

In our prior example, we assumed that the two business owners we compared continued to live in the same house and spend the same amount of money. But, what might the Texan do with after tax income $7,344 higher than his California counterpart? He could expand his business more quickly, hiring more people or giving greater benefits so as to improve employee retention. He could invest in equipment, improving his productivity. Or, he could decide to buy a better car or a larger house or the latest big screen TV—in which case, he's going to pay more sales tax or property tax.

The point being this: California taxes *success* while Texas taxes the *results* of the success.

Thus, the lack of an income tax and the low overall tax rate of Texas matters greatly when it comes to fostering entrepreneurship. This low tax philosophy is a big driver of Texas' consistently high growth in both population and in income.

2006: Did Texas Raise Taxes?

In 2006, a major lawsuit over the equity of public school funding threatened to upend the entire tax structure of Texas. The judicial branch ruled that funding schools through local property taxes resulted in unequal funding for education, with Texans residing in low real estate value areas getting far less per student funding than those from wealthy neighborhoods.

Less than three years before, Nevada, one of nine states without an income tax, faced a similar judicial showdown over taxes and school funding. Facing slowing revenues in the wake of the post-9/11 decline in tourism, Nevada's governor, Kenny Guinn, a moderate Republican, asked the Legislature for a massive tax increase to fund schools. Nevada has a two-thirds legislative vote requirement to raise taxes, and the Legislature fell short, so Guinn sued the lawmakers: he wanted his taxes. The Nevada Supreme Court intervened to give the Governor his tax hike, saying that the governmental duty to fund schools was higher than the state constitutional requirement, approved by 70 percent of the voters via initiative in 1996, for a two-thirds vote to approve taxes. A countersuit in Federal court threatened to upend the tax increase by judicial fiat under the Republican Guaranty Clause of the U.S. Constitution. But, before the case could be settled, the Nevada State Senate provided the two-thirds vote needed for $836 million in new taxes.

With events in Nevada providing a fresh understanding of what a state supreme court might do to demand compliance with its mandates, elected officials in Texas were faced with a choice: they could take the easy way out and simply raise taxes, as did the Nevadans, or they could try to meet the court's demands while keeping Texas as competitive as possible. They chose the latter course.

All states except Alaska generate the vast majority of their tax revenue from three sources: income taxes (personal and corporate); sales taxes; and property taxes. Lacking income taxes, Texas relied far more heavily on property taxes. The challenge with the court's education funding equity demand was to develop an alternative funding mechanism while maintaining Texas' historically low tax rates.

The true test of success would be the measure of state and local taxes paid as a percentage of personal income before and after the dust settled on the tax law changes. As mentioned previously, the Tax Foundation estimated that the total state and local tax burden of Texans in 1977 was 7.9 percent of income, the 48th-least taxed state. In 2005, the year before the changes, Texas ranked as the 45th-least taxed state with residents paying 7.5 percent of income. The 2006 tax law changed Texas' ranking to 47th-least taxed state with 7.5 percent of income paid to state and local governments. By 2009, Texas ranked 45th, with 7.9 percent of income paid to state and local government, the same level it was 22 years previously, causing the Tax Foundation to remark that taxes in Texas "remain(ed) relatively constant."

The 2006 tax changes were as follows: school property taxes were cut by $7 billion as much as one-third, while a new margins tax was levied on business (replacing a franchise tax that many businesses avoided altogether by structuring themselves as limit liability partnerships), nearly tripling their tax obligations. Taxes on tobacco were also increased by $1.5 billion per year—but even after the increase, Texas ranked 23rd in cigarette taxes among the states.[86] This totaled $5.9 billion in new taxes, offset by $7 billion in property taxes.

Conservative critics of the tax plan called it the largest tax increase in Texas history. But, this criticism rings false as the total amount taxed didn't go up; it went down—the source of the revenue simply changed under pressure from the courts from property taxes to taxes on the gross margins of business. Disproving the notion that the 2006 tax law changes amounted to a tax increase, State Representative Jim Dunnam, the House Democratic Leader, said that all of the new revenue generated from the business tax and tobacco tax would go to offset property taxes, observing, "This tax bill provides not one penny for public education, and it never will."[87]

---

[86] "State Cigarette Excise Tax Rates, as of January 1, 2011," The Tax Foundation, http://www.taxfoundation.org/taxdata/show/26076.html.
[87] "Business tax plan OK'd by House," *The Dallas Morning News*, by Terrence Stutz, April 25, 2006.

Beyond the rhetoric of whether or not 2006's tax law changes amounted to an increase in taxation, economic growth in Texas marched on, consistently outperforming the rest of the nation.

Economic Development: The Lure of Picking Winners and Losers

Lastly, a word on special tax breaks, credits, and state-run investment programs, generally known under the rubric of "economic development." The Tax Foundation correctly notes that, as a state tax code becomes more complex and the rates go higher, the impact on business gets more onerous, often leading lawmakers to approve targeted incentives for favored businesses (read, the ones most connected to political power, usually through campaign donations and lobbyists).

A high-profile example of this are film production credits to entice Hollywood out of California (or, in California's case, to keep Hollywood in Hollywood). New Jersey Governor Chris Christie recently cancelled a $420,000 subsidy for MTV to film Jersey Shore in Jersey, the so-called "Snooki" tax credit. The problem with such subsidies is that they are a symptom of a larger problem—in New Jersey's case, that they rank 48th in the nation in their Tax Foundation business climate index.

So, as business feels the pressure, and some close up or leave the state, the temptation grows in legislative halls to "do something." Because creating special rules, programs, and credits looks more like "doing something" than lowering tax rates for everyone, without playing favorites (plus, there's the benefit of raking in campaign donations from favored interests), that's what lawmakers tilt towards doing.[88]

As is often the case in things political, there has been a fair amount of attention of late on Texas' economic development programs, as if they are a prime driver of Texas' huge job growth. But, while Texas has such programs, their scale is minor compared to other states. For example, the much talked about Texas Enterprise Fund has disbursed about $363 million since 2003, about $45 million per year in a $1.3 trillion economy—about 3/1,000[ths] of one percent of Texas' output. Texas spends one-tenth the amount on this program as Michigan does on their equivalent state-run effort—but Texas' population and economy is some three times larger, meaning that the Michigan program is about 30 times larger proportionally. Yet, Michigan is hemorrhaging jobs while Texas is adding them.

The bottom line is that targeted incentives and time-limited subsidies are a poor substitute for a broad-based tax reform that lowers rates while simplifying the tax code.

Lawmakers, influenced by big campaign donors and tax lobbyists, make very poor deciders of economic winners and losers. No matter the temptation, they should resist the urge and follow the Texas model of a modest level of taxation, simply administered.

---

[88] Again, perhaps not unsurprisingly, Ibn Khaldun saw this as a problem in his time too, warning of the negative effects of governments intervening in the marketplace when government spending exceeded tax revenues, *Al Muqqadima*, Chapter 38.

CHAPTER FOUR—THE LAWSUIT CLIMATE IN TEXAS

Why does frivolous lawsuit reform matter? Because, according to one study, America spends 2.2 percent of its GDP on lawsuits, double that of Germany and more than triple that of economic competitors France and the United Kingdom.[89] While another study pegs lawsuit costs even higher, at $589 *billion* per year.[90] Or, put another way, almost $2,000 per year for every man, woman and child in America in the form of higher prices, greater insurance costs, more taxes, fewer doctors, smaller paychecks, and fewer patents.

Because most civil actions are filed in state courts, frivolous lawsuit reform at the state level is the prime driver in reducing the economic drag caused by excessive use of the courts by people looking to get rich off of an accident or an error.

A Brief Texas Legal History[91]

The nature of Texas' origin impacted the development of the state's legal system. As a territory of Spain, then Mexico, the Texas legal system operated under Spanish rules, then the Mexican Constitution of 1824. It wasn't until 1840, when Texas operated as an independent nation, that some aspects of English common law were adopted. The 1876 post-Reconstruction-era Texas constitution featured an "open courts" provision, construed to grant access to the legal system for all Texans. Further, neither English common law, nor Texas legal experience up to that time, countenanced non-economic damages—the classic "pain and suffering" awards—these being developed over more than 100 years, not by the Legislature, but by the judicial system itself.

It's this latter point, the internal development of the civil law, which likely walled off the legal system from efforts to reform it for many years. Without direction from the people's elected representatives, the courts saw creation of the legal concepts of class action lawsuits, contingency fee contracts for plaintiffs, strict liability for product manufacturers, expanded claims for noneconomic damages, punitive damages and other legal mechanisms that saw a rapid increase in the volume and value of lawsuits beginning in the 1960s.

Prior to this ramping up of lawsuits, accountants and architects, contractors and corporate directors alike found it unnecessary to carry liability insurance. But today, all practicing doctors and most professionals carry liability policies and, with a policy in place, the incentive to sue ironically became greater as lawyers and their clients now had reliably deep pockets to pick. This vicious circle placed ever greater resources into the hands of the trial bar while increasing the economic cost of doing business in Texas. It even began to impact the lives of every day Texans as people adjusted their behavior to avoid even the slightest risks.

---

[89] "U.S. Tort Costs and Cross-Border Perspectives," Tillinghast–Towers Perrin.

[90] "Jackpot Justice," Pacific Research Institute.

[91] For this section and a subsequent summary of the 2003 legal reforms passed by the Texas Legislature, the author is indebted to former State Representative Joseph M. Nixon and his May, 2008 paper, "A History of Lawsuit Reform in Texas," Texas Public Policy Foundation, http://www.texaspolicy.com/pdf/2008-05-RR04-tortreform-jnixon-posting.pdf.

Growing mindful of the unintended economic consequences of rampant use of the civil justice system, the Legislature passed a bill in 1977 limiting damages to $500,000 in medical malpractice suits. The law was overturned in 1988 by the Texas Supreme Court which ruled a medical liability cap a violation of the 1876 "open courts" provision of the state constitution. Further, the Texas Supreme Court ruled that only the courts, not the Legislature, had the standing to amend common law practice. In making the ruling the judges appeared to forget that it was the Legislature itself that incorporated the part of English common law that didn't conflict with the positive laws that they themselves had approved.

As public awareness of the lawsuit problem grew, three significant legal reform groups sprang up from 1986 to 1994: the Texas Civil Justice League, Citizens Against Lawsuit Abuse, and Texans for Lawsuit Reform. The latter group, Texans for Lawsuit Reform, formed a political action committee that provided a needed political counterweight to the prohibitive power of the trial bar—power protected by both money and legal precedent. The trial attorneys' power was further strengthened by a 1988 Texas Supreme Court ruling which prevented the Legislature from passing laws aimed at reforming lawsuits. In effect, the courts ruled that they were immune from legislative branch oversight. This left a state constitutional amendment voted on by the people as the sole route for civil justice system reform.

The drive for lawsuit reform became a major political issue in the gubernatorial campaign of 1994, pitting Governor Ann Richards against George W. Bush. Bush won, partly because of his commitment to tackle lawsuit reform—welcome news in a state that was already known as the lawsuit capital of the world.

While the public easily grasped that the civil justice system needed fixing, the complexities of the system itself defied easy answers. Texans for Lawsuit Reform offered a detailed, 11-point program for 1995 Legislative Session. Eight major tort reforms were passed during the session, despite the collaboration between the Democratic majority and trial bar which blocked more extensive reforms.

Despite these reforms and others passed in 1999, by 2003 Texas remained a "judicial hell hole" and a "lawsuit Mecca" with lawsuits national in scope being brought in Texas for resolution because of tightened Federal Court rules. Medical malpractice insurance premiums were driving doctors out of the state, as getting sued became a bigger part of the practice of medicine than healing patients. The U.S. Chamber of Commerce ranked Texas' legal system 46th-worst in the nation, alongside states such as: California, 45th; Louisiana, 47th; Alabama, 48th; West Virginia, 49th; and Mississippi, 50th.[92] Texas' challenges were manifold. According to detailed surveys returned to the U.S. Chamber of Commerce every year, the Texas legal system lagged behind its counterparts, with complaints about excessive damage awards, runaway juries, and judicial fairness and competence.

---

[92] "2010 State Liability Systems Ranking Study, Table 70," U.S. Chamber of Commerce, http://www.uschamber.com/sites/default/files/reports/2010LawsuitClimateReport.pdf.

Governor Rick Perry declared the medical liability situation a state-wide crisis. Importantly, prior to this declaration, a historic political shift had occurred in the Legislature, with the 2002 legislative district boundary redistricting leading to Republican control of the state House and Senate for the first time in 130 years. The trial attorneys' allies were out of power; reform was possible.

House Bill 4 was introduced in 2003 to address the growing lawsuit problem. The 96-page bill dealing with a broad array of legal reforms was debated in the House for two weeks—the longest debate in Texas history. Some 375 amendments were offered on the floor, most by the trial bar's allies with the intention of weakening the bill. Very few passed. In the end, strong bi-partisan majorities in both houses approved the bill and it went to the governor's desk for approval with the *Wall Street Journal* calling the law, "Ten Gallon Tort Reform." The medical malpractice lawsuit reform law didn't go into effect until September 1, 2003 with the needed amendments in the state constitution being approved by voters via ballot initiative on September 13, 2003.[93]

With some regional exceptions, such as east coastal Beaumont near the Louisiana border,[94] the legal climate in Texas is wholly different, and better, today than it was in 2002.

The U.S. Chamber ranked Texas' legal system 36th in the nation in 2010. More importantly, as the average legal survey score improved from 52.7 in 2002 to 57.9 in 2010, Texas' score went from 45.2 to 56.3—from 7.5 points below average, closing the gap to 1.6 points below the national mean, an improvement of 11.1 points and 10 places in the national ranking. Texas' pace of legal system improvement was more than double the national average, joining only four other states in seeing a relative ranking increase of 10 or more from 2002 to 2010.

An alternative ranking by the Pacific Research Institute completed in 2010, looks more narrowly at the issue of lawsuit awards, or torts. This "U.S. Tort Liability Index" ranks Texas 18th in the nation, with Ohio the only state among the eight largest states to rate more highly than Texas at 15th. The other six large states are a trial lawyer's dream, according to the study, with California ranked 41st, Michigan 43rd, Pennsylvania 46th, Illinois 47th, Florida 48th, and New York 49th.[95]

Clearly, something remarkable happened in Texas courtrooms over the past nine years.

Most observers name two reasons for the Lone Star State's legal metamorphosis: 2003's lawsuit reform law that broke the political hammer lock of the Texas trial bar, and the appointment of hundreds of judges over ten years by the governor.[96] Regarding the latter, six of the nine jurists on the Texas Supreme Court were appointed by Governor Rick Perry, with only one of the ten

---

[93] After noting the 10-year battle in the courts in California over the constitutionality of California's medical malpractice lawsuit reform law, Texas lawmakers decided to link their statutory changes with a constitutional amendment to be approved by the voters so as to provide certainty for both doctors and insurance carriers.
[94] Ibid. p. 12.
[95] "U.S. Tort Liability Index: 2010 Report," by Lawrence J. McQuillan and Hovannes Abramyan, June 2010, Pacific Research Institute, http://www.pacificresearch.org/docLib/20100525_Tort_Liability_Index_2010.pdf.
[96] Judges in Texas stand for election as they have since the 1870s, but most resign before their term is up, allowing the governor to appoint to fill the vacancy, and, once appointed, can run as a hard-to-defeat incumbent.

appointments he's made over the years, Xavier Rodriguez, losing an election. Supreme Court Justice Don Willett said Perry's judicial appointments reflect an "unabashedly conservative" judicial philosophy.

House Bill 4 encompassed a broad range of reforms, the most controversial of which was medical malpractice reform.

Lawsuit Reform: Good Medicine

Perhaps the most studied and controversial lawsuit reform in Texas was the 2003 law that limited non-economic medical malpractice awards from $250,000 to $750,000, depending on the defendants in the case.[97] Awarding damages for non-economic claims—pain and suffering—was the prime driver in spiraling medical malpractice insurance premiums. The rising cost to obtain medical malpractice insurance, needed for any doctor to practice medicine without the prospect of lawsuit-driven bankruptcy hanging over his head, served as growing disincentive for doctors to practice medicine in Texas prior to 2003. Further, the higher costs for insurance, in many cases, well over $60,000 per year in premium payments, had to be passed along to patients.

As with any significant reform, there were powerful interests on both sides of the issue. The trial bar claimed that limited non-economic damages would make it more difficult for patients who had been harmed by medical error to seek economic relief. Doctors said it would lead to more doctors practicing medicine and greater healthcare access. Insurance companies claimed that medical liability insurance premiums would decline. These claims and counter-claims are fairly measurable. With it being eight years since the reforms were passed, it should be easy to see what happened in Texas.

Further, Texas wasn't the first state to enact such reforms. Uncharacteristically, in light of its recent political drift, California led the way with the Medical Injury Compensation Reform Act of 1975 (MICRA). In the early 1970s in California, medical malpractice insurance rates rose more than 300 percent in a few years because liability claims grew more frequent and awards grew larger. Doctors, especially those in higher-risk practices, such as neurosurgery and obstetrics, were unable to obtain insurance or couldn't afford it. They left medicine. There was even a widespread physicians strike in 1975. Californians were beginning to find it more difficult to access healthcare.

In 1975, California's once and future governor, Jerry Brown, called a special legislative session to address the medical "malpractice crisis." The result was a bipartisan agreement to limit attorney contingency fees on a sliding scale, limit so-called pain and suffering damages to $250,000, focus compensation on true economic damages, such as medical costs and lost wages, and other reforms.

---

[97] The non-economic exposure for physicians is $250,000, a similar $250,000 cap applies to a hospital or nursing home, and a third $250,000 cap applies if a third, unrelated institution is brought into the case. In most instances the practical cap is $500,000 since one or more physicians and a hospital are enjoined in most medical liability lawsuits. At least thirty states place a non-economic or total dollar cap on awards in medical liability lawsuits. The $500,000 practical cap places Texas in the mean when compared to other state caps.

As with Texas, California's powerful trial bar claimed that there would be severe repercussions for patients in reforming medical liability rules. But, to the contrary, California's reform has increased patient access to healthcare, by providing some of the lowest malpractice insurance premiums in the nation. This has saved California's healthcare system billions of dollars annually while getting patients injured through medical error their financial compensation 26 percent more quickly than in states without similar reforms (this, due to the ability to have binding arbitration among other reasons). More significantly, after reform, injured patients, not lawyers, get the majority of the financial payout.

Not unsurprisingly, trial attorneys and their allies claim that Texas' success in reforming medical liability rules hasn't benefitted patients and hasn't resulted in higher numbers of doctors practicing medicine in Texas. An October 2011 article by an academic who once aided lawyers who cashed in on the nationwide multi-billion dollar tobacco lawsuit as an "ethics" advisor asserted that the rate of per capita growth of doctors in Texas was actually higher *before* the 2003 reform than in the years afterwards.[98] Further, the academic asserted that Texas had 61 fewer doctors per 100,000 people seeing patients than the national average in 2002 slipping to 76.5 doctors below the national average in 2010. If true, these allegations would make a serious dent in the case for tort reform.

The data is correct, but highly misleading in that the years chosen to calculate the number of doctors and the impact of medical liability reform don't account for the delayed response in medical insurance premiums following passage of the law and doctors' response to the reality of their changing premium costs or even the very availability of insurance to begin with.

Similar to the timeline seen in California in the years leading up to the medical malpractice insurance crisis that resulted in the passage of its 1975 reform law, Texas also saw a growing crisis in the years leading up to 2003, with growth in number of doctors per capita slowing to a crawl by 2003 then showing a sharp decline in 2004, the year *after* the reform became law. Other than a huge influx of new people moving to Texas (which was happening), why would the number of doctors per capita decline after passage of a reform meant to boost their numbers?

According to Jon Opelt, the Executive Director of the Texas Alliance for Patient Access, the cost of medical liability insurance in Texas doubled from 1999 to 2003. By the summer of 2002, 6,200 Texas physicians, mainly in high-risk fields such as obstetrics, found themselves dropped from their liability coverage by insurance companies that were losing money to the surge in lawsuits. Without insurance, a doctor cannot obtain hospital privileges.

Soon after passage of the reforms, only one major insurance carrier reduced rates by 12 percent. Other carriers, financially weakened and wary of Texas' legal climate, didn't follow suit until February 2004.

---

[98] "Guest Column: No Better Care, Thanks to Tort Reform," by Charles M. Silver, *Texas Tribune*, October 24, 2011, http://www.texastribune.org/texas-health-resources/health-reform-and-texas/guest-column-no-better-care-thanks-tort-reform/.

By 2004, the number of doctors dropped from coverage by financially drained insurance carriers had risen to 9,000—the cause of the crisis had been addressed, but the damage was still working its way through the system. Further, the statistics didn't capture the fact that half of the physicians in high-risk fields had restricted their practices: refusing to deliver babies, for example. It wasn't until 2005 that the number of doctors in Texas began to rise significantly.

Thus the critics of the Texas lawsuit reforms cynically choose to measure 1996 as the starting point for their claims, years before Texas fell into crisis. (As Mr. Opelt observes: a mathematical sleight of hand allowed them to gloss over the downturn numbers in the crisis period, in the same way one could measure GDP in the mid 1920's, renew the count in the early 1940's and thus explain away The Great Depression as if it were a mere nuisance.)

That doctors would respond to cost incentives, just like most people or businesses do, should be a given: people change their behavior when money is involved. With that in mind, it is interesting to note that City of New York Mayor Michael Bloomberg contacted the Texas Alliance for Patient Access to inquire about why it was that almost 1,300 doctors had left New York for Texas from 2003 to 2011. The Texas Alliance for Patient Access noted that, in 2003, Texas physicians were paying slightly more in medical malpractice insurance than doctors in New York. Today, Texas doctors pay half of what they did in 2003 for liability insurance, with rates returning to their 1999 levels while New York doctors pay 63 percent *more*—and that amount is subsidized by the state.[99] The total insurance savings for Texas doctors amounts to $1.6 billion in reduced premiums since 2003.

In Houston, for example, a doctor practicing family medicine paid $11,127 for a liability policy in 2001 to Texas Medical Liability Trust, Texas' largest medical liability firm. By 2003, that premium soared to $17,044. In 2011, with a renewal dividend, the cost for insurance dipped to $7,827, a reduction of 54 percent. For the high-risk fields of obstetrics and neurosurgery, the numbers were even more dramatic. Ob/Gyn rates spiked from $35,091 in 2001 to $53,752 in 2003 then retreated to $25,667 in 2011, eight years after passage of the reform law, a decline of 52 percent while rates for a neurosurgeon went from $68,177 in 2001 to $104,433 in 2003 then $47,959 in 2011, a decline of 54 percent, a savings of more than $56,000 per year.

Figure 27 clearly tracks the positive results of 2003's lawsuit reforms as it charts the medical liability cases in the greater Houston area of Harris County. Note the spike in cases in 2003 as lawyers rushed to file lawsuits before the new law went into effect—yet another reason why doctors continued to flee Texas through 2004. In the three years leading up to reform, there was more than one lawsuit for every three doctors in Harris County—defending against medical malpractice claims had to have grabbed the attention of the region's doctors. In 2009 the lawsuit rate was one lawsuit for every 12 doctors in the prior three years, a four-fold decline from the trial attorney feeding frenzy of 2001 to 2003.

Another claim made by those opposed to Texas' medical malpractice reform law is that the number of doctors per capita in Texas has fallen further behind the national average than it was

---

[99] Source: Medical Liability Monitor.

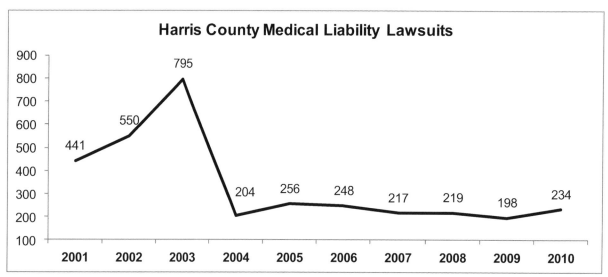

Figure 27—Lawsuits against doctors soared in Texas' largest county, home to Houston, but are now half of what they were before the lawsuit reforms.

in 2003. Again it is important to note that the exodus of doctors fleeing the toxic lawsuit environment in Texas didn't reverse until 2005—things had gotten so bad that doctors who had made the decision to leave in 2003 made the move in 2004, a year when Texas saw the largest drop in direct patient care physicians per capita in 20 years.

Since 2004, however, Texas has shown strong gains in the growth of doctors. That said, the population of Texas grew by 20.6 percent from 2000 to 2010, about double the national average. As a state's population expands and the need for medical services grows, doctors respond to the increased demand for their services—but this is a lagging phenomenon, especially among established doctors who have to uproot their existing practices and start over in another state.

According to the Federal Department of Health and Human Services, Texas ranked 10th in the nation in the percentage per capita growth of patient care physicians from 2003 to 2008. It was 23rd five years before.

Further, since 2006, Texas has licensed at least 60 percent more new doctors each year than was the case in the years before lawsuit reform. This surge in physician interest in practicing in Texas has taken its own toll, as the licensing bureaucracy has struggled to process new applications with waits up to six months.[100] Figure 28 charts the number of physicians licensed in Texas since 2001 as well as new physician applications, the latter having risen 72 percent since 2001, showing a healthy increase in the desire to practice medicine in Texas.[101] The bottom line is this: the number of new doctors in Texas has exceeded population growth by 84% since 2003's lawsuit reforms. From 2003 to 2011, Texas' population grew by 17 percent while the number of

---

[100] "More Doctors in Texas After Malpractice Caps," by Ralph Blumenthal, *New York Times*, October 5, 2007, http://www.nytimes.com/2007/10/05/us/05doctors.html?pagewanted=all

[101] Source: Texas Medical Board – Fiscal Year-End Reports as compiled by the Texas Alliance for Patient Access.

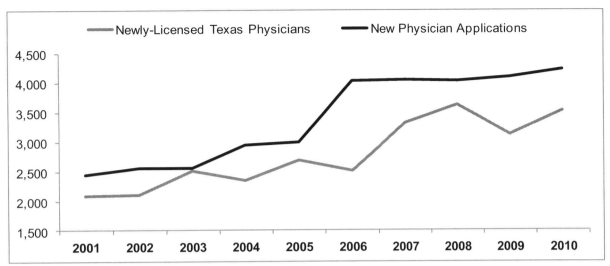

Figure 28—Applications to practice medicine in Texas have ballooned 72 percent since 2001, leading to a backlog in physician application approvals.

actively practicing doctors grew by 31 percent in the same period. Texas' remarkable medical turnaround can be seen in the number of New York-trained doctors who have moved to Texas. According to the Texas Medical Board, in response to a public records request, there have been 22,166 newly-licensed physicians in Texas since September 1, 2003 with 1,271 of these having attended medical school or completing their residency in New York. As mentioned before, this caught the attention of New York Mayor Michael Bloomberg who said in a January, 2011 speech to the New York State Bar Association:

> *"We have all seen how the fear of litigation has forced people to act defensively. Just take health care. Fear of litigation too often makes doctors afraid to choose the best treatment options, and so they over prescribe drugs, tests, and surgeries, which lead to unnecessary treatments... This fear of litigation drives up the cost of health care, and it can lead to a shortage of doctors in certain specialty fields... New York was one of just nine states to receive a failing grade from the American Medical Association for our medical malpractice environment. So the question we must ask ourselves is: How can we remove the straightjacket our law is placing on our doctors and instead use the law to improve our treatment options and our health?*

> *"The low hanging fruit is malpractice reform. After Texas enacted malpractice reform, the shortage of doctors they had long suffered from disappeared. And can you guess which state the most doctors came from? You got it—New York. Reforming our medical malpractice laws would help drive down costs, improve care, and improve access to doctors..."*

The reduction in costs cited by the mayor of New York City has another tangible benefit: increased charity care. Charity care provided by Texas hospitals rose 24 percent from 2004 to 2010, with the value of the services delivered increasing 36 percent, an increase of $594 million. Were it not for the more than $100 million per year in insurance premiums saved by the 109 hospitals surveyed by the Texas Hospital Association in 2008, this increase in charity care not only would not have been financially possible, dozens of hospitals would have likely had to close their doors.

Further, according to the Texas Hospital Association, hospitals have used their $100 million annual savings in a variety of ways beneficial to the general public: 58 percent expanded patient safety programs; 51 have maintained or expanded coverage or services for uninsured or underinsured patients; 46 percent of hospitals have subsidized Medicaid and Medicare payment shortfalls; 41 percent of hospitals have met monthly obligations, improved salaries for nursing personnel, maintained or increased nurse staffing levels, or funded staff education; 39 percent of hospitals invested in new capital, buying new medical equipment; and 37 percent of hospitals used their reduced liability coverage costs to pay on-call physicians.

When money isn't flowing into the pockets of lawyers via greater lawsuit activity, it can and will be spent to improve the quality of healthcare. This was one of the lost opportunities in the sweeping national healthcare law passed in 2010 as the Patient Protection and Affordable Care Act, the so-called ObamaCare. By not enacting medical liability reforms along the lines of those passed in Texas and California, the 2010 Federal law missed an opportunity to save some $54 billion over 10 years, according to the Congressional Budget Office.[102]

Class Action Reform

While the medical malpractice reforms generated most of the attention, a second key aspect of House Bill 4 addressed the growing problem of class action lawsuits.

Class action lawsuits involve consolidating people who may have been harmed by a product or service into one legal action. The court's acknowledgement of a "class," known as "certification," is considered the most important step in the legal process. With certification comes a court's finding that the plaintiff, the person suing, has a probable right of recovering damages. Because a class action case could involve many thousands of people, rather than just one, certification of a case expands the potential liability exponentially making defendants far more likely to settle so as to limit their losses. So, certification dictates outcome.

Before passage of House Bill 4, trial courts could certify a class action and defendants could appeal the certification. Few cases ever made it to the Texas Supreme Court leaving little guidance for lower courts in class certification precedence. This lead to an exploitation of class actions by the trial bar in which lawyers often won huge fees while the individuals harmed received very little: a few dollars, or even a coupon to buy a product from the same company they sued.

Today class certification can be immediately appealed to the Court of Appeals and then to the Texas Supreme Court with the proceedings in the trial court stayed pending the resolution of the certification appeal. Further, the trial court must dismiss without prejudice a class-action case if administrative remedies are available through government action.

---

[102] "CBO: Medical Malpractice Reforms Could Save Up to $54 Billion," *Washington Post*, October 9, 2009.

But the biggest change to class action procedures is the awarding of attorney's fees. Now class action fees in Texas follow the Federal court model and are based on the number of hours actually worked at a customarily charged hourly rate that cannot exceed 25 percent of the amounts collected for the harmed class. Further, if the attorney negotiates coupons as a means of making the class whole, then the attorney gets paid with those same coupons.

Other Reforms

There were other significant reforms contained in the 2003 effort that impacted pre-trial settlements, venue shopping, multi-district litigation and further areas.

Before 2003, the civil procedure rules discouraged out of court settlements. This had the impact of making nuisance lawsuits common as companies would simply pay "go away" money to attorneys who brought lawsuits with little merit.

The Legislature developed new rules which allowed a defendant the ability to make an offer to the person suing him, to make him whole, early on. If the plaintiff refused to accept the offer, then it put him at risk for paying the defendant's legal fees if the settlement offer was larger than what was awarded in going to trial. This reform presaged the loser pays reform passed into law in 2011.

Venue shopping—looking for a friendly court in which to file a lawsuit—was another way trial attorneys skewed outcomes in their favor. But, allowing venue shopping violated the legal tradition that a case should be brought only where the injury occurred or where the defendant or plaintiff resides. But in Texas before 2003, any number of plaintiffs from all over the U.S. could join a suit by filing together with a plaintiff who lived in Texas.

Seeing their state court system used for what were essentially federal cases, the Legislature tried to stem this practice in 1995, but some trial judges maneuvered around the law and it became moot. The 2003 law closed the loophole created by the trial judges, mandating that each plaintiff in a case must establish proper venue.

Multi-district litigation arises when similar cases are pending before multiple courts. To streamline the results and prevent inconsistencies in outcomes, the U.S. Congress created a system that allows transfer of similar cases to a single court for consolidated pre-trial proceedings. The process proved consistent, cost-effective and fair. But Texas lacked a similar mechanism. Before 2003, it was common to see thousands of cases dealing with the same product or claim filed all over the state resulting in huge inconsistencies dealing more with venue than with the actual merits of the case. The costs on the entire civil justice system were huge.

The Legislature addressed this challenge by modeling a multi-district litigation system on federal lines, creating a multi-district litigation panel made up of judges selected by the Texas Supreme Court. This panel can transfer similar cases to a single court charged with managing pre-trial activity. As an example, there were more than 65,000 asbestos-related lawsuits in the Texas court system before 2003. These have all been consolidated to one court. In the 2009 legislative session there was an attempt to repeal many of the gains seen with the adoption of the multi-district litigation system, but it failed.

Other fixes enacted by the Legislature included the assignment of proportional responsibility in damages, rather than simply going after the entity with the deepest pockets; product liability reforms that eliminated the exposure of retailers to the defects of the manufacturers; reducing the financial burden of taking out prohibitively large bonds, called supersedeas bonds, so as to appeal a judgment; applying common sense to so-called "successor liability" rules where a firm that long ago briefly owned a subsidiary or piece of land that was later found liable for damages found itself on the hook for harmful actions it never took itself; and volunteer immunity changes that make it safe for people to serve their neighbors, whether it be a volunteer firefighter or stopping to aid someone in an auto accident.

Site Selection Magazine, in explaining why Texas is now the nation's number one state in which to locate a business, cited the 2003 lawsuit reforms as one compelling reason:[103]

> *As for the 2003 reforms, (Governor) Perry says he can cite concrete evidence that they produced the desired results: "There are 23,000 more physicians practicing medicine in Texas, [Corpus Christi-based] CHRISTUS Spohn Health System saving almost $100 million in legal defense costs that they can put back into their system for more doctors and technology. Premiums have gone down for doctors, and more importantly, 30 counties have emergency room physicians today that did not have them in 2003."*

> *"Tort reform and protection from frivolous lawsuits is a story that does not get its due, but the Dallas Fed chairman said earlier this year that one of the most important things that has happened in Texas is tort reform, meaning the measures passed in 2003," Gov. Perry told Site Selection in an interview… "One of the great things about the 10th Amendment, the concept the Founding Fathers had that these units of government within the United States would compete against each other, was that you can't just live on what you did last year or yesterday. You have to continuously improve your game, to be looking at your tax structure, your regulatory climate and your legal system. That's why we passed loser pays, which took effect the first of September."*

Loser Pays

In the 2011 legislative session (the Texas Legislature meets on odd years only) a bill was approved and signed into law that continued Texas' ongoing efforts at lawsuit reform. House Bill 274, the 2011 Omnibus Tort Reform Bill, incorporated some fairly non-controversial changes to civil procedure as well as a significant change opposed by the trial bar.

Among the legal system changes were joining 42 other states in allowing judges to immediately dismiss frivolous lawsuits. The limit for using the small claims court process was lifted from

---

[103] "A Better Mousetrap," *Site Selection Magazine*, Nov., 2011, www.siteselection.com/issues/2011/nov/cover.cfm.

$10,000 to $100,000, meaning that larger claims can be pursued quickly and with less of a discovery burden, saving Texans money while boosting access to the legal system.

Modifications to the offer of settlement incentivize the parties in a lawsuit to make and accept settlement offers earlier in the litigation process, again, saving court costs. In addition, changes to the motions to dismiss and interlocutory appeals process are expected to reduce costs by streamlining courtroom time.

The most controversial change to the Texas civil justice system was the introduction of "loser pays" in cases of frivolous lawsuits, a priority for the Texas governor that he said would, "…set Texas on the path toward greater economic prosperity in the years to come." In cases where a judge dismisses a lawsuit as having no merit, the party that loses the dismissal motion must pay the legal fees their opponent incurred arguing the motion. This reform built on the effort in 2003's House Bill 4 to encourage use of the "offer of settlement" tool to reduce nuisance lawsuits. This was one of the underused disappointments of House Bill 4 and the Legislature set out to revisit the matter.

U.S. loser pays legal provisions originated in Britain and have become common in America's economic competitors, none of which even remotely approaches the per capita number of lawyers that America enjoys. A December 2008 study by the Manhattan Institute reviewed the results of the five-year period from 1980 to 1985 in which Florida instituted a loser pays regime solely for medical malpractice lawsuits—the law being repealed by sustained trial bar lobbying.[104] The Manhattan Institute study found that the number of lawsuits dropped went from 44 percent to 54 percent upon adoption of the rule, signifying a reduction in frivolous claims, while the rate of settled cases went from 46 percent to 40 percent and the number of cases making it to court went from 11 percent to 6 percent, almost halving the number of cases coming before a judge. Interestingly, the average value of the cases settled out of court under loser pays went up, from $73,786 to $94,489 while the average trial damage awards almost tripled, from $25,190 to $69,390 (adjusted for inflation) with the plaintiffs more frequently prevailing at trial. These results suggest that more substantive claims were being addressed by the court system than was the case before—in effect, improving the efficiency of the legal system, itself a costly system populated by well-paid professionals.

Given that the U.S. now spends about 2.2 percent of its economy on lawsuits, ensuring that the civil actions that are brought have merit and result in proper compensation to the damaged party is paramount, not only for justice, but for prosperity as well.

Follow the Money
In Texas it isn't just members of the Legislature who raise money to run for office, judges do as well. And, as with any human system, it has its vulnerabilities. The First Amendment to the U.S. Constitution protects free speech. Speech takes many forms and in elections, speech often takes

---

[104] "Greater Justice, Lower Cost: How a 'Loser Pays' Rule Would Improve the American Legal System," by Marie Gryphon, Manhattan Institute for Policy Research, December 11, 2008, http://www.manhattan-institute.org/html/cjr_11.htm.

the form of costly television and radio advertisements. Many states limit campaign donations, balancing concerns about undue influence purchased by political donors with concerns over limits placed on speech. Texas has no such limits, preferring instead to allow vigorous speech attended by disclosure of who is spending the money.

That there are enormous sums of money to be made in civil cases has lead, naturally, to enormous sums of money being spent to influence both elected representatives in the Texas Legislature even the judges themselves who must periodically stand for election. That large sums of money are at stake is one explanation for why Texas' lawsuit reforms took so long to implement in the face of mounting evidence that frequent recourse to lawsuits were harming the Texas economy as well as the lives of average Texans.

Further, as is the case with most government spending programs as well as a spiraling lawsuit environment, the benefit accrues to a distinct group of people while the costs are distributed more widely, making it very difficult to convince the larger number of people who bear the burden to contribute towards addressing the problem.

Fortunately, in the instance of medical malpractice reform, the legal predations of attorneys had touched a cohesive, well-organized and empowered group: doctors. Roughly 21,000 Texas lawyers, only some of whom were engaged in civil litigation, took on 43,000 doctors, many of whom faced statistical certainty in being sued multiple times in their careers. The venue in this battle would be a statewide ballot initiative, Proposition 12, during a September 13, 2003 special election.

Proposition 12 passed by 51.1 percent of the vote after some $18.2 million was spent by nine political action committees with $9.76 million being spent to defeat the measure by the trial bar and $8.45 million being spent by the yes side, almost all of it from the medical community.

The surprising fact is that the attorneys benefiting from the lax lawsuit rules didn't spend more, after all, Texas was home to John Eddie Williams, one of the legendary "Tobacco 5" attorneys who cashed in on $3.3 *billion* in fees from Texas alone for his role in the nationwide class action case against the tobacco industry.

Aside from one-time spending to defeat Proposition 12 in 2003, the Texas trial bar engages in a more sustained, partisan effort to buy friends and influence enemies. According to campaign finance records, trial lawyers donated almost $9 million to competitive legislative campaigns in Texas in the 2010 election cycle, the largest of any single industry or group. Further, 90 percent of the money raised by the Texas Democratic Party comes from trial attorneys with some 97 percent of the crucial finals weeks' funding for the Democratic Party in the 2008 campaign cycle coming from personal injury attorneys.[105]

---

[105]"High wattage: Trial lawyer Mikal Watts funds Democrats' resurgence," by Matt Pulle, *Texas Watchdog*, November 17, 2008, http://www.texaswatchdog.org/2008/11/high-wattage-trial-lawyer-mikal-watts-funds-democrats-resurgence/.

From 2000 to 2008, the law firm of Mikal Watts plowed $4.5 million to candidates—virtually none of it to Republicans with half a million dollars going to the state Democratic Party alone in 2008.[106]

Watts himself offered a rare glimpse into the world of money and law when a letter he wrote surfaced in which he tried to pressure the opposing lawyers in an auto accident case to accept a $60 *million* settlement by predicting that he'd win on appeal because his law firm heavily financed the winning campaigns of the judges sitting on the court of appeals in Corpus Christi. Watts wrote, in part, "This court is comprised of six justices, all of whom are good Democrats… The Chief Justice, Hon. Rogelio Valdez, was recently elected with our firm's heavy support, and is a man who believes in the sanctity of jury verdicts."[107]

According to Sherry Sylvester spokesperson for the group Texans for Lawsuit Reform, in 2009 Texas lawmakers introduced over 900 pieces of legislation that would weaken existing lawsuit reforms or create new opportunities to sue.

Lastly, according to a report authored by Ms. Sylvester, trial attorneys in Texas fund a vast network of front groups whose objective is to build public support for lawsuits.[108] For instance, the anti-lawsuit reform group Texans for Insurance Reform receives 97 percent of its multi-million budget from trial attorneys while Texans for Public Justice, a liberal public interest group the produces reports in support of trial attorneys, receives its funding from asbestos and tobacco class action lawyers.

Texans for Public Justice frequently supports a so-called campaign finance reform bill that would restrict contributions from corporations, but leave intact the ability for personal injury lawyers to give as much as they want.

Texas Watch is yet another front group—this one designed to interact with the press. It was cited over 400 times since 2003 advocating for more lawsuits. Called an independent watchdog by the press, it is anything but.

Lastly, trial attorneys fund studies by researchers to boost the case for more lawsuits.

---

[106] Ibid.
[107] Ibid.
[108] "Covert Operations: The Texas Trial Lawyer Message Machine," by Sherry Sylvester, Texans for Lawsuit Reform.

CHAPTER FIVE—THE DIVERSITY OF THE TEXAS ECONOMY

Some people who ought to know better explain Texas' economic success as due to oil and gas, or minimum wage jobs, or even Mexican drug cartels.[109] Mainly liberals, they are deeply invested in the concept that bigger government is better. They believe that central planning from an educated cadre of elites is needed to bring order and fairness out of the chaos of the free market. For these folks, the simple, sometimes preposterous, explanations of Texas' success *must* be true for if the truth were otherwise their cognitive dissonance would threaten cranial explosions.

In Chapter Two we compared Texas to the seven largest states in the U.S., making the case through data that Texas is doing better while taxing and spending less than its fellow states. In that discussion we briefly touched on the fact that the share of non-petroleum manufacturing as a percentage of the Texas economy grew from 2000 to 2009 and that manufacturing produces a bigger share of the economy than do oil and gas, contrary to some of the myths about the nature of Texas' success. This chapter will delve deeper into the nature of the Texas economic dynamo.

Texas is Not an American Version of a Persian Gulf Statelet

Figure 29 examines the relative diversity of the economies of two nations and two states.

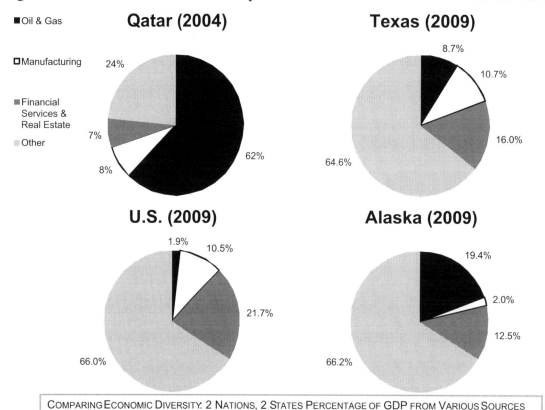

COMPARING ECONOMIC DIVERSITY: 2 NATIONS, 2 STATES PERCENTAGE OF GDP FROM VARIOUS SOURCES

Figure 29—The Texas economy looks more like the U.S. economy than it does the Alaskan economy or that of Qatar: far more diversified than its critics claim.

---

[109] "The Stimulant Stimulus: Could something other than Rick Perry's business-friendly policies be keeping the Texas economy buzzing?", by Tina Rosenberg, *New York Magazine,* July 10, 2011.

shows that Texas is not as dependent on oil as the critics would like people to believe. As mentioned before, oil and gas extraction and refining together accounted for 8.7 percent of the Texas economy in 2009, with manufacturing, minus oil refining, coming in at 10.7 percent of the Texas GDP. Figure 30 presents these two basic measures, along with the financial service sector, including real estate, and the rest of the economy, comparing Texas to the Persian Gulf oil state of Qatar, the U.S. and the state of Alaska. As the chart shows, Texas' share of manufacturing is a bit above the U.S. national average, its financial service sector is smaller by about six percent and its oil, gas and refining sector is larger by a little less than seven percent. Importantly, the rest of the Texas economy, about 65 percent, compares closely to the national average of 66 percent. The economy of Qatar, on the other hand, is almost two-thirds oil driven. So, the Texas economy looks far more like the U.S. economy than it does Alaska's economy or that of Qatar's.

Does oil play a role in the Texas economy? Of course it does. But the part it plays is far less than critics looking for a reason to dismiss Texas' job creation record over the past few years.

As Figure 30 shows, in 1981, 30 years ago, oil and gas extraction and refining played a much larger role in the Texas economy—almost 21 percent of the state's output. Further,

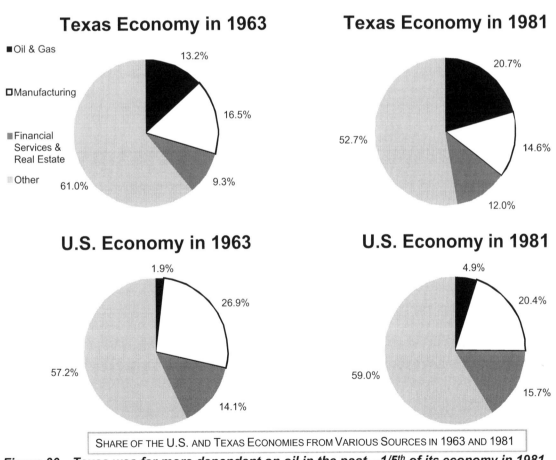

SHARE OF THE U.S. AND TEXAS ECONOMIES FROM VARIOUS SOURCES IN 1963 AND 1981

Figure 30—Texas was far more dependent on oil in the past—1/5th of its economy in 1981.

manufacturing generated almost 15 percent of the Texas' wealth then, compared to just over 20 percent nationally. Texas actually increased its reliance on the oil industry from 1963 to 1981.

This happened because of a series of oil shocks to the U.S. economy caused by the Arab oil embargo of the mid-70s, subsequent missteps in U.S. energy policy, and the 1979 Islamic revolution in Iran. World oil prices skyrocketed and Texas obliged, drilling new wells.

But, in 1985, the price of oil plummeted as Saudi Arabia maximized production. Weaknesses in the Texas economy manifested themselves. Several Texas financial institutions went bankrupt. Real estate values sank and the unemployment rate went from 6.1 percent in September 1984 to 9.3 percent two years later—at a time when the U.S. unemployment rate declined from 7.3 percent to 7.0 percent.

But, rather than panic and raise taxes, as other states frequently do when tax revenue declines sharply, Texas soldiered through it, keeping their tax and regulatory structures attractive to business in general. As time went on, Texas' dependence on the oil and gas industry waned while other sectors waxed in importance.

Texas oil producers even asked for rent-seeking government protection, whether it was subsidies, tax breaks, or tariffs on imported oil. Elected officials did nothing and the market corrected itself. By 1990, unemployment rates in much of Texas were once again below the national average.

The Roots of Economic Growth
Today, the Texas economy is diversified and growing strongly. Understanding "why" has significant ramifications to the rest of the nation.

As cited in Chapter Two, *Site Selection Magazine* ranked Texas the best place to locate a business in 2011, after nine years as #2 to North Carolina with its fabled "Research Triangle" high-tech area anchored around Raleigh-Durham.[110] This national magazine, a key resource for business leaders looking to expand operations, uses both objective data and survey information from executives in charge of business site selection to arrive at its rankings. Being national in scope and headquartered in Georgia, the magazine's findings are useful in discovering why Texas has prospered, while other states have lagged.

Site Selection gathers objective data and equally weights each category, then considers survey information as well. The data-driven part of its ranking consisting of five categories: new and expanded facilities; total per capita projects; the state's Competitiveness Ranking; new plant projects year-to-date; and the Tax Foundation's business tax climate ranking. The value of this analysis and the attendant survey results is that it deals with real business leaders making real decisions about where to conduct business. Unlike economists, journalists, and politicians who express an opinion about Texas, these business leaders make decisions that can benefit or harm their firms' bottom line as well as impact their personal earnings when time comes to award

---

[110] "A Better Mousetrap," *Site Selection Magazine*, November, 2011, http://www.siteselection.com/issues/2011/nov/cover.cfm.

bonuses, stock options, and salary raises. As such, some of the survey comments about Texas reported by *Site Selection* bear repeating:

> *"a pro-business, entrepreneurial, right-to-work state"*
> *"no state income tax, ease of pulling permits, available work force"*
> *"the government makes it easy to do business"*
> *"the state fights OSHA, EPA and other negative, useless regulations; no state income tax"*
> *"work-force availability, existing facilities and good economics for labor and facilities"*
> *"cooperation and flexibility of state and local officials; proactive in growing the economy"*

Site Selection also favorably mentions Texas lawsuit reform efforts and light regulatory burden, quoting Governor Rick Perry about 2011's loser-pays reform, "People instinctively understand that if you get sued frivolously the other side picks up your court costs and legal fees. That is a huge win for the business environment. It's about confidence that you can risk your capital and know that you'll have a chance to have a return on that investment. I can't tell you how important that is to the job creators in this country. Groups like the Texas Association of Manufacturers know that a fair and efficient legal system is a very important consideration when manufacturers look for locations in which to invest. We lead the nation in the value of manufactured goods, and we added more net new manufacturing jobs—19,000—than any state in the nation between July 2010 and July 2011."

Typical of the observations by business relocation experts is this, from a Dallas relocation analyst: "Corporate relocations and expansions to the market remain a positive catalyst for Dallas with several companies announcing plans to move headquarters and other significant office operations to the market due to a combination of lower costs, business-friendly environment and strong, diversified work force. Most announced relocations are from California (but other relocations are from not-surprising states). This trend is expected to continue for the foreseeable future. All current economic indicators (positive job growth, strong population growth, healthy corporate profits) point to a much more robust Dallas office market in late 2011 and beyond, especially compared to the national landscape."[111]

The *Wall Street Journal's* Daniel Henninger added to the anecdotal evidence of Texas as a place to do business, interviewing several business leaders who made the move:[112]

> *...Alan Boeckmann, until recently CEO of Fluor Corp., the engineering and construction firm, says regulatory and legal hassles pushed Fluor out of California. Congress passed Sarbanes-Oxley, but "California had its own version." There were constant class-action suits over Fluor's benefits. "It could have been settled, but not in California. That's how the game is played there."*
>
> *When word of the 2006 move got out, "California made no attempt to keep us." In Texas, "things started to happen quickly, without us initiating them."*

---

[111] Ibid.
[112] "The Perry Paradox," by Daniel Henninger, *Wall Street Journal*, November 3, 2011.

Ed Trevis ...moved Corvalent Corp. to Austin for similar reasons. He had to hire a firm just to do California's compliance. "In California," he says, "you are always doing something wrong."

"What I found in Texas is that from the standpoint of running a business, cost of living, education, the labor pool, quality of life, it just blew other states out of the water." I heard this constantly—people enjoy being in business in Texas.

David Booth, who moved Dimensional Fund Advisors's headquarters to Austin from Santa Monica in 2008, puts Rick Perry's role in perspective: "He understands his job isn't to get in the middle of everything." (Fluor's Alan Boeckmann seconded that.) But Mr. Booth and others said this is also true of the Texas lieutenant governor, its attorney general and the comptroller.

"They are very supportive of business," says Lee Raymond, "in the sense of moving things along. If there is a rock in the road, they want to know what they can do to move it out of the way."

This isn't merely the "pro-business" bias of a Rick Perry or any other governor. Texas' pro-business bias goes back about 175 years—and never died. "It's just that they believe in the whole Horatio Alger myth down here," said Mr. Booth. "It's hard to understand if you haven't lived here."

Texas: Business Friendly or Competition Friendly?

In California, high taxes and complex labor laws have hurt the ability of business to operate profitably. Rather than reduce taxes for everyone, allowing the free market to choose winners and losers, the Legislature, led by Hollywood actor and then-Governor Arnold Schwarzenegger, passed a movie tax break. Other firms were leaving the state, but the beautiful people of film were incentivized to stay.[113]

In Michigan, high taxes and stultifying unions made it hard for the auto industry to thrive: they got bailouts and tax breaks.

In Texas, uncompetitive businesses get little sympathy from government; rather, they are likely advised to consult the bankruptcy code. In this sense, Texans aren't "business friendly" as they like to brag, but "competition friendly."

Like most states, Texas has an economic-development fund, but it's a small one: Since it was created, the Texas Enterprise Fund has disbursed slightly less than $363 million. That's one-tenth the amount Michigan has spent on economic development in recent years, and Texas has

---

[113] The saying that "Politics is show business for ugly people," may explain why so many elected officials across the nation are willing to bend their tax codes to benefit the film industry—most everyone likes hanging out with the "cool kids."

almost three times the population. In other words, the government of Texas spends about one-thirtieth as much per resident of the state on corporate-welfare projects as Michigan.

Some economists and tax code observers note that large government-directed economic development efforts, special tax breaks, and government sponsored national television ad campaigns such as Michigan's Economic Development Corporation commercials with actor Jeff Daniels promising to give businesses "The Upper Hand" are symptoms of a complex, high rate tax code. The simple thing to do would be to cut taxes. But, politicians and tax law lobbyists know that tinkering with a complex code preserves their power while wholesale tax reform helps a wide array of people who then feel no gratitude to the elite.

As mentioned in the chapter on taxes in Texas, the Legislature passed a major school funding tax reform in 2006. Property taxes were cut by about $7 billion and a gross business receipts tax and higher tobacco taxes replaced the lost revenue. A hotly contested aspect of this change in the tax code was that the state's business franchise tax unevenly taxed businesses. Limited liability partnerships were able to steer profits to their owners as salaries, a business expense, and thus avoid business taxation, while traditional corporations were unable to shield their profits. The 2006 tax code changes were designed not to raise taxes overall, rather shifting the burden from one form of taxation (property) to another (business gross margins). The final result was a more level playing field for business in Texas, with businesses paying similar rates based on their size rather than different rates based on the legal paperwork that created them.

That Texans would rather government just stay out of their business is summed up by a longtime Houston oilman, George Strake, who said, "Give me wide open spaces. Let me enjoy the good times, and don't feel sorry for me in bad times."

Energy for Growth
Texas produces and consumes the most energy of any state. Oil, gas, coal, and even wind energy serve to generate revenue while spinning the electrical generators that power the state's economy. There's an important distinction to be made here between simply extracting crude oil and selling it for others to refine and use, as some claim drives the state's economy, and producing large amounts of affordable and reliable energy that modern manufacturers require.

The Texas Public Policy Foundation commissioned Drs. Steven Hayward and Kenneth Green of the American Enterprise Institute to examine the synergy of Texas energy extraction and generation. They concluded in *"Texas Energy and the Energy of Texas: the Master Resource in the Most Dynamic Economy,"*[114] that new oil and gas extraction technology, linked with highly productive applications of energy to make goods, have been a key driver of the Texas economy and its diversification over the past decade.

The study linked Texas' emergence as America's industrial and manufacturing powerhouse to its consumption of energy. Texas' energy use dwarfs most other states, a fact often misleadingly

---

[114] http://www.texaspolicy.com/pdf/2011-01-RR02-TexasEnergyandtheEnergyofTexas-CEE-Hayward-Green.pdf.

attributed to inefficiency. The manufacturing output of Texas, however, is now larger than the output of former industrial titans Michigan and Ohio combined.[115]

Affordable energy from coal-fired plants, natural gas, and America's largest amount of wind generation has attracted a concentration of energy-intensive industries. Manufacture of chemicals, plastic, petroleum products, metals and machinery requires copious energy. Further, the profit incentive encourages these industries to make their product with the least amount of energy possible. Such market-driven innovation has reduced energy use per dollar of economic output in the U.S. by 50 percent from 1973 to 2006.[116]

Texas: America's Export Leader

Foreign trade has consistently increased in importance to the U.S. economy over time. The U.S. exported $1.8 trillion in goods and services in 2010, contributing 12.6 percent of America's economic output.

The export of goods is easy to understand: Americans make stuff that people overseas buy; things like computers, cars, aircraft and corn. In 2010, goods comprised almost $1.3 trillion of U.S. exports, or, about 70 percent; services, $549 billion for almost 30 percent. Service exports are less visible by nature and include financial services, films, tourism, and airfare on U.S. carriers. For example, the U.S. earned almost $106 billion on royalties and license fees, mostly from software, in 2010 (that's why software piracy is such a big deal to the U.S.) while foreign tourists left about $104 billion behind in the U.S. that year.

In prior chapters we discussed how Texas successfully competes with other states for job-creating capital based on its relative economic strengths. Of course, the same can be said about competition with other nations. Measuring Texas' international exports of goods is one way to see how Texas stacks up.

The value of the U.S. dollar and the strength of overseas economies have a huge impact on U.S. exports. When the dollar is strong, foreign goods are cheaper for Americans to buy. When the dollar is weak, American goods become more attractive to foreigners. In addition, U.S. goods have to provide value for foreigners to want to purchase them: quality and price, which are affected by productivity, matter greatly in the vigorous race to compete internationally. So, the year-to-year value of exports is dependent on a number of factors, both external, and domestic.

While the amount that the U.S. exports can fluctuate significantly, the share of each state's exports relative to one another, is more stable. Thus, the value of Texas' exports relative to the

---

[115] And for this manufacturing job-creating engine, liberal critics, such as the New York Times columnist and author Gail Collins, attack Texas for emitting the most carbon dioxide of any state—as if CO_2 was a deadly toxin, rather than the gas trees must have to grow.

[116] "The Potential of Energy Efficiency, An Overview," by Lester B. Lave, *The Bridge*, Summer 2009, Volume 39, Number 2, National Academy of Engineering, http://www.nae.edu/Publications/Bridge/EnergyEfficiency14874/ThePotentialofEnergyEfficiencyAnOverview.aspx.

U.S. and to California, the largest state, serves as another indicator of strength and diversity of the Texas economy.

Figure 31 tracks the value of the exports shipped out of Texas and California over four years. Surprisingly, even though California, due to its sheer size, remains America's largest manufacturing state, Texas actually exports more abroad than does California. Texas' total goods exports in 2010 came to almost $207 billion, 16.2 percent of the goods America sold abroad, almost $64 billion more than second-place California.[117]

Must be due to all that Texas oil and gas, right? Wrong!

Remove refined oil and gas products from the mix and Texas still exports some $33 billion more than does California.

Further, the relative share of America's exports made in Texas have been rising over the years compared to California and to the nation as a whole. Every year from 2007 to 2010, the share of U.S. exports produced by Texas has risen, going from 14.7 percent of all U.S. exports in 2007 to 16.2 percent of all U.S. exports in 2010. California has seen its competitive position erode, with its market share of U.S. goods exports declining from 11.7 percent of all U.S. goods sent abroad in 2007 to 11.2 percent in 2010.

After refined oil products, Texas' next-largest export categories were: $5.6 billion of drilling machinery, $4.5 billion in computer parts, $4.3 billion in computer chips, $3.8 billion in aircraft and aircraft parts, $3.8 billion in video and audio equipment, and $3.2 billion in machine tools for making computer chips. California's top goods exports were: $4.6 billion in aircraft and aircraft parts, $4.0 billion in cut diamonds, $3.4 billion in computer parts (even with Silicon

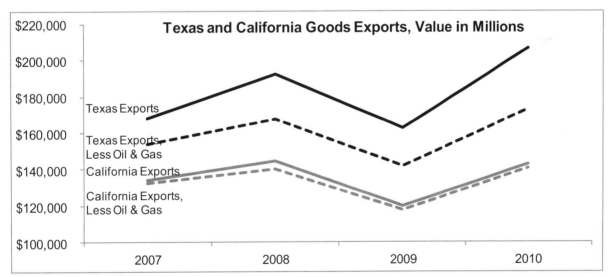

Figure 31—Texas is America's export machine, outpacing runner-up California by $64 billion.

Source: U.S. Census, Total U.S. Exports (Origin of Movement) via Texas and Total U.S. Exports (Origin of Movement) via California.

Valley, $1.1 billion *less* than Texas), $3.2 billion in video and audio equipment (less than Texas), and $2.9 billion machine tools for making computer chips (again, less than Texas).

Looking at the top U.S. markets for exports, we see that Canada purchased the most U.S. goods, followed by Mexico, China, Japan and the United Kingdom. One explanation for Texas' export prowess might be that it is better situated geographically to export than its large state rival, California. But, the top five export destinations for Texas goods were: Mexico, Canada, China, Brazil and South Korea. California's top five customers were remarkably similar: Mexico, Canada, China, Japan and South Korea. Brazil being #14 for California, situated, as it is, on the other side of the Panama Canal or the Straits of Magellan while Japan is #10 for Texas, so, it would appear that geography has a bit of an impact, but is not by itself determinative.

Since 2000, trade between the U.S. and Mexico has grown by 60 percent (the North American Free Trade Agreement went into effect in 1994, accelerating trade between the two neighbors). Electronic component manufacturers in the Texan border city of El Paso have added shifts to meet demand in Mexican vehicle and electronics assembly plants.[118]

The share of the Texas economy generated from manufacturing has risen over the years while California's manufacturing base has been trending towards being a smaller part of its economy. So, Texas is likely to continue its dominance as America's export champion.

As mentioned earlier, services account for about 30 percent of U.S. trade exports. This is where California does well, especially in the roughly 19 percent of service export earnings generated by tourists visiting America, totaling some $103.5 billion in 2010. California estimates that domestic and international visitors spent $95 billion in California in 2010 from 199 million domestic person-trips to California and 13.6 million international person-trips to the Golden State.[119] Tourism accounted for about five percent of California's economy in 2010.

But Texas is no slouch when it comes to the hospitality industry either, with the Texas Economic Development and Tourism office reporting visitor spending at $48 billion in 2010.[120] This amounts to four percent of the Texas economy.

So, relative to Texas, tourism in California is about 20 percent more important to the economy.

Some Californians argue that their stringent environmental regulations (Texans might call them "burdensome") have made California a beautiful place to visit and that California's environmental assets make California a top tourist destination. But, this is an arguable claim. Due differences in geography and history, some 42 percent of the land in California is owned by the Federal or state government, the seventh greatest percentage in the U.S. Texas, on the other hand, government owns less than two percent of the land, ranking 47th in the nation.[121] It's

[118] "In Texas Jobs Boom, Crediting a Leader, or Luck," by Clifford Krauss, *New York Times*, August 15, 2011.
[119] California Tourism Industry Website: http://industry.visitcalifornia.com/Research/.
[120] State of Texas, Office of Governor, Economic Development and Tourism: http://www.deanrunyan.com/TXTravelImpacts/TXTravelImpacts.html.

doubtful that California's regulatory climate has impacted the environment of Yosemite National Park to a degree appreciable enough to affect tourism.

Lastly, boosters of the economic line of reasoning that claims that a higher regulatory burden leads to a cleaner environment (we'll dispute this claim in Chapter Seven—Regulation in Texas) which leads to more tourism miss out on a key fact: mean annual wages in the hospitality industry are $22,440, less than half of the mean annual wage, $45,680, earned by workers in the manufacturing sector.[122] In other words: good luck trying to build a middle class on the tourism industry.

One last aspect of trade that often goes unnoticed should be discussed before we move on: the value of international trade in the transportation sector. The value of the goods transported over Texas' border with Mexico or through its ports passed $100 billion in 2010.[123]

As with all goods, unless made and consumed onsite, there is some cost associated with transportation. In today's economy, transportation has become so efficient that it no longer constitutes a large percentage of the final cost of most products. In 2010, transportation and warehousing constituted 2.8 percent of the U.S. GDP of which trucking had the largest share at 29 percent.

Transportation and warehousing was 2.3 percent of the California economy in 2010 and 3.4 percent of the Texas economy the same year.

One of the larger portions of this segment of the economy in California is centered on America's largest container port complex: the twin Ports of Long Beach and San Pedro in Southern California. The Port of South Louisiana and the Port of Houston ship the greatest tonnage, the bulk of it oil. But crude oil and refined product don't need much in the way of labor to load and unload from a tanker. Container ships, on the other hand, do, with labor consuming as much as 75 percent of a general cargo terminal's operating costs and up to 50 percent in a well-capitalized container cargo facility.[124] According to a report commissioned by the Port of San Pedro, of the cost to operate a container vessel between Asia and Los Angeles, port costs made up seven to nine percent of operating costs.[125]

Now, here's where things get interesting from a policymaker's attitudinal standpoint.

Elected officials in California view the ports as providing a national service, and, as such, frequently see them as a burden that adds to regional congestion and pollution. Port tonnage taxes have been proposed in the California Legislature, ostensibly for the purpose of reducing

---

[121] Source: National Wilderness Institute.

[122] U.S. Bureau of Labor Statistics, May 2010 National Industry-Specific Occupational Employment and Wage Estimates.

[123] "In Texas Jobs Boom, Crediting a Leader, or Luck," by Clifford Krauss, *New York Times*, August 15, 2011.

[124] "Adding up the Costs," *Port Strategy Magazine*, June 7, 2011.

[125] "Forecast of Container Vessel Specifications and Port Calls Within San Pedro Bay Final Report," Mercator Transport Group, February 22, 2005, Table II-25 - Slot Costs For 5-Vessel Asia-USWC Services.

pollution, even though such port taxes are unconstitutional.[126] One such tax hike, passed in 2008 only to be vetoed, would have more than doubled the cost to use California's ports.

Add to this taxing attitude the devastating labor strike by the International Longshore and Warehouse Union at California's largest port in 2002, costing some $2 billion dollars per day while idling some 100,000 port-related jobs. Throw in the political refusal to significantly upgrade the transportation infrastructure in the region. Then tack on the ongoing upgrade to the Panama Canal, expected to double its capacity by 2015, and you understand the optimism at the Port of Houston, America's seventh-largest container port and second-largest by tonnage. Shipping experts see container cargo traffic almost doubling at Houston, as ships from Asia bypass costly West Coast ports, use the newly-widened Panama Canal, and then unload their cargo in Texas for destinations in the Midwest.[127] Almost doubling the number of containers using Houston would result in it having America's fourth-business port, behind San Pedro, Long Beach, and New York, and ahead of Savannah, Georgia and Oakland, California.

Adding a note of irony, California, which no longer smelts steel, will lose out to Texas as the Panama Canal comes to completion on the tensile strength of 15,800 tons of Texas steel, manufactured at the Gerdau Long Steel North America mill in Midlothian and shipped to Panama through the Port of Houston.

Texas: Reasonable Regulation Lowers Costs for Manufacturing
Along with taxes, labor and land costs, energy costs can be a factor in business decisions to locate or expand in a state, especially for energy-intensive industries such as aluminum smelting, chemicals, steel, and glass manufacturing. Electric power generation claims about 40 percent of U.S. energy consumption with coal providing 48 percent of that power.[128]

But, regulations can greatly impact the cost of electricity. Clean air rules make coal power more expensive—or, in the case of a 2006 California law, effectively illegal.[129] And, statutory or regulatory requirements to use ever greater amounts of government-approved, but more costly electricity generation means, such as solar power, also drive up the cost of electricity.

---

[126] Ending the practice of port taxes was one of reasons the Constitution was proposed and ratified. For example, Connecticut and New Jersey were heavily dependent on the port of New York, a fact that the State of New York was well aware of as it ramped up taxes to use the port, generating tax revenue on goods destined for neighboring states. For an example of such legislation, see California Senate Bill 974 of 2008, vetoed by Gov. Schwarzenegger, it sought to levy a tax of $30 per twenty-foot equivalent unit on each shipping container processed in the Ports of Los Angeles, Long Beach and Oakland. For the bill language, see: http://www.leginfo.ca.gov/pub/07-08/bill/sen/sb_0951-1000/sb_974_bill_20080805_enrolled.html.

[127] "Panama Canal expansion means big changes at Port," by Jenalia Moreno, *Houston Chronicle*, June 19, 2011.

[128] *Annual Energy Review 2010*, U.S. Energy Information Administration, October 2011, Tables 1.3, 2.1b-2.1f, 10.3 and 10.4.

[129] California's Senate Bill 1368, passed in 2006, made it illegal for the state's power companies to renew electricity contracts from traditional coal-fired providers that provide the majority of the 28 percent of the electricity that California imports from other states. For bill language, see: http://www.leginfo.ca.gov/pub/05-06/bill/sen/sb_1351-1400/sb_1368_bill_20060929_chaptered.html.

According to the U.S. Department of Energy, energy costs, much of it for electricity, account for 8-12 percent of glass production costs, 5 percent of metal casting expenses, and 15 percent of steel manufacturing costs, while petroleum refining is the most energy-intensive industry in America.

In the case of electric arc steelmaking, electricity accounts for about 7 percent of the cost to make the steel, at $0.10 per kilowatt hour.[130] But, the average cost of electricity for industrial users in Texas was $0.0674 per kilowatt hour in 2009, slightly above the national average of $0.0670. In heavily regulated California, the industrial cost of electricity was $0.1007 with only seven states seeing higher costs: Hawaii and Alaska and the Northeastern states of New Jersey, Connecticut, Rhode Island, Massachusetts, and New Hampshire.[131] The difference in electrical costs for a steel manufacturer in California vs. Texas, all other factors being equal, would be about $11 per ton, or about 2.2 percent of the delivered cost of the steel, year in and year out.

California energy policymakers, both elected officials and unelected bureaucrats with the California Public Utilities Commission, the California Independent System Operator Corporation, and the California Energy Commission claim that California's regulatory policies have resulted in fairly flat per capita increases in electricity use in California compared to the U.S. at a time when big screen TVs and air conditioning are increasing electricity use. In fact, since 1973, per capita residential electricity use in California has only increased 14 percent, as compared to 60 percent nationwide, making California the most electrically efficient state in America.

But, has this efficiency, largely driven by higher electrical costs, come at the price of jobs?

The U.S. Energy Information Administration states that in 2010, residential use of electricity accounted for 39 percent of U.S. usage. With that in mind, residential electricity savings accounted for 42 percent of the difference between California's overall electrical savings as compared to the U.S.—and, much of that can be explained by the benign coastal climate zone that the majority of the California population lives within as well as heavy residential use of natural gas for heating, water heaters, and cooking vs. the higher use of electricity for those household applications in other parts of the nation.

California's industrial sector accounted for 39 percent of the difference between the U.S. and California's per capita electrical consumption, with more than half of reduction occurring since 1999, when electrical prices began a sharp rise in California due to public policy. During the same time measured, 1973 to 2005, American industrial consumption of electricity was up 6 percent overall, but, as with California, the industrial sector has seen declines in consumption from 1999 to 2005.

---

[130] Electric Arc Furnace Steelmaking Costs 2011, Steelonthenet.com.
[131] Source: U.S. Energy Information Administration, Form EIA-861, "Annual Electric Power Industry Report," 2009.

How much of California's energy-intensive manufacturing decline that can be linked to high electricity costs can be difficult. What can be measured, however, is the total electricity use in Texas vs. California and the extra cost paid by Californians for their higher cost electricity. In 2009, Texas paid $34.1 billion to consume 345,296 gigawatt hours of electricity. California paid $34.4 billion to consume 259,584 gigawatt hours of electricity. If California charged the same for its electricity that Texas does, then California residential, commercial and industrial users could have saved $10 billion per year, or about $270 per capita—money that could be spent on other parts of the economy or to make lower cost products to improve competitive positioning.

Over time, the cost differential for electricity impacts the competitiveness of certain industries, just as other cost inputs do, from labor, to land to taxes and regulatory costs. California policymakers may believe that, on balance, the state comes out ahead by forcing energy-intensive industries, and their higher emissions, off shore or out of state. But, such policies are not without negative consequences, as manufacturing jobs typically pay more for those without a college education than do service jobs that don't require higher education.

An interesting example to follow is the fate of primary metal manufacturing in Texas, California, and the U.S. as a whole. Primary metal manufacturing occurs when steel or aluminum is made from ore or scrap. It's energy-intensive. And, the jobs in the industry often pay well.

Due to changes in the way the U.S. Bureau of Economic Analysis compiled its data, 1997 is a break point. Looking at U.S. primary metal manufacturing from 1990 to 1997, we see fairly strong growth in output from $68 billion to $99 billion. California showed growth slightly below the national rate, with value rising from $1.9 billion to $2.5 billion, while in Texas, the rate of growth was slower than California, going from $1.6 billion to $1.9 billion. Figure 32 charts the output of this basic industry through 1997, a time before California really began to crack down on high energy use industries.

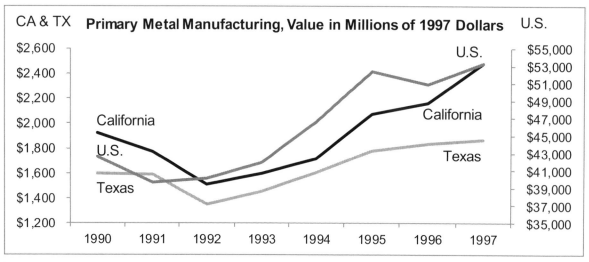

Figure 32—Texas primary metal manufacturing grew in the 1990s, but below both the national average and the rate of growth within California.

One of California's largest steel manufacturing plants was Kaiser Steel, once employing 9,000 workers. It ceased operations in 1984, under pressure from Japanese competition, as well as California clean air rules. In 1993, California Steel Industries, a firm which used Kaiser's old facility in Fontana, asked for the State of California's assistance in expediting a stalled permit to build a $220 million electric arc furnace, keeping the 1,000 workers employed on the site and making the firm more competitive. Today, the firm fabricates its product from imported steel. It does not operate an arc furnace in California, meaning that a significant part of the value added for their products is produced elsewhere.[132]

Figure 33 looks at the primary metal manufacturing output in Texas, California and the U.S. from 1997 to 2009. Here we see the trend lines reversed, with growth in the U.S. and California stalled while the trend in Texas is strongly up.

As Figures 29 and 30 showed earlier, the share of manufacturing, not including oil refining, as a percentage of the U.S. economy dropped from 26.9 percent in 1963 to 10.5 percent in 2009. During the same period, manufacturing as a share of the Texas economy went from 16.5 percent to 10.7 percent, a decline, but today slightly larger than the U.S. as a whole. California, with its greater regulatory, tax and cost burden, saw manufacturing's importance in the economy drop from 20.0 percent in 1963 to 9.6 percent.

People create businesses to make money. They do this by offering a superior product or service for a competitive price that consumers willingly purchase—and by ensuring that the cost to design, develop, and offer the product is less than its cost over time. Costs include the cost to

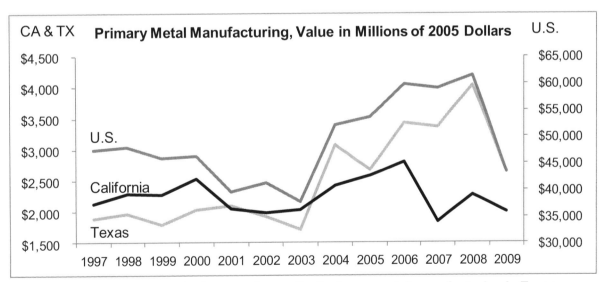

Figure 33—From 1997 to 2009, the rate of growth of primary metal manufacturing in Texas outpaced that in California and the U.S. as a whole—the California electricity crisis (2000-2001) hit energy-intensive industries hard, while in 2006 two significant California laws were passed that are expected to steeply increase electricity costs.

---

[132] California has one remaining steel refinery, the TAMCO mini mill at Rancho Cucamonga, which uses an electric arc furnace to turn scrap steel into concrete reinforcing bars (rebar).

borrow money, land, physical plant such as building and machines, labor, energy and taxes. Regulations also take a toll, although they are harder to quantify. Over time, states with high taxes and burdensome regulations will, all other factors being equal, lose business to states with lower taxes and regulations. Likewise, countries compete for business-creating capital as well.

Manufacturing, more so than services anchored to a state, such as retail stores, is more sensitive to state costs. If a steel manufacturer can lower its costs by moving to another state or nation, it will—or risk going bankrupt in the face of fierce competition.

For this reason, Texas is likely to see continued growth and diversification of its economy; as long as it maintains its competitive edge relative to other states.

CHAPTER SIX—ENERGY AND THE ENVIRONMENT IN TEXAS

In a modern economy, energy is tightly tied to output and quality of life: energy is used to boost our ability to manufacture things, to heat and cool our homes, get us to work, and allow us to vacation far afield if we wish.

How we obtain energy and use it also impacts the environment. Strip mining coal can level a mountain and, if done incorrectly, contaminate groundwater. Burning coal releases harmful chemicals and particulates into the air as well as greenhouse gases which some fear might be driving global warming. Crude oil can spill while extracting it or shipping it by tanker or pipeline. When refined into gasoline and burned in cars, oil can contribute to that orange-brown urban haze called smog, a photochemical brew that irritates lungs and makes the eyes water. Nuclear power, while free from chemical emissions, produces radioactive materials that, if not recycled, can be dangerous for 200,000 years. Even wind power has its issues, with unsightly and noisy pylons looming over the landscape holding aloft massive blades that, with 150 mph wingtip speeds, make mincemeat of rare raptors and bats without remorse.

But, unless humanity wishes to reduce its numbers by a factor of 100 and return to living in caves, the intensive use of energy is here to stay. Fortunately, modern technology can mitigate many of the ill-effects of our energy use—and, in many cases, make the environment even better. The examples are all around us: the New York City of 120 year ago was far smaller, but the streets were daily covered with tons of horse manure that had to be removed and dumped at sea by barge; the Los Angeles Basin, frequently plagued with thick, choking smog in the 1970s today has clear air; while in parts of Africa, untouched as yet by modernity, people forage for fuel to cook their food, denuding forests and causing desertification.

As detailed in previous chapters, Texas has vaulted to becoming America's foremost export state and second-largest manufacturing state. Texas' success can be attributed to many things: the light hand of government, geography, an abundance of natural resources, and, increasingly, the policies of other states that discourage industry. This latter issue has a heavy note of irony attached to it, for, as California drives out manufacturing as a result of its restrictivist energy policies in the name of a cleaner globe, the manufacturing doesn't go away, it merely moves.

Today California imports ever larger amounts of electricity, practicing electrical colonialism by shifting the jobs and the emissions associated with power plants to other states. Further, as manufacturing has fled America's most energy efficient and, in many respects, cleanest state, the overall environmental damage which so concerns California's policymakers actually increases. How? To the extent that the things once manufactured in California are now manufactured elsewhere in places such as China or even Texas, the emissions associated with these goods increases many fold, as these items are often being produced with industry energized by coal power plants, many without even basic pollution control devices, then shipped around the planet in emissions-belching container vessels. The tyranny of unintended policies consequences is particularly harsh in this realm.

Texas' rise in manufacturing has coincided with a rise in critics who claim, correctly, that Texas emits the greatest amount of air pollution. That America's second-largest state with a vibrant manufacturing base would produce more emissions than nuclear-powered Vermont or other smaller states is a given—the problems come when those same critics then make the dubious leap to asserting that Texas is a polluted, dirty state—that the jobs generated by industry come at too high a price for the environment.

So, what are the facts? Is Texas dirtier than other states because of its economic success? Or, does the wealth generated by success, with attendant advances in technology, allow Texas to produce more things of value to the rest of the world while reducing the negative impacts often associated with producing such things?

Texas Energy Overview

Texas produces and uses the most amount of energy of any state in America. Its energy production from oil, gas, coal, and wind provides industry with the needed foundation to produce goods consumed around the world.

According to the U.S. Energy Information Administration, Texas leads the nation in oil production (although offshore Federal waters produce more than any single state); Texas' 27 refineries produce more than a quarter of America's domestically-produced fuel; 30 percent of America's natural gas comes from Texas; and Texas' more than 2,000 wind turbines make more wind power than any state.[133] Texas is also the top coal consuming state in America with about a third of the coal being mined in Texas and most of the remainder imported from Wyoming.

The Energy Information Administration also ranks Texas' industrial emissions. But much of what it measures the critics. When measured by the amount of emissions per megawatt hour of electricity produced, Texas is 30th in Sulfur Dioxide emissions, 33rd in Nitrogen Oxide, and 23rd in Carbon Dioxide.[134] So, Texas is number one in emissions due to the massive size of its industrial base, but it ranks well in the emissions produced to make all that stuff, meaning its manufacturing is both clean and efficient, compared to other states. Perhaps that's why, as Figure 1 showed up in the front of the book, that out of the 20 U.S. cities with the worst air pollution in 2011, none were in Texas while California hosted five, Ohio four and Pennsylvania two.

Pennsylvania, the fifth-largest state with a large number of aging coal-fired power plants, produces the second-highest amount of Sulfur Dioxide emissions, ahead of number three Texas, as well as the second-greatest amount of Nitrogen Oxide and Carbon Dioxide emissions, just behind Texas.[135]

The area with the most air emissions relative to the amount of electricity it produces? The "do as I say, not as I do" city of Washington, D.C.: scoring a triple play in Sulfur Dioxide, Nitrogen

---

[133] Source: http://www.eia.gov/state/state-energy-profiles.cfm?sid=TX.
[134] Source: http://www.eia.gov/cneaf/electricity/st_profiles/texas.html.
[135] Source: http://www.eia.gov/cneaf/electricity/st_profiles/pennsylvania.html.

Oxide, and Carbon Dioxide emissions.[136] This is even more shocking when one stops to consider that D.C.'s economic output almost entirely consists of laws and regulations for the rest of us.

Vermont, known for its environmental sensitivities, has the least air emissions per megawatt hour because, as with France, 80 percent of their electricity comes from nuclear power, with most of the remainder generated by hydroelectric dams.[137]

Texas Electricity Market Deregulation: Doing it Right

Texas and California both moved to deregulate the wholesale electric market in the late 1990s. Today, Texas consumers pay less for their electricity, after deregulating the market even more in the years since, while California consumers pay far more after their lawmakers rolled back the reforms and reregulated the market. How did this happen?

In 1996, California Governor Pete Wilson, a Republican, signed a partial deregulation of the Golden State's electric market. In four years, wholesale electric prices were up 800 percent in California. Blackouts began hitting California in the summer of 2000 with two of California's three major public utilities filing for bankruptcy as a result of rampant market manipulation caused by the botched half-deregulation (the government only deregulated a portion of the market, leading to even larger market distortions than was the case under full regulation). Blackouts again hit California in 2001. By November, 2003, Democratic Governor Gray Davis declared an end to the electric state of emergency—he had been only the second governor in U.S. history to have been recalled just five weeks earlier, partially due to fallout from the partial deregulation of the electric market. Californians in the vast Pacific Gas & Electric service region paid an average of 9.7 cents per kilowatt hour in 2000 for their electricity; by 2011 the system-wide rate had risen to 15.1 cents, an increase of 56 percent.[138]

In contrast, Texas began restructuring its electricity markets to encourage wholesale competition about the same time California did. Unlike California, Texas then extended the deregulation to the retail market six years later. Then, three year ago, Texas eliminated all electricity price controls.

What a novel thought—allowing the free market to deliver a vital commodity, electricity, with as little interference from government as possible!

Naturally, there was a heated debate about whether or not the free market could perform in supplying a reliable product at a competitive price to Texas consumers. But, the numbers tell the story of success: in 2001, the average electric price in Texas was 8.77 cents per kilowatt hour. By 2009, the price was 9.27 cents per kilowatt hour, an increase of 5.7 percent over eight years.

---

[136] Source: http://www.eia.gov/cneaf/electricity/st_profiles/dc.html.
[137] Source: http://www.eia.gov/cneaf/electricity/st_profiles/vermont.html.
[138] California Public Utilities Commission, Rate Charts and Tables – Electricity, 2000 to 2011, ftp://ftp.cpuc.ca.gov/puc/energy/electric/rates+and+tariffs/Average%20Rates%20by%20Customer%20Class%20Years%202000-2011.ppt.

Adjusting for inflation, electricity in Texas in 2009 was 11.3 percent *below* 2001 prices. The national average increase in that time span was 41.6 percent.

Further, Texas, unlike California which must import up to a quarter of its electricity, has ample reserve margins. This is because in states such as California, generating firms must get regulatory permission to build new facilities—they have to prove need. In Texas, generating companies build facilities when they believe a new generator might turn a profit.

Imagine: a company being allowed to make decisions about investments free from government control.

Allowing the profit incentive to function has resulted in more than $25 billion in generation investments totaling 39,000 megawatts of power into the grid since 1996. Further, under the Texas model, investors, not consumers, assume the risk. In California, and most other states, by contrast, public utilities are guaranteed a rate of return by a regulatory body—this removes much of the incentive to produce inexpensive power.

Texas electric market competition broke up five regional monopolies. Together, these five electric giants lost between 56 and 80 percent of their market share. The average Texan within the state's electrical grid can now choose from 138 plans offered by 29 providers. This consumer choice has resulted in about 82 percent of Texas electrical users changing their rate plans.

Of course, this singular success story is threatened by Federal market distortions, including subsidies to favored "green energy," taxes and fees, market disruptions caused by environmental lawsuits or regulations, and other forms of government market intervention. These threats from law or regulation could increase costs to Texas consumers by as much as $3 billion per year.[139]

While the deregulation of the Texas electric market has been an unqualified success for Texas consumers and the Texas economy, there were a few monopolistic islands left intact—artifacts of political reality that resisted the deregulation effort. Municipal utilities and electric cooperatives were allowed to maintain their hold on consumers in their service areas.

Cooperatives operate along the lines of the credit union model. An electric cooperative's consumers are the investors in the firm. As such, they may get a dividend from the electric cooperative's operations. They also have a say in its operation, with larger consumers usually having a larger say. Some cooperatives have allowed competition in their service region.

Municipal utilities are another issue entirely. The City of Austin, Texas' capital, is well known as one of the non-conservative areas in Texas. Their government-run electric utility, Austin Energy, has a monopoly on the delivery of electric service to almost one million customers. The electric deregulation law gives Austin Energy the option of allowing competition, but they don't. With a captive mass of customers, Austin Energy, driven by the Austin City Council, has been striving

---

[139] "Regulation of Electricity Markets," by Bill Peacock, Texas Public Policy Foundation. http://www.texaspolicy.com/pdf/2011-RegulationofElectricityMarkets-CEF.pdf.

to increase its use of expensive "green energy" with the predictable result being large rate increases.

Profit making electric utilities and cooperatives make business decisions to maximize return to their shareholders: how much and what type of generation capacity to build or invest in; when and where to build additional transmission lines; when up upgrade or retire generation; what rates to charge; and the like. In a competitive market, making these decisions badly will result in loss of market share and, if not corrected, bankruptcy.

A municipal utility faces no such pressure. If they make a profit, the money generated can subsidize city operations. In California, the Los Angeles Department of Water and Power is a massive example of this, with their monopoly over Los Angeles generating $2.8 billion a year in revenue of which about a quarter-billion in profit is sent to underwrite some 8 percent of the City of Los Angeles' operating budget. Alternatively, if a municipal utility generates a loss, opaque government accounting practices might hide this fact for some time, allowing city leaders to defer critical maintenance and upgrades, putting both consumers and taxpayers at risk.

Further, with large sums of money and literal power at stake, elected officials often can't help themselves in making statements with their public companies. This was the case when, in mid-November 2011, Austin Mayor Lee Leffingwell announced his reelection bid at an elementary school where he promised to end Austin Energy's use of coal, one of the least expensive ways to generate power, and shift the city towards renewable energy, after a "dialogue with the community."[140] One wonders how much the "community" really knows or cares to know about electric system cost and reliability. In the meantime, the mayor could act on his promise by ending Austin Energy's monopoly, allowing consumers the choice of paying more for "green" energy if they so choose from one of several "green" energy providers in Texas.

Oil and Fracking

In 2009, Texas had the nation's largest proven increase in oil reserves (529 million barrels) and total oil discoveries (433 million barrels). But, as recently as 2006, petroleum experts were claiming that Texas' best oil days were behind it—that production had peaked and was going into an irreversible decline.[141] Technology and the free market regularly makes fools out of people predicting scarcity and doom: Texas oil production was 934,000 barrels a day in 2006, but rose to over 978,000 barrels a day in 2010, a five percent increase, with proven reserves in Texas higher today than in 2006.[142]

Texas gas production tells a different story; one that's even more dramatic from a technology impact. In 2006, Texas produced 6.08 trillion cubic feet of natural gas. By 2010, production rose

---

[140] "If Austin Goes Coal-Free, Could the Rest of Texas Follow?" by Terrence Henry, *State Impact*, NPR, November 17, 2011.

[141] "Has oil peaked?: Yes," by Jeffrey J. Brown, Post Carbon Institute's *Energy Bulletin*, June 10, 2006, http://www.energybulletin.net/node/17009.

[142] "Oil Production and Well Counts (1935-2010)," Texas Railroad Commission, http://www.rrc.state.tx.us/data/production/oilwellcounts.php.

to 7.25 trillion cubic feet, an increase of 19 percent in only four years. Natural gas production in 2009 was the higher than it was since 1976—so much for irreversible declines.[143]

Much of the reason for the continued strength in oil and gas production in Texas is due to advancements in technology and policymakers who allow the benefits from those advancements.

Hydraulic fracturing, aka "fracking," has been around since the 1940s. It involves pumping water, sand, and a small amount of chemicals under high pressure into a completed well to create fissures in the rock deep underground. The cracks in the rocks allow the oil and or gas embedded in them to escape into the well. The sand is used to keep the fissures from closing up under the great pressure from the millions of tons of rock overhead. Combined with advanced horizontal drilling at depths of one to more than two miles below the earth's surface, hydraulic fracturing has unlocked enormous amounts of natural gas in Texas, as well as in places like the Appalachian region of Pennsylvania.[144]

Government estimates of the amount of recoverable oil and natural gas have soared. Global natural gas supplies rose 40 percent in 2010. From 2010 to 2011, the Energy Information Administration increased its estimate of Texas' natural-gas reserves by 70 percent. Due largely to fracking, producers now have access to two billion barrels in the Wolfberry formation in the Permian Basin of West Texas. While the Eagle Ford fields in south Texas increased oil production fourfold in the first ten months of 2010. And the Haynesville-Bossier fields, straddling Texas' border with Louisiana, reserves of natural gas increased by 9.4 trillion cubic feet while production jumped twelvefold.[145] Proven natural gas reserves in Texas have increased 100 percent in the last 10 years. Since 1990, exports of Texas natural gas have increased 1,400 percent.[146]

Most of the currently surging oil and gas production is on private land, where federal permission is not required and state governments are supportive.

The Federal Government's Assault on Texas: The EPA and Fracking[147]
The U.S. Army had simple phrase for junior soldiers: *If it moves, salute it; if it doesn't move, pick it up; if you can't pick it up, paint it.* Army veteran Ronald Reagan adapted this to government's view of the economy: *If it moves, tax it. If it keeps moving, regulate it. And if it stops moving, subsidize it.* The Federal government has moved from the "tax it" to the "regulate it" phase of Texas' oil and gas production efforts.

---

[143] "Natural Gas Production and Well Counts (1935-2010)," Texas Railroad Commission, http://www.rrc.state.tx.us/data/production/gaswellcounts.php.
[144] "The Fracas About Fracking," by Kathleen Hartnett White (of the Texas Public Policy Foundation), *National Review*, June 20, 2011.
[145] Ibid.
[146] "Texas Energy and the Energy of Texas: the Master Resource in the Most Dynamic Economy," by Drs. Steven Hayward and Kenneth Green, American Enterprise Institute.
[147] Much of this discussion is drawn from a Texas Public Policy Foundation paper entitled "The Case of Range Resources," by Mario Loyola, September, 2011, see: http://www.texaspolicy.com/pdf/2011-09-PP15-TheCaseofRangeResources-CTAS-MarioLoyola.pdf.

On December 7, 2010, the U.S. Environmental Protection Agency's office for the south-central U.S. announced that they were hitting Range Resources Corporation, a Texas-based natural gas company, with an endangerment finding and remedial order for contaminating the drinking water in Parker County, Texas.

The trouble began in December 2009, when Parker county resident Steven Lipsky claimed he had problems with his well water. Parker contracted to have a water well drilled on his property in 2005, but asserted methane contamination when he began using his well for domestic consumption at the time he moved into his new, and much larger, home in 2009. Lipsky suspected that the source of his problems was a nearby natural gas well that Range Resources had built and "fracked" earlier that year to exploit a part of the massive Barnett Shale nearly a mile underground.

Environmental activists tracked Lipsky down and encouraged him to watch "Gasland," an anti-fracking propaganda film filled with fraudulent claims. Once fortified, the enviro-activists encouraged him to file suit with the EPA and Texas regulatory authorities.

Testing showed that there indeed were trace amounts of methane in Lipsy's drinking water. And, like the methane found a mile deep in the Barnett Shale formation where Range Resources was drilling, it was "thermogenic," meaning it formed deep underground, rather than "biogenic," created by microbes. The testing simply proved that both samples had come from deep underground.

That was all the proof the EPA needed to proceed. They concluded that Range Resources "caused or contributed to" the trace amounts of methane in Mr. Lipsky's well. "We know they've polluted the well," Al Armendariz, then EPA's regional administrator, alleged in a television interview at the time the order was issued. "We know they're getting natural gas in there."[148]

However, it quickly became clear that the EPA hadn't a clue as to how the company could have caused the contamination. A week *after* the EPA accused Range Resources, EPA staff met with the company, which wanted to find out just how the EPA thought it had polluted the well.

The gas from the company's well could only have infiltrated Mr. Lipsky's well in one of two ways: either it migrated vertically over 5,000 feet up to the Trinity Aquifer as a result of 10 days of fracking the new well, a geologic impossibility, or it migrated into the aquifer from a mechanical integrity failure in the well pipe.

EPA staff agreed that fracking could not have caused the contamination, because there were no faults extensive enough to permit migration of gas over such a great distance. And they did not

---

[148] Armendariz resigned in April 2012 after remarks he made to his EPA colleagues came to light in a video showing him advocating "crucifying" oil companies for alleged regulatory violations. See: "EPA official resigns over 'crucify' remark," by Lesa Jansen and Todd Sperry, *CNN*, April 30, 2012, http://www.cnn.com/2012/04/30/us/epa-crucify/index.html, accessed on June 16, 2012.

dispute the veracity of the pressure-testing that confirmed the mechanical integrity of the well. In fact, they couldn't propose a single theory, viable or otherwise, as to how the gas had contaminated the well.

Weeks later, in a sworn deposition, regional EPA enforcement chief John Blevins was questioned about internal emails in which an EPA engineer warned that the simple methane isotope test EPA had conducted was not "conclusive" proof. Range Resources' lawyers (Recall the chapter on lawsuit reform which set U.S. lawsuit costs at 2.2 percent of the economy, triple that of the U.K. or France?) asked Mr. Blevins whether he was aware that many of the water wells in the area had contained natural gas long before any drilling. He was. Had he seen the email from an outside scientist telling the EPA that it had to "evaluate the potential for other sources that would be thermogenic and the geology or structures that would store or transmit the gas from origin to aquifer"? He had. Had the EPA considered other possible geological sources of the gas in the Lipsky well such as the Strawn formation, a shallow layer of rock infused with salt water and natural gas? It had not. Mr. Blevins had indeed heard of the Strawn formation, although he was unaware of both its exact nature and whereabouts. No one at the EPA had considered the Strawn formation as a source of gas, either.

The freshwater Trinity Aquifer, from which the Lipsky well drew its water, extends about 200 feet underground. Just beneath that is a rock strata laden with natural gas and salt water called the Strawn formation, which extends down to about 400 feet underground. Over 5,000 feet below that is the Barnett Shale, from which Range Resources was extracting natural gas.

The Trinity Aquifer and Strawn formation overlap in places. This allows gas and salty water to migrate from the Strawn to the aquifer; particularly when increased pumping of ground water for human consumption draws in gas and saltwater from the formation underneath the aquifer. It doesn't help that the migration pathways for this gas-infused saltwater have been increased as a result of drilling of dozens of water wells through the Trinity into the Strawn; sometimes by as much as 50 feet.

With the EPA now under oath, Blevins unsurprisingly backed away from the original bureaucratic order against Range Resources. He would not affirm that the company had "caused or contributed to" the endangerment; only that the company "may have" done so.

Sadly, in the modern administrative state, "caused" endangerment and "may have" don't have a practical difference when it comes to sanctions and fines.

A complex and expensive battery of chemical fingerprint testing, focused particularly on nitrogen content, irrefutably demonstrated that the gas in the Lipsky well was the same as that in the Strawn formation, and different than that in the Barnett Shale—which explained why area residents had found natural gas in their water wells years before any drilling for oil and gas. In fact, some water wells were even "flared" for days after drilling, to release dangerous levels of methane. One area subdivision's water tanks warn, "Danger: Flammable Gas."

But, of course, for the "Gasland" enlightened environmentalists, Lipsky, Armendariz, and Blevins, facts don't much matter. While the scientific case for EPA's claims imploded, they persisted in suing Range Resources for refusing to obey its original order, and asking a federal district court to levy up to $15 million in fines. Lewis Carroll's Queen of Hearts would find a home in today's EPA: "Sentence first, verdict afterwards."

The list of environmental hazards assigned to fracking is long: drinking water contamination, pollution of rivers, groundwater depletion, air emissions of toxic pollutants and greenhouse gases, radiation, and even earthquakes. But, with the exception of groundwater depletion, no connection between hydraulic fracturing itself and any of these environmental problems has been demonstrated. Faulty well construction, breaches in cemented and heavy-steel-encased wellbores, and accidents could, of course, lead to adverse environmental impacts. But there is no evidence that fracking itself is inherently damaging. Which, is a fairly common sense proposition, given that fracking usually occurs a mile underneath the aquifers from which people draw their well water.

The Society of Petroleum Engineers estimates that more than 1 million oil and gas wells in the U.S. have used hydraulic fracturing over the past 60 years. During this time, the process has never been connected to groundwater contamination.[149]

Worries about some other dangers are equally unfounded. Air emissions from drilling sites have been the most persistent public concern in the Barnett shale area. Studies by the Texas Department of Health and the Texas Commission on Environmental Quality have confirmed that the emissions do not exceed levels protective of human health.[150]

Risk can be managed and reduced, but never eliminated. Over the last 30 years, the on-shore oil and gas industry has had a sound environmental record. The many risks—more uncertainties than palpable dangers—attributed to hydraulic fracturing have not occasioned serious environmental harms. But, in only a few years, fracking has allowed recovery of approximately 7 billion barrels of oil and 7 trillion cubic feet of natural gas. Vast stores remain, and almost all new wells will need hydraulic fracturing.[151]

The Federal Government's Assault on Texas: The EPA vs. Cleaner Air
While fracking in some form has been around for decades, its greater use and complex underground science may excuse some of the EPA missteps. Air quality is another matter. Measuring air quality is a fairly straightforward premise: you figure out what you want to measure then measure it. If a concentration of some molecule is deemed unhealthful to humans, you figure out where it comes from and in what quantities—then you figure out how best to mitigate it. This last part is the challenge.

---

[149] The Fracas About Fracking, supra.
[150] The Fracas About Fracking, supra.
[151] The Fracas About Fracking, supra.

Before detailing the struggle between Texas and the EPA over how best to clean the air in Texas, recall the very first figure of this book. In the second line from the bottom, we cited the number of cities in Texas that were in the top-20 most polluted cities in America for 2011. There were none. California had five in the top 20.

Unelected bureaucrats in the regulatory agencies typically prefer command and control regimes: they simply order a region or an industry or particular companies to reduce or stop emissions of certain substances. Problem solved.

Except that the problem is rarely solved so easily. If command and control rules result in mass layoffs as entire industries, unable, or unwilling to adapt in place either close down or move, elected officials will often enter the fray, pressuring the bureaucrats to back off in the name of jobs.

Alternatives to command and control regulatory approaches to reducing air pollution have been tried with some success. Levying a tax on the unhealthful emissions is one approach to reduce their volume. Another approach is to auction off permits to emit with the overall amount of permits determining the total acceptable emissions for a region or industry. As the permits decline over time, industry will face an increasing cost to buy the right to emit, allowing them to factor in the costs as they calculate when would be the best time to upgrade or close down older facilities. The Texas Flexible Permitting Program is a variant of this latter strategy.

As mentioned earlier in this chapter, because Texas produces the most electricity in the nation, it has the largest amount of emissions within the electrical sector. The Texas fleet of coal-fired power plants is one of the youngest in the nation and has invested $16 billion in emission control technology over the last 20 years. The emission rates at these plants are extremely low. According to EPA's acid rain database, the nitrous oxides (NOx) emission rate at Texas power plants is 38 percent less than the national average. Texas also attains the National Ambient Air Quality Standards for nitrogen dioxide, sulfur dioxide and carbon monoxide.[152]

But, many kinds of manufacturing generate emissions of their own, especially in the petrochemical industry. Reducing these emissions while improving prosperity has been a tough challenge for Texas policymakers—and one that they've succeeded quite well at over the years—at least until the EPA began to interfere.

Texas has become a national leader in effective and innovative environmental programs. Between 2000 and 2008, Texas lowered ozone levels by 22 percent compared to a national average of 8 percent; and this, while the state's population grew at double the national average. In the same period, Texas lowered nitrous oxides (NOx) levels by 46 percent while they declined nationally by only 27 percent. In fact, Texas has emission rates for most pollutants that are among the lowest in the nation.

---

[152] Susana Hildebrand, TCEQ Chief Engineer, Update of Air Quality in Texas (presented at Oct. 29, 2009 Commission Work Session) http://www.tceq.com.

All major urban areas in Texas currently meet the Federal eight-hour ozone standard of 85 parts per billion (ppb), with the exception of the Dallas-Fort Worth area at only 1-2 ppb above the limit. Even the Dallas-Fort Worth region, however, reduced ozone levels from 96 ppb in 2006 to 86 ppb in 2009, a remarkable improvement in air quality with tangible benefits for the area's residents.

The oil refining and chemical manufacturing hub of Houston offers a case in point. Over the last decade, as the Texas population grew by over 4 million people and the state economy grew by a rate of 40 percent, Texas air quality dramatically improved—thanks in large part to the Texas Flexible Permitting Program. The Houston region, in years past vying with Los Angeles as the most ozone polluted part of the country, reduced ozone levels from 119 parts per billion in 1999 to 84 parts per billion in 2009. Houston, the home of the nation's greatest concentration of petrochemical plants, met the legal requirement of 85 parts per billion federal ozone standard.[153]

The Texas Flexible Permitting Program significantly contributed to the dramatic improvement in air quality in this heavily industrialized area. Coal and petroleum coke-fired power plants with flexible permits have decreased sulfur dioxide (SOx) by 25,803 tons per year and NOx by 10,330 tons per year and particulate matter by 795 tons per year. For refineries, flexible permits decreased SOx by 3.9 tons per year, NOx by 15,844 tons per year and volatile organic compounds by 920 tons per year.[154] Stationary emissions sources in the Houston area decreased ozone-forming NOx emissions from 650 tons per day in 1993 to 156 tons per day in 2008. Houston also decreased highly reactive volatile organic compounds (HRVOCs) by 50 percent. In 2008, all benzene monitors in and around Houston measured levels below the long-term level for healthy air. These volatile organic compounds are the chief ingredient in the photochemical smog that appears at daybreak in many industrialized cities around the world. And, unlike in economic competitor California, Texas managed to achieve these reductions while *growing* its industrial base.

Stringent, innovative, and targeted controls along with voluntary efforts based on cutting-edge science drove these improvements in Texas air quality. Thousands of Texans worked on this effort. The Governor, the Texas Legislature, Texas Commission on Environmental Quality (TCEQ), local governments, industry, business, private organizations, and individual Texans rolled up their sleeves and cleaned the air of Texas. Even the Federal EPA was on board in the formative years.

The distinguishing feature of the Texas Flexible Permitting Program is the use of pollutant-specific emission caps. This contrasts to the Federal EPA approach of limiting emissions for certain pieces of equipment as required in traditional Federal New Source Review permitting programs such as Prevention of Significant Deterioration and New Source Non-Attainment

---

[153] Comments attachment from Texas Commission on Environmental Quality on EPA proposed rulemaking, Approval and Promulgation of Implementation Plans; Texas; Revisions to the New Source Review (NSR) State Implementation Plan (SIP); Flexible Permits, 74 Fed. Reg. 48,480 (Sept. 23, 2009) Docket ID No. EPA-R06-OAR-2005-TX-0032.

[154] TCEQ, supra note 1.

Review permits. With Texas Flexible Permits, the emission caps are established according to Best Available Control Technology limits for all facilities contributing to the cap, and then use worst case scenarios to calculate the caps.[155]

Actually stricter than federal rules, the Texas Flexible Permitting Program requires Best Available Control Technology emission controls even on minor sources of emissions. Emission caps are set for specific emission categories, typically for Federal criteria pollutants and Volatile Organic Compounds (VOCs). Individual emission limits for specific pollutants, such as toxics, may also be applied.

Where the "flexibility" in the Texas permits process comes is in the use of control technology and operation. Control flexibility means the permit holders may "over control" one facility by going beyond Best Available Control Technology (BACT) established emission caps "in order not to add additional controls at another facility, provided that the net sum of emissions is at least as stringent as BACT being applied to each existing facility."[156]

Operational flexibility is allowed "to the extent that a permit holder may vary throughput rates, charge rates, firing rates, etc., as long as control requirements are met and compliance with emission caps and/or individual emission limits is maintained."[157]

In other words, rather than micro-managing to the individual piece of equipment level, as the EPA does, the regulatory process in Texas allows industrial facility owners to best plan how to reduce emissions from the entirety of their operations. This encourages them to apply scarce resources to achieving the goal of reducing pollution, rather than straitjacketing them into replacing or upgrading specific items.

In the face of overwhelming evidence that the Texas Flexible Permitting Program reduced pollution to Federally required levels while allowing the economy to grow, the U.S. EPA intervened anyway.[158] On June 15, 2010, the EPA ruled that the Texas Flexible Permit Program violated the federal Clean Air Act.[159]

The EPA claims the Texas Flexible Permit Program "hides" emissions, shields industrial facilities from more stringent Federal requirements and lacks enforceability. These are interesting charges, given the track record of success in pollution reduction in Texas.

---

[155] 30 Tex. Admin. Code §§ 116.710 et seq. (2010).
[156] TCEQ, supra note 1.
[157] TCEQ, supra note 1.
[158] Much of this discussion is drawn from a Texas Public Policy Foundation paper entitled "EPA Process vs. Texas Results," by Kathleen Hartnett White, September, 2010, see: See: http://www.texaspolicy.com/pdf/2010-09-PP18-FlexPermits-khw.pdf.
[159] EPA, Approval and Promulgation of Implementation Plans; Texas; Revisions to the New Source Review (NSR) State Implementation Plan (SIP); Flexible Permits; Final Rule, 75 Fed. Reg. 41,312 (July 15, 2010) Docket ID No. EPA-R06-OAR-2005-TX-0032.

This disagreement between EPA and the Texas Commission on Environmental Quality is technical—really more of an argument over process rather than results—but the stakes are high for Texas' environment and economy. The EPA's invalidation of the Texas Flexible Permit Program leaves hundreds of Texas businesses without a solid legal authorization to operate, putting thousands of jobs at risk.[160]

The first and ultimate refuge of the bureaucrat is process. Institutional inertia and mindset conspire to squelch innovation. Innovation in government, unlike in business, carries high risks and few rewards. No one gets fired for following process, even to the point of losing sight of the agency's founding rationale for existence.

The EPA's disagreement with the Texas Flexible Permit Program emphasizes the "how," as in how the permit details every mandate and how legal compliance is proved. And, while the EPA says it doesn't like the Flexible Permit Program, they can't exactly say what will make it legally acceptable. It comes down to this: *Texas, we don't care if you've been wildly successful in reducing pollution, we want you to do it our way. Impose prescriptive dictates for individual pieces of equipment instead of your flexible facility-wide emission caps.*

The legal relation between the EPA and TCEQ involves overlapping authorities. EPA's rejection of the state's Flexible Permit Program rests on an EPA power to approve all state rules relevant to the State Implementation Plans. Yet the EPA, acting under State Implementation Plan authority, is superseding the state authority otherwise federally delegated to TCEQ. The Federal Clean Air Act (CAA), Federal New Source Review (FNSR) permitting rules, Federal Title V operating permits rules, Texas State Implementation Plans for Ozone, and the Texas Clean Air Act are all interwoven in the current dispute.

The Federal Clean Air Act sets out different roles for the Federal and state governments. Once characterized as an example of cooperative federalism, the Clean Air Act directs EPA to establish standards and gives states discretion to establish the path to attain them. In an early iteration of the Clean Air Act, Congress found "that prevention and control of air pollution at its source is the primary responsibility of the States and local government."[161] Subsequent amendments increased EPA's oversight authority over state decisions, but always re-affirmed the state's role in implementing federal dictates.

For decades, EPA and TCEQ have cooperated as partners. In recent years, however, EPA has assumed a heavy-handed and adversarial role, treating the state agency more as an instrument of the Federal government than as a partner, contrary to stated Congressional intent.

TCEQ has long been in discussions with EPA about Federal approval of the Flexible Permit Program. But, in 2007, instead of acting on the Flexible Permit Program rules, EPA sent letters

---

[160] Valero Energy Corporation Vice President Rich Walsh, Oral Testimony to the Texas Senate Natural Resources Committee, August 18, 2010.
[161] 42 U.S.C.S. § 7401. (For original language on "primary responsibility of States and local governments" see "Amendments—1990—Subsec. (a)(3)" in the annotations to §7401).

to all flexible permit holders in Texas, implying their flexible permits were not valid under U.S. rules.

This put Texas employers in a bind. Faced with uncertainty about the legal status of their permits, a business group filed suit in 2008 to compel EPA to make a final decision on the Flexible Permit Program as well as 30 other state rules which EPA had suspended in legal limbo for years.[162] Federal law requires EPA's final decisions on these State Implementation Plan-related state rules within 18 months of the state's submission. But, EPA's decisions were over 10 years late for many of the 30 state rules in question (only government can blow a legal deadline by more than eight years with no consequences).

In a settlement of the litigation, EPA agreed to a schedule for final action through a Consent Decree issued by a Federal court in Dallas.[163] This lawsuit quickened TCEQ's negotiations with EPA about the state's Flexible Permit Program. Trying to accommodate EPA's concerns, TCEQ proposed revisions to the rules in question on May 28, 2010.[164] But, rather than consider TCEQ's proposal, the EPA met its court-ordered consent decree in the easiest manner possible for them: they simply issued their final rule disapproving the Texas Flexible Permit Program. EPA's invalidation of the state rules acknowledged but gave no consideration to TCEQ's proposed rule changes.[165]

On July 23, 2010, Texas Attorney General Greg Abbott challenged EPA's disapproval in a Petition for Review before the U.S. Court of Appeals for the Fifth Circuit.[166]

TCEQ continues negotiating with EPA to resolve this dispute. In addition to changes in the Flexible Permit Program rules, TCEQ has proposed an alternative permitting mechanism to "de-flex" the current flexible permits—intended as a quick means of putting the many businesses with flexible permits back into compliance. In the meantime, EPA has created a cloud of regulatory uncertainty that can only reduce business activity, weaken the state's economy, and eliminate jobs.[167]

The full consequences of EPA's action are still unclear. EPA's final disapproval, however, apparently suspends the permitting authority delegated to the state by EPA as Congress intended.

---

[162] Complaint, BCCA Appeal Group v. EPA, No. 3-08CV1491-G (N.D. Texas 2008). A large group of businesses filed a citizen's suit under the CAA to compel EPA to perform a non-discretionary duty to take final action on the over thirty state rules requiring EPA approval. The CAA dictates that EPA must take final action on the state rules within 18 months after the state submits the rules for EPA consideration. Many of the state rules at issue had been pending before EPA for over a decade.

[163] Consent Decree, BCCA Appeal Group v. EPA, No. 3-08CV1491-G (N.D. Texas 2008).

[164] TCEQ, Flexible Permit Program Revisions, 2010-007-116-PR (June 16, 2010) http://www.tceq.state.tx.us/rules/prop.html.

[165] Supra Note 3. EPA could have delayed final disapproval of the FPP and given full consideration to TCEQ's changes to the flexible permit rules. The Consent Decree explicitly provides for modification of the stipulated schedule: "Any motion to modify the schedule established in this Consent Decree may be accompanied by a motion for expedited consideration. Neither Party to the Decree shall oppose such a motion for expedited consideration."

[166] Petition for Review, Texas v. EPA, No. ___ (5th Cir. July 23, 2010).

[167] Letter from Bryan Shaw, Chairman, TCEQ, to Alfredo Armendáriz, Regional Administrator, EPA (Aug 9, 2010).

In addition, EPA has asserted federal control over several flexible permits and threatened enforcement against over 120 entities operating under state flexible permits. These permits cover most refineries, chemical plants, large manufacturing plants and some power plants, a large portion of the Texas industrial base. Thousands of Texas jobs flow from these industries. Among the many businesses left hanging are the new $6.5 billion Motiva Refinery in Port Arthur and Total's $3 billion investment in a refinery expansion. As a result of EPA's action, the predictable regulatory system that business needs to remain efficient and competitive is now fractured.

Although the dispute between EPA and TCEQ is about rule language, EPA now considers the hundreds of facilities, although in full compliance with state rules, to be in violation of the Federal Clean Air Act and subject to enforcement if EPA so chooses. Even before final invalidation of the TCEQ rules in the middle of 2010, EPA brandished the coercive club of enforcement authority. EPA proposed in the Federal Register, the 75,000 page and growing volume of U.S. regulations that have the force of law, an Audit Program for Texas Flexible Permit Holders accompanied by a Consent Agreement and Final Order; i.e., an enforcement decree. Labeled as voluntary, the audit agreement to allow continued operation "is not subject to negotiation," requires an admission of violating Federal law, and mandates payment for a "community project," none of which is required by Federal law.[168]

EPA's stated concerns revolve around two primary issues: Federal applicability and Federal enforceability. EPA claims the Texas flexible permits process conceals the full volume of pollutants at issue and thus shields business from more onerous Federal requirements. EPA also maintains that the permit terms are not detailed enough to prove compliance—remember, Texas has successfully reduced pollution using its own innovative regulatory means. TCEQ's extensive responses to EPA have explained in detail how the state rules do, in fact, prevent the flexible permit holder from circumventing Federal New Source Review rules and establish enforceability.[169]

In truly cooperative Federal-state programs, a measure of mutual trust and cooperation is necessary. Although the dispute is between EPA and TCEQ about rule language, EPA now considers the hundreds of facilities, although in full compliance with state rules, to be in violation of the Federal Clean Air Act and subject to enforcement if EPA so chooses.

As mentioned, later Congressional amendments to the original Clean Air Act diminished the basis for Federal trust of state decisions. As David Schoenbrod, former senior litigator for the Natural Resources Defense Council and current professor at the New York Law School, has observed, "The EPA is built on the premise that no one below it in the chain of command, including state and local government, can be trusted."[170]

---

[168] EPA, Audit Program for Texas Flexible Permit Holders, 75 Fed. Reg. 34,445 (June 17, 2010).
[169] TCEQ, supra note 1.
[170] "Saving our Environment from Washington," by David Schoenbrod, Yale University Press, 2005, p. 64.

Under the Texas Flexible Permit Program, when a permit application for new emission source or an amendment to an existing permit triggers additional Federal requirements because of emission volumes, pollutant type or location in a non-attainment area, TCEQ imposes all the Federal requirements. As an example, one of the facilities whose flexible permit was recently federalized by EPA had its emission cap for NOx, over time, lowered 90 percent from when the first emission cap was set in 1994. If the analysis triggers more stringent limits, such as for Federal Prevention of Significant Deterioration requirements, the tighter limits, such as Lowest Available Emission Rate, are plugged into the emission cap and offsets are stipulated to the emitting business. TCEQ consolidates the state flexible permit and the Federal New Source Review permit into one document with different permit numbers. Nothing in the CAA prohibits this use of emission caps.

TCEQ's rules require flexible permit holders to conduct detailed monitoring and record-keeping to assure compliance. Special conditions set forth the methods to verify compliance. TCEQ requires the same methods used in traditional Federal permits: compliance stack testing, periodic stack testing, continuous emissions monitoring and other parametric monitoring, as well as record keeping. Because of the wide variety of industries authorized under flexible permits in Texas, the TCEQ tailors the compliance requirements to the specific facility, process and equipment involved, using common sense in understanding that not all facilities in all locations are the same. EPA, however, views site-specific adaptation with suspicion.

The EPA's action in overturning Texas' successful pollution control process jeopardizes the planned construction of a new $6.5 billion Motiva refinery in Port Arthur and Total's planned $3 billion refinery expansion. Thousands of new highly-skilled and well-paying jobs are at risk.

And it's not just Texas that suffers. EPA's heavy-handed response to a dispute over permit rules strikes the heart of the state's industrial base, one of the U.S. economy's few healthy engines. It's no accident that Texas produces more than 25 percent of the country's transport fuel and more than 60 percent of its industrial chemicals while creating the lion's share of jobs in America as the nation slowly recovers from the deep recession.

EPA's actions are even more puzzling when one realizes that they have supported flexible permitting schemes identical in concept to the Texas program for years. EPA even *required* states to create permitting programs that allow operational flexibility.[171] An EPA authored regulation stated: "It is possible to use … these regulations to allow for operational flexibility around federally enforceable emission limits or caps."[172]

Before Texas implemented the Flexible Permit Program in 1994, EPA carried out a study on the effectiveness of regulating under emission caps versus individual emission limits. "Regulators had set limits on the amounts of pollution that could come out of each of [the refinery's] many smokestacks, pipes, and vents and, further, prescribed the methods to be used to achieve those limits (*Note: the old command and control way of regulating*). Researchers asked the refinery

---

[171] 40 C.F.R. § 70.4 (b)(12)(iii).
[172] 57 Fed. Reg. 32,250 at 32, 627 (July 21, 1992).

managers whether, if freed from these highly particular instructions, they could achieve similar environmental results more economically."[173]

The refinery proved that it could get 97 percent of EPA's required emission reductions when it chose the methods of control and at 25 percent of the cost of EPA's detailed approach. "These savings could be achieved if a facility-wide release reduction target [emission cap] existed […] if regulations did not prescribe the methods to use, and if facility operators could determine the best approach to reach that target."[174]

EPA introduced a Federal Plant-Wide Applicability Limit permitting mechanism similar to the Texas Flexible Permit Program in 1996, described as "an emissions cap or an emissions budget, an annual emissions limit that allows managers to make almost any change anytime as long as the plant's emissions do not exceed the cap."[175]

In a subsequent rule making, EPA again underlined the benefits of emission caps. "Overall, we found significant environmental benefits [….] We found that in a cap-based program, sources strive to create enough headroom [under the emission cap] for future expansions by voluntarily controlling the emissions."[176]

And as recently as October 2009, EPA promulgated rules for a *Federal* Flexible Air Permitting (FAP) system. "The purpose of this rulemaking is to clarify and reaffirm opportunities within the existing regulatory framework to encourage the wider use of the FAP approaches."[177]

Why has EPA invalidated the Texas Flexible Permitting Program, assumed control over several major facilities' permits, and threatened enforcement against more than 100 major Texas businesses in full compliance with their Flexible Permits? If Texas air quality were declining, EPA's actions might be warranted. But measured levels at the many Texas air quality monitors, however, demonstrate the success of the state's air quality programs.

Most of the flexible permits are held by large industrial facilities in the Houston region where the greatest air quality improvement has occurred. EPA should be applauding Texas as an example for other states rather than going after Texas.

The conflict between EPA and TCEQ about permit terms absorbs time and money that could be productively focused on actual environmental improvement. Federal law, however, gives EPA broad authority to trump state authorities—if EPA elects to fully use the Federal club. As Schoenbrod observes, "EPA talks flexibility but generally practices rigidity."[178]

---

[173] Schoenbrod, supra, p. 183, quoting, Howard Klee, Jr. and Mahesh Podar, Amoco/USEPA Emission Prevention Project: Executive Summary (Amoco & EPA, May 1920, at v).
[174] Schoenbrod, supra, p. 183, quoting, Howard Klee, Jr. and Mahesh Podar, Amoco/USEPA Emission Prevention Project: Executive Summary (Amoco & EPA, May 1920, at v).
[175] 61 Fed. Reg. 38,250 at 38,251 (July 23, 1996).
[176] 67 Fed. Reg. 80,186 at 20,027 (Dec. 31, 2002).
[177] 75 Fed. Reg. 51,418 (Oct. 6, 2009).
[178] Schoenbrod, supra, p.184.

Over the last four decades, the scope of EPA's regulatory authority has steadily increased to the point where regulation of environmental impact is tantamount to regulation of basic economic activity. Doubt this? Recall the U.S. Supreme Court's 5-4 2007 decision finding carbon dioxide a pollutant under the Clean Air Act giving the EPA authority to, in effect, regulate everything.

While a Federal air quality permit may directly control only emissions it can indirectly control what is produced and how it is produced. In the words of a founding trustee of the Environmental Defense Fund whose view of EPA has changed over the years: the EPA's regulation "has grown to the point where it amounts to nothing less than a massive effort at Soviet-style planning of the economy in order to achieve environmental goals."[179]

The Federal Government's Assault on Texas: The EPA and Greenhouse Gases[180]

Sadly, EPA's actions regarding the flexible permitting program are far from unique. EPA's "Endangerment Finding," that carbon dioxide (CO_2) is a pollutant under the Clean Air Act, wins top honors for reckless bureaucratic overreach. As Iain Murray noted in *National Review*, the Endangerment Finding demonstrates "the administration's contempt for the Constitution," and is "an act of legislative thuggery and an economic suicide note, all in one package."[181]

Many proponents and opponents of carbon limits agree that the Clean Air Act is wholly unsuited to regulate CO_2, a ubiquitous by-product not just of all economic activity but indeed of oxygen respiration in all forms of life. CO_2 constitutes a significant fraction of the Earth's atmosphere, ranking fourth behind argon (if water vapor is excluded). This fact led U.S. Supreme Court Justice Scalia to argue in his dissent from the landmark Supreme Court's ruling in Massachusetts vs. EPA, that something cannot "pollute the air" if it is the air.

In fact, the average human being exhales about 800 pounds of CO_2 annually, slightly less than 1/250 of the 100 tons per year threshold for pollutants under the Clean Air Act. In other words, every business that emits as much CO_2 as 250 persons exhale in a year would need an EPA Title V operating permit, which would include millions of buildings and restaurants. By the EPA's own estimate, the number of Title V permit holders would increase from 14,000 to more than 6 million, at a cost to permit holders of $49 billion over three years, just in the costs of securing the permits, on top of the $23 billion administrative cost for the agencies issuing the permits.

Even the EPA recognized that the result of regulating greenhouse gases under the literal terms of Clean Air Act would be "absurd," "infeasible," and "adversely affect national economic development."

---

[179] "Controlling Environmental Risks through Incentives," by Richard B. Stewart, 13 Columbia Journal of Environmental Law 153, 154. (1988).

[180] "EPA's Regulatory Barrage and the Lone Star State," by Kathleen Hartnett White and Mario Loyola, Inside ALEC, November/December 2010: http://www.texaspolicy.com/pdf/InsideALEC-FINALPDF.Nov.Dec10-extractedpages.pdf.

[181] "Air Power: In Which the EPA Mistakes Itself for Congress," by Iain Murray, *National Review*, Dec. 31, 2009.

To avoid this, the EPA simply re-wrote the law in rule, changing the blackletter regulatory triggers in the Clean Air Act and substituting its own vastly higher thresholds to narrow the number of entities affected in the initial phase of implementing the new regulation. In this "Tailoring Rule," EPA changed the statutory thresholds that trigger Title V and Preventions of Significant Deterioration (PSD) permits from 100 tons per year (tpy) and 250 tpy, respectively, to 100,000 and 75,000 tpy for carbon dioxide.

Through an illegal change to Federal law, duly passed by Congress and signed by the President, this comically strained interpretation of existing rules combined with a six-hundred word new definition of what "subject to regulation" now means to state agencies, the EPA declared regulation of CO_2 automatic January 2, 2010.

If states are unwilling or legally unable to meet this effective date, the EPA will immediately take over with Federal Implementation Plans. EPA's Federal Register notice of early September lists 13 states as the most likely candidates for a Federal takeover, with Texas among them. As Texas Gov. Rick Perry said recently, to accept EPA's greenhouse gas lawless initiative would be "following flawed science down a road that will lead to the loss of hundreds of thousands of Texas jobs, while doing nothing more to protect human health."[182]

In a August 2, 2010, letter to EPA, the Texas Attorney General Greg Abbott and TCEQ Chairman Bryan Shaw communicated the categorical refusal of the state of Texas to comply with the new regulation. "The State of Texas," they wrote, "does not believe that EPA's 'suggested' approach comports with the rule of law. The United States and Texas Constitutions, United States and Texas statutes, and EPA and TCEQ rules all preclude TCEQ from declaring itself ready to require permits for greenhouse gases from stationary sources as you request."

As the stakes increase dramatically in this showdown between Texas and the EPA, what hangs in the balance is not just the autonomy and economic future of all the states, but the very balance of shared sovereignty and rule of law that is essential to our federalist Constitutional framework. The Obama administration's assault against economic freedom and Constitutional constraints must be resisted.

The Federal Government's Assault on Texas: The EPA and the "Cross-State Rule"[183]

By 2012, there may be less electricity generated in Texas—at higher prices. And, for a state that has built much of its manufacturing success on having abundant supplies of competitively-priced electricity, this is a big problem. The trigger for this economic headwind is a new, poorly-crafted EPA rule. The Cross-State Air Pollution Rule, adopted in mid-2011, threatens the use of lignite coal from Texas for electrical generation—and, therefore, threatens more than one-tenth of the state's electricity supply.

---

[182] Office of the Governor Rick Perry. Statement by Gov. Perry Regarding Proposed Revision of National Ozone Limits. Jan. 7, 2010, http://governor.state.tx.us/news/press-release/14128/.

[183] "EPA's Capricious Lignite Rule Threatens Texas' Electricity Supply," by Kathleen Hartnett White, Texas Public Policy Foundation, July 12, 2011, http://www.texaspolicy.com/commentaries_single.php?report_id=3948.

Sulfur dioxide emissions from coal-fired power plants are the EPA's main concern. Sulfur dioxide is the main ingredient of what was once a big problem in the Northeast: acid rain. Although Texas power plants have reduced this pollutant by 33 percent over the past ten years, the new rule orders a larger reduction of sulfur dioxide by the end of 2011 than was accomplished in ten years.

The EPA emission reductions are unachievable for most coal-burning generators because rapid fuel-switching is logistically and legally impossible. Texas electric companies say the rule may force plant closures and limited operation of other plants.

Retrofitting plants that now use Texas lignite coal would involve three to four years of engineering, fabrication, boiler reconstruction, new rail construction and complex new permits—at multibillion-dollar costs. Once retrofitted, the plants would use lower-sulfur coal from Wyoming; coal that costs twice as much as Texas coal.

The average price of Texas lignite coal in 2009 was $16.67 per ton compared to a national average from all sources of $33.15 per ton. Coal's comparatively stable and lower prices have made coal an anchor for base-load electricity generation in Texas.[184]

Lignite coal provides 11 percent of electricity generation in Texas. Abrupt elimination of lignite in the fuel mix risks 7,000 to 13,000 megawatts of generation across the state, reducing the Electric Reliability Council of Texas' targeted reserve margin of 13.75 percent of surplus capacity to 5.2 percent at best—and at worst, it takes Texas into deficit, risking rolling blackouts and other service interruptions. This is a sobering statistic on hot summer days when the council has issued energy emergency alerts because electricity demand may exceed available generation.

The lignite industry is also vital to the Texas economy. Directly and indirectly, lignite mining supports 10,000 to 14,000 jobs and supports many local tax bases and business. Lignite contributes $1.3 billion to the state's economy and $71 million to state revenues.

The International Brotherhood of Electrical Workers told the EPA that their rules threaten the jobs of 1,500 union members working at six power plants in Texas.

The target of the EPA's complex rule is emissions that drift across state lines. The EPA is concerned that sulfur dioxide emissions from Texas plants may make it more difficult for St. Louis to achieve EPA standards for fine particulate air pollution. Yet this St. Louis meets Federal standards—as does Texas. In addition, the EPA's own modeling demonstrates that Texas emissions do not trigger ill-effects in Missouri or any other state for that matter.

---

[184] Base-load electricity generation refers to the constant base of power needed to supply an electrical grid from day-to-day; by its nature, it should be reliable and cost-effective. This is contrasted with peaking power, often generated by natural gas or other easily modulated sources, that come on to provide extra power needed during the day, especially on long, hot summer days.

The EPA justifies saddling Texas with this onerous regulation based on speculation of what *may* happen the future.

When drafting its anti-lignite rule, the EPA requested comments on Texas but did not include Texas in the rule nor did they provide any information about specific Texas requirements. Instead, they wrote Texas in at the last hour, flouting the Constitutional due process guaranteed in the Administrative Procedures Act for all rulemaking.

Asserting Federal power without formal notice to those entities coerced by that power is not a use of government power that would be associated with a federal republic governed by rule of law. Further, the EPA has no environmental basis for subjecting Texas to this rule. It is using the Clean Air Act, intended to protect human health, to force an energy policy to suppress coal regardless of economic consequences.

The bureaucratically-driven legal uncertainty can be devastating to prosperity. To grow and be profitable, businesses need to plan. When planning, businesses do consider business cycles, changing technology, competition, and customer responses to their products and services. If a unpredictable regulatory and attendant legal climate is layered on top of that, out of self-defense business tends to hold on to its money. Thus, when business carefully follows environmental regulations, even at great expense, but this no longer secures clear and reliable clearance from the government, legal uncertainty freezes business decisions.

This regulatory risk has an adverse impact on investment. "Regulatory uncertainty is the enemy of economic development," says one Valero executive.[185] "If you can't estimate the value of a project, you don't make the investment."

The new EPA rules do not merely impose added marginal costs on production; they threaten entire sectors of the economy. If the Obama Administration's real goal is "to end the era of fossil fuels in our generation," as President Obama has repeatedly declared, the EPA is blazing the path. There's just one problem: no alternative to fossil fuels yet exists that can replace 85 percent of our energy with remotely comparable supply, efficiently and affordably.

The sheer number of recent EPA actions is staggering, but the revised Federal standards for ozone and fast-tracked greenhouse gas regulation are the most heavy-hitting. These rules would impact large industry and small business across the country on a scale that would pressure U.S. manufacturing activities to foreign countries that operate without the EPA's regulatory burden. In a June 2010 report, the Business Roundtable, which represents companies that employ more than 12 million people, warned of the economic harm posed by the EPA's new agenda. "As the U.S. manufacturing sector continues to struggle and is shedding jobs overall, the EPA's actions will … create uncertainty and place U.S. companies at competitive disadvantage compared with foreign firms."[186]

---

[185] Valero, a $14 billion Texas-based refiner, is America's largest independent oil refiner.
[186] "Policy Burdens Inhibiting Economic Growth," Business Roundtable, June 2010.

Organized labor, historically not a regular opponent of EPA rules, has formed Unions for Jobs and the Environment to resist EPA's job-killing plans. In response to the proposed rule for industrial boilers, the United Steel Workers commented: "Tens of thousands of these jobs will be imperiled. In addition many more tens of thousands of jobs in the supply chain and in the communities where these plants are located will also be at risk."[187]

The Federal Government's Assault on Texas: The Attack of the Dunes Sagebrush Lizard

A West Texas lizard may shut down a large amount of Texas' oil extraction efforts. How a small reptile can do what competition and 85 years of oil pumping in West Texas failed to do is an interesting tale.

The three-inch-long reptile, known as the dunes sagebrush lizard, is under consideration for listing as an endangered species by the U.S. Fish and Wildlife Service. Such a listing might endanger some 20 percent of America's oil production while axing thousands of jobs.

The oil industry claims that research proves that the lizard which ranges the West Texas Permian Basin should not be listed as an endangered species. But, a scientist whose studied the lizard since 1994 thinks otherwise and this is the man to whom the Fish and Wildlife Service is listening.

Beyond the dispute about the lizard's status is this fact: oil drilling activities cover a tiny fraction of the region, especially now that modern drilling techniques allow multiple wells to be dug from the same, small footprint.

The oil industry points to a recent scientific survey that found the lizard in 28 of 50 locations across West Texas. Environmentalists counterclaim that the lizard *wasn't* found in 22 of 50 locations.

The lizard lives in shallow depressions and a variety of scrub oak in West Texas and the southeastern New Mexico. Foes of the oil industry content that oil field development comes with roads that disrupt the lizard habitat. New Mexico has already declared the lizard endangered.

Opponents of the endangered listing for the lizard say that it relies on shaky science, that the U.S. Fish and Wildlife Service is essentially picking its own conclusion from conflicting scientific findings.

The fight is an important one, however, as the U.S. Fish and Wildlife Service, the administrative custodian of the Endangered Species Act, has made devastating economic decisions in the past. In the Clinton-era, it acted to protect the spotted owl, even though the same species lives in abundance in Mexico, resulting in the loss of about 20,000 jobs in the Pacific Northwest as well as the increased importation of lumber from abroad. California's delta smelt also received Federal protection, resulting in the shutting down of massive water pumps that fed large swaths

---

[187] United Steel Workers Union. Comment: Proposed Rule, National Emission Standards for Hazardous Air. EPA-HQ-OAR-2002-0058-2964.1.

of California's vibrant fruit, nut, and vegetable production. Later studies showed that the pumps in question might not be the real threat to the delta smelt, but instead, other hungry fish—ironically California's own Department of Fish and Game is constantly restocking largemouth bass for anglers to catch—a non-native fish introduced to California by sport fishermen some 100 years ago that voraciously feeds on the little delta smelt.

As with the spotted owl and the delta smelt, Texas might be dealt an economic blow—but on an industry far larger and of greater national import than was the case in the previous endangered species rulings. The region in Texas that might be affected is among the most productive oil-and-gas area in Texas. Further, with a ruling, significant new costs would be imposed on drilling activity and road construction. Even electrical lines needed to carry "green" electricity from wind farms in West Texas to cities in the east would be threatened.

And the dunes sagebrush lizard isn't the sole reptilian challenge to Texas prosperity. A spot-tailed earless lizard might impose heavy costs on producers in the Eagle Ford shale in south Texas as well, in effect, putting most of Texas' onshore oil production at risk.

In both cases, regulatory uncertainty alone discourages prospective developers.

Beyond the potential listing of these two lizards is a deadline for Federal compliance with a court-ordered consent decree requiring the Fish and Wildlife Service either to list 50 new species as endangered or to designate "critical habitats" for them, imposing further costs on industry.

In the meantime, Americans struggling with a lackluster recovery now have to contend with a pair of lizards they've never met.

(As this book was going to press, the U.S. Fish and Wildlife Service announced on June 13, 2012 an agreement with Texas to keep the dunes sagebrush lizard off the endangered species list. The agreement, brokered largely by Texas state Comptroller Susan Combs, prevents the endangered species listing from denying access across the Permian Basin region, which produces in excess of 1 million barrels of oil per day, about one-fifth of the crude oil extracted in the lower 48 U.S. states.)

Since becoming a state in 1845, Texas has consistently outpaced the U.S. in population growth. The same can't be said of other states in the South, Midwest or West. For instance, since 1850 Alabama outpaced the national growth rate once, during the decade of the 1970s. Texas' Midwest neighbor to the north, Oklahoma, surpassed the national growth rate in five of the last 12 decades, but since the Dust Bowl of the 1930s, has only seen one period of above average growth: in the 1970s. In the West, Oregon has been more steady, showing higher growth than the U.S. as a whole for ten of the past 12 Census reports. California, as with so many other factors, joins Texas in growing more quickly than the nation since its birth as a state in 1850.

Figure 34 compares Texas' population growth rate to California and the U.S. since 1900. The impact of the Great Depression can clearly be seen for all three in the 1940 Census, which measured the growth of the nation in the 1930s. California grew more quickly than did Texas in ten of the last 16 decades, but, more recent times tell a different story.

In the decade of the 1970s, the high price of oil due to the Arab oil embargoes, combined with Texas' peak oil output, meant healthy times for Texas economy. Texas added 27.1 percent to its numbers by 1980. California, on the other hand, only added 18.6 percent, falling behind Texas for the first time since the 1900 Census. The reasons aren't too hard to fathom: taxes and aerospace. Governor Ronald Reagan, before he came to understand just how damaging high taxes are, presided over two large tax increases, one in 1967, the other in 1971, which together tripled tax revenue to the state over his eight years in office ending in 1975. In addition, the end of the Vietnam War meant a downturn in defense spending, hitting California particularly hard.

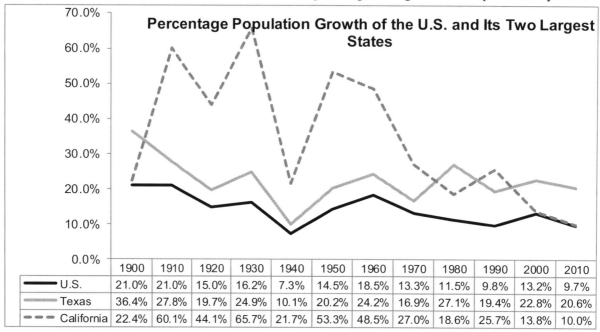

	1900	1910	1920	1930	1940	1950	1960	1970	1980	1990	2000	2010
U.S.	21.0%	21.0%	15.0%	16.2%	7.3%	14.5%	18.5%	13.3%	11.5%	9.8%	13.2%	9.7%
Texas	36.4%	27.8%	19.7%	24.9%	10.1%	20.2%	24.2%	16.9%	27.1%	19.4%	22.8%	20.6%
California	22.4%	60.1%	44.1%	65.7%	21.7%	53.3%	48.5%	27.0%	18.6%	25.7%	13.8%	10.0%

Figure 34—While outpacing U.S. population growth since statehood in 1845, in recent years Texas has overtaken perennial growth leader California.

The decade of the 80s saw California back on top as oil prices retreated and the Texas economy, more dependent on oil than today, suffered. Reagan, now President, instituted the largest peacetime military buildup in history helping to win the Cold War over the former Soviet Union leading to a boom in the California economy where taxes, as a percentage of personal income, were lower than usual.

But, for the past twenty years, Texas has grown more rapidly than California, and this trend is not likely to be reversed soon. Since the 1990 Census, Texas has almost *doubled* California's growth rate: 48 percent to 25 percent. America grew 24 percent over the same period.

Prior chapters detailed why Texas has become the destination of choice for Americans looking for the freedom to make a living as they see best. This chapter will examine more closely what is popularly known in the Lone Star State as the "Texodus"—the massive ongoing migration to Texas of Americans seeking economic freedom—economic refugees, in a sense.

Who Are the New Texans?

In many respects, moving 1,500 miles to an unknown land, leaving behind family and friends and the familiar comforts of home is easier than it was back in 1835 when Davy Crockett, freshly defeated for reelection to the U.S. House of Representatives said, "…you may all go to hell and I will go to Texas." Crockett's dramatic departure kicked off a wave of emigration from Tennessee to Texas, with "G.T.T." painted on abandoned cabins indicating the former residents had "Gone to Texas." While transportation over long distances is more reliable than it was then, would-be Texas residents in Crockett's era were merely leaving self-built cabins in expectation of gaining cheap land—today, many Americans are frozen in place by upside-down mortgages and a sluggish real estate market that makes the financial aspect of moving more difficult than at any time since the Great Depression.

Before the Great Recession depressed housing values, leaving many Americans underwater in their mortgage, in 2007, Texas received an average of *1,353* people every day from other parts of America.[188] This pace slowed considerably in 2010 and 2011, as the Census reported that only 11.6 percent of Americans changed residences then, the lowest recorded rate in 63 years due to the burst of the housing bubble and high jobless rate. For at least a decade, the plurality of new arrivals to Texas have been Californians, with the Census reporting that 32,377 more Californians moved to Texas than Texans moved to California in 2010, with Texas gaining a net of 74,917 interstate arrivals in 2010 while California lost 129,239.

Broadly speaking, there are three categories of people moving to Texas: those who move because their work brings them to Texas, those who move to Texas in expectation of finding work, and retirees.

---

[188] Source: IRS data as quoted by *Politifact* in analyzing a December 29, 2009 press release from Texas Governor Rick Perry: http://www.politifact.com/texas/statements/2010/jan/13/rick-perry/perry-says-1000-people-move-texas-daily/.

One family representing the first category was profiled by Voice of America:[189]

> *"It's exciting, looking forward to getting out there and it's a new adventure," said Taki Pappas. He and his family of four are packing and leaving the western state of California for the south central state Texas. After being laid-off more than six months ago, Pappas recently got a job in Austin. His wife Mabyn says housing in Texas is half of what it costs in California. "The biggest thing is that we're not buying immediately but we can actually afford to buy in Austin where as we really can't afford to buy out here," she said.*
>
> *"There's no state income tax there which also helps," said Takki Pappas.*

In a few brief lines, the Pappas family mentioned three key facts: they have work in Texas while in California they did not, housing is half the cost in Texas as it is in California, and Texas has no income tax.

Even people without a firm job lined up move to Texas in the hopes of finding one. This person posted a query on a website intending to move to Texas from the San Francisco Bay area:[190]

> *Hi, So I'm a young single mom whos moving with her son to Texas. Im currently living in california (bay area) and have so my whole life! This is definetly will be a change for me, but thats one reason im moving, but mostly, The job market and the price of living is just terrible! Ive had no luck finding a job so far and i cant afford to live out here anymore (sic).*

Her post, a plea really, again cites the same factors: no work in California attended by a high cost of living. As mentioned in Chapter Two, Texas has America's second-lowest cost of living, at 90 percent of the U.S. average, while California ranks behind only Hawaii and New York as having the third-highest cost of living, with an index of 132 percent of the U.S. average. The same dollar in California will buy a Texan about $1.54 in goods and services.

Across America 58.8 percent of the people live in the states of their birth. Texas, due to its size, abundance of jobs, and higher birthrate, is composed of 60.5 percent natives. Figure 35 examines the origins of Texas residents compared to the U.S. and to California.[191] So, while Texas has benefitted from interstate migration, it's striking to see that Texas' strong economy has allowed native Texans the luxury of staying put, if they so choose. Further, contrary to recent reports about Texas job growth mainly going to foreign immigrants, we see that Texas only has 3.5 percent more foreign born residents than the U.S. as a whole and 10.8 percent fewer foreign born

---

[189] "Researchers See Trend of People Moving Between Texas, California," by Elizabeth Lee, *Voice of America*, July 24, 2011, http://www.voanews.com/articleprintview/163236.html.

[190] Posted March 1, 2011 on http://www.city-data.com/forum/texas/1214202-single-mom-kid-moving-texas-but.html.

[191] "Table 1 – Place of Birth for the United States and Puerto Rico by Region and State: 2010," U.S. Census Bureau.

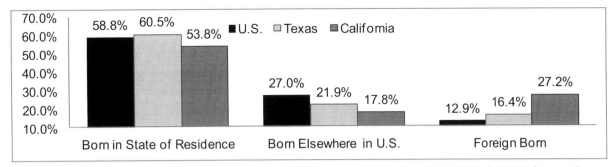

Figure 35—With a strong economy, Texans don't have to leave the state of their birth for work.

residents than does California.[192] Put another way, one of eight people in America were born abroad, one of six people in Texas were and more than one in four Californians claim a foreign nation as their birthplace. U.S. Census data shows us the typical new arrival to Texas is a Californian. Other than non-working family members, the new Texan is likely a trained professional such as a doctor or a teacher, earning more than $75,000 per year.[193]

Why Are People Moving to Texas? Jobs!

Interactive online programs allow anyone to map American out and in-migration by county. These tools show a consistent pattern of Americans leaving high-tax states for lower-tax states, for instance, from super-high-tax New York to high-tax California and low-tax Texas; and from high-tax California to low-tax Texas. Using a tool provided by *Forbes.com*, the American Enterprise Institute's Ryan Streeter wrote about his findings in 2010:[194]

Texas's low-cost, liberty-loving atmosphere has become an attractive alternative to California's oppressive public sector and dysfunctional policy environment. No amount of heart-melting vistas, celebrity sightings, or traipses through wine country can make up for what almost appears a strategic attempt by one of the nation's largest states to drive businesses and productive people away.

Thanks to an interesting interactive map at Forbes.com, we now can see some visual evidence of the trends we have been discussing. The map shows county migration in the United States in pictorial form. Black lines show inward migration to a county, and red lines show outward migration. The thicker the line, the higher the volume.

---

[192] A Center for Immigration Studies September 2011 report claimed that 81 percent of jobs generated in Texas from 2007 to 2011 went to foreign immigrants who had arrived in the U.S. in the past three years, up to half of them illegal. The Texas Public Policy Foundation disputed these findings in "The Texas Model: Who Really Gets Texas Jobs," by Chuck DeVore, October, 2011, http://www.texaspolicy.com/pdf/2011-10-PB45-TexasModel-WhoReallyGetsTexasJobs-CFP-ChuckDeVore.pdf.

[193] "Current Population Survey, 2011 Annual Social and Economic Supplement, Geographical Mobility: 2010 to 2011, Migration Flows Between Regions, by Income in 2010, Labor Force Status, Major Occupation Group, and Major Industry Group: 2010 to 2011 – Table 14," U.S. Census Bureau, http://www.census.gov/hhes/migration/data/cps/cps2011.html.

[194] "America as Texas vs. California: Who's Moving Where Edition," *The Enterprise Blog*, June 18, 2010.

If we look at Harris County, Texas, where Houston is located, we can practically hear a giant sucking sound as the state's largest city pulls people southward from the northeast, the Midwest, and elsewhere. Most of the outmigration is regional... You get a similar picture when you look at the migration patterns to Dallas and Austin.

For example, Travis County, home to Austin, looks similarly like a bull's eye on the dartboard of appealing places to live. It's hard to find any distinct patterns of where people in Austin go when they leave the state...

Now let's look at California. Aside from the appeal of Los Angeles to people living in the high-cost northeast (you might as well have good beaches and sunny weather if you're paying high taxes for bad services), it appears the city of angels is losing its heavenly radiance in a massive way. San Diego also looks very red...

The Census provides backup to Streeter's observations, reporting that from 2007 to 2009 more than two million people moved out of California with the top destination being Texas. An analyst with the California-based Milken Institute reports that the business climate is driving this, citing the example of a permit to build a new mall: what takes three to four months in Texas takes three *years* in California.[195]

How Emigration to Texas Increases Texas' Official Unemployment Rate While Lowering Other States' Rates

The U.S. Census data shows some interesting distinctions between the sorts of Americans that move between regions. People moving to the South, of which Texas is one of 16 states comprising about a quarter of the regional population, are the most likely to be unemployed compared with people moving to other regions, with 20.1 percent of people wanting to work not having a job at the time of their move.[196] By contrast, only 12.8 percent of adults in the labor pool who move to the Northeast are unemployed at the time of their move. Further, 32.2 percent of all people moving to the South aren't in the labor pool at all, most of them children or retirees. This compares to 22.3 percent in the Northeast.

The region showing the greatest percentage of unemployed people moving to a different area is the Northeast, with 22.2 percent of people in the labor pool being unemployed at the time of their move. Of Northeasterners in the labor pool who moved to the South, a staggering 27.6 percent of them were unemployed when they moved.

This means that people immigrating to Texas are far more likely to be looking for work. When they move, they cease counting on the unemployment rolls of the state they moved from and

---

[195] "Researchers See Trend of People Moving Between Texas, California," by Elizabeth Lee, Voice of America, July 25, 2011.

[196] "Current Population Survey, 2011 Annual Social and Economic Supplement, Geographical Mobility: 2010 to 2011, Migration Flows Between Regions, by Income in 2010, Labor Force Status, Major Occupation Group, and Major Industry Group: 2010 to 2011 – Table 14," U.S. Census Bureau, http://www.census.gov/hhes/migration/data/cps/cps2011.html, data extrapolated from Census table by authors.

start counting on Texas' unemployment rolls, assuming they still have time remaining on their up to 99 weeks of unemployment insurance compensation from the government.

Examining Census data for the number of people who move between California and Texas and the employment status of those people who move between the West and the South, we can extrapolate how the employment rates in those states might have differed had people not moved at all and remained unemployed.

The Census estimates that 68,959 people moved from California to Texas in 2010 while 36,582 people made the reverse move for a net of 32,377 in Texas' favor.[197] Of the people who moved, using Census data, we can estimate that 34,985 had jobs as they moved into Texas from California while 19,234 employed Texans moved to California for a net of about 15,751 employed people to Texas. The movement of unemployed people is smaller, with about 7,685 out of work Californians moving to Texas while 3,520 unemployed Texans moved to California, for a net of 4,165 unemployed people to Texas. Considering solely the movement of people in the labor pool between the two largest states, we estimate that the unemployment rate in California in 2011 was 0.01 percent lower due to migration to Texas while the Texas unemployment rate is 0.02 percent higher because of unemployed Californians moving to Texas.

When considering people moving to Texas from the rest of America, the impact to Texas' unemployment rate is two to three times greater than when looking at California alone. About 75,000 more people moved into Texas than moved out of it in 2010. Of these, about 10,200 were unemployed on their arrival in Texas or about 850 people every month added to Texas' unemployment rolls from other states throughout 2010. Texas pays about $17.5 million per year in unemployment insurance to these new arrivals, a burden that comes out of business payroll expenses. Texas' official unemployment rate in October 2011 was 8.4 percent. Were it not for out of work Americans moving to Texas, the rate would have been about 8.35 percent—a perceptible difference, but not particularly determinative in 2011. The impact on the Texas unemployment rate was likely greater in years' past before the bust in housing values greatly slowed interstate migration.

Over many years, the effect of migration on employment and unemployment rates compounds, especially when people who are periodically unemployed, for instance, in the construction trades, pick up their tool belts and move to Texas.

Looking at interstate domestic migration's impact on the unemployment rate over longer periods of time is an interesting thought exercise. One would have to assume that the economy is static— that individuals and businesses don't change their behavior because of taxes and regulations— and that when a state suffers job losses and its residents didn't move that they'd remain unemployed. With these caveats in mind, we know from Chapter Two that about a net of two million Californians vacated the Golden State in the ten year period between the 2000 and 2010 Census. We also know that almost 800,000 people moved into Texas in that time. Meanwhile,

---

[197] "2010 American Community Survey, Table 1. State-to-State Migration Flows: 2010," U.S. Census Bureau.

over an 11-year period ending August 2011, Texas added a net of almost 1.1 million jobs while California lost a net of just over a half-million jobs.

Using the Census data for the demographic profile of the people who migrate from region-to-region, we can come up with a rough estimate of how many of the two million people California lost were in the labor market, how many were employed at the time of their move and how many were unemployed. Similarly, we can do the same with the people who moved into Texas.

The numbers indicate that of the two million more Californians who left the state than residents of other states who moved into California, about 300,000 were unemployed when they moved out, 1.2 million had work and were leaving for an out-of-state opportunity, and 500,000 were non-working family members or otherwise not in the labor pool.

Similarly, of the 800,000 people who moved into Texas, we can calculate that about 161,000 were unemployed, 381,000 had a job in Texas as they moved, and 258,000 were not in the labor pool.

If the 300,000 people who were unemployed and left California had remained in the state without work, they would have boosted California's 2011 unemployment rate by 1.4 percent, a significant amount.

In Texas, had the 161,000 unemployed workers who moved into Texas from other states not moved, and people already in Texas been able to fill the needed positions, the 2011 Texas unemployment rate would have been 1.3 percent lower. Figure 35 illustrates what the unemployment rate would have been in America's two largest states if the unemployed were somehow forced to remain in states suffering the most in our current economic downturn.

Again, thought exercises such as these are extremely limited in their application to the real, dynamic world—but, nonetheless, the massive amounts of immigration to Texas and similar emigration from California have had an impact on local job markets and unemployment rates.

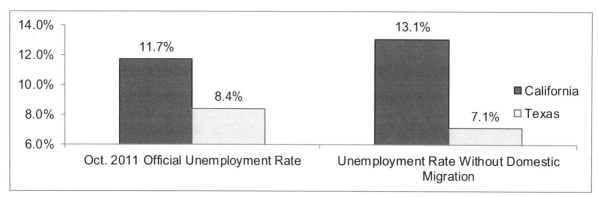

Figure 35—California's unemployment rate would be far higher if people without work hadn't taken the big step of moving out of state to find a job, similarly, Texas' already below average unemployment rate would be lower still had it not provided employment for so many out of work Americans.

Texas has a reputation of being a rough, tough on crime state. The story goes that, in Texas, they lock up and execute a large number of criminals. Further, critics say that minorities and the poor suffer disproportionately from a remorseless criminal justice system costing Texas taxpayer hundreds of millions of dollars that could best be spent elsewhere.

The truth, as has been the case throughout this book, is otherwise.

With a higher-than average violent crime rate (recall from Chapter Two that crime rates are closely linked to demographic factors such as age, race and ethnicity) Texas has had the unenviable distinction of having the nation's second highest percentage of its residents locked-up. Some ten times the official rate of the People's Republic of China (where prisoners are often held in labor camps without formal charges, or swiftly executed). Living up to its reputation as a "lock-em-up" state, from 1978, when "tough-on-crime" legislation became popular, to 2004, the number of Texas inmates grew by 278 percent while its general population expanded by 35 percent—almost eight *times* the rate growth in the state.

But, in spite of Texas' well-deserved reputation as a tough on crime state, or perhaps because of it, in recent years Texas lawmakers have approved alternatives to incarceration for both adult and juvenile offenders. These reforms have avoided more than $2 billion in taxpayer outlays and saved the state from building 17,000 more prison beds. In 2011, with evidence of the previous reforms' effectiveness, the Legislature approved a recommendation from Gov. Rick Perry and the Texas Public Policy Foundation to shutter the Sugar Land Central Unit, the first such prison closure in state history, saving taxpayers approximately $10 million per year, in addition to the one-time proceeds from the sale of the property.

Texas' Shift from Tough on Crime to Right on Crime[198]
How Texas became smart on crime, rather than merely tough on crime, paradoxically achieving significant declines in both crime rates and incarceration rates, is a story that needs telling.

Some politicians maintain that the main purpose of government is to ensure the safety of their people. This isn't what the Founders' believed. Any king or dictator can claim any number of oppressive actions in the name of security. Rather, America's founding premise was that government exists to ensure liberty. Clearly, liberty can be threatened by external forces or internal chaos and crime. That's why criminal justice is so important and so difficult to balance at the same time. Crime hurts innocent, law-abiding people, robbing them of the peaceful enjoyment of their liberty. But, on the other side of the ledger, we must take care when we lock people away, depriving them of their liberty, at great expense to the taxpayer—that it not be overdone.

---

[198] Much of this section has been derived from "Adult Corrections Reform: Lower Crime, Lower Costs," by Marc Levin, Texas Public Policy Foundation, September, 2011.

Policymakers in Texas have consciously tackled this fundamental criminal justice dilemma, much to their credit. Since 2005 the Texas Legislature approved greater alternatives to imprisonment holding nonviolent offenders accountable while providing effective supervision. From 2005 to 2010, Texas has seen a double-digit reduction in crime, reaching its lowest crime rate since 1973.[199,200] Similar reductions in crime happened nationally. But, Texas and Massachusetts had the sharpest drop in their incarceration rates from 2007 to 2008—and this while Massachusetts experienced out-migration and an aging population while Texas continued to grow. Texas' incarceration rate fell 4.5 percent while the average state incarceration rate increased 0.8 percent in the period. Relative to other states, Texas had the second highest rate of incarceration in 2004, declining in 2010 to number four due to a 9 percent per capita decline in the prison population.[201]

In 2005, lawmakers reformed the criminal justice system by boosting local probation departments with $55 million, provided they agreed to a 10 percent reduction in probation revocations for technical infractions and to implement graduated sanctions. Graduated probation sanctions sought to match the penalty with the violation, such as missing a meeting with a parole officer and included steps such as increased parolee reporting, extended parole terms, electronic monitoring, or weekends in jail. The bulk of the added funding went towards reducing the parole agent caseload from almost 150 in urban areas to 110 while also carving out special caseload levels for parole officers dealing with mentally ill probationers or other challenging subgroups. This closer supervision and new approach to penalties short of a return to prison, saved taxpayers $119 million.[202]

By 2007 it became apparent the alternatives to prison were becoming overloaded. Judges, prosecutors, and corrections officials, fortified with criminal justice system data, alerted lawmakers to a problem: increasing numbers of low-level, nonviolent offenders were being sent to prison after sentencing or probation revocation because of long waiting lists for alternative sentencing programs. Compounding matters, parolees frequently remained in prison because halfway houses were full and mandatory rehabilitative programs had waiting lists as well.[203]

This catalyzed the Legislature to follow up their 2005 efforts in the next session, appropriating $241 million in 2007 to create prison alternatives such as additional non-prison sanctions, drug abuse treatment beds, drug courts, and mental illness treatment programs. This marked a fundamental change of direction for lawmakers facing a pending need to build 17,332 prison beds at a cost of $2 billion.[204] Texas legislators added 4,000 probation and parole treatment beds,

---

[199] Source: Texas Crime Rates, FBI Reports.
[200] National crime rates peaked in 1980 for both violent and property crime, about 3 times higher than the rates in 1960.
[201] "Texas Criminal Justice Reform: Lower Crime, Lower Cost," by Marc Levin, Texas Public Policy Foundation, January 2010.
[202] "2011-12 Texas Legislators' Guide to the Issues," section on Adult Probation, page 110, Texas Public Policy Foundation.
[203] "Justice Reinvestment in Texas: Assessing the Impact of the 2007 Justice Reinvestment Initiative," Council of State Governments Justice Center, April 2009.
[204] "Adult & Juvenile Correctional Population Projections Fiscal Years 2007-2012," State of Texas Legislative

500 in-prison treatment beds, 1,200 halfway house beds, 1,500 mental health pre-trial diversion beds, and 3,000 outpatient drug treatment slots in the two-year 2008-09 budget.

With increased emphasis on non-prison aspects of punishment and rehabilitation, judges, juries, and prosecutors responded with a six percent reduction in prison sentences in 2009 as more nonviolent offenders were diverted from prison to probation.[205] This trend reversed a long-standing six percent per year increase in the number of people being sentenced to prison.[206] In addition, only half of the number of people being sent to prison are sent there due to a crime being committed with the attendant judge and jury—the other half are people on probation or parolees who run afoul of what are often technical violations. People convicted of a crime, but not sent to prison, can be put on probation—a kind of supervised punishment with certain restrictions. Similarly, people who have done time behind bars can be paroled—released early— remaining free so long as they meet requirements. Since the increased supervision from the 2005 reforms, revocations of parole and probation have declined.[207]

The probation revocation rate declined from 16.4 percent in 2005 to 14.7 percent in 2010.[208]

The parole revocation rate declined sharply from 11,311 in 2004 to 6,678 in 2010 with the number of new crimes being committed by parolees down by 8.5 percent from 2007 to 2010.[209] This is out of a population of 76,607 parole-eligible cases in 2009 of which 23,182 Texas inmates were released with parole supervision. The parole system has benefitted from enhanced supervision, graduated sanctions, instant drug testing, and a restored parole chaplaincy program. Parole resource centers coach parolees in decision-making skills based on concern for others and the victim. In addition the parole board has greater access to an option to put parolees who commit rules violations or a minor misdemeanor in an intermediate sanctions facility, a lower-cost but secure facility, usually for 60 to 70 days, until their parole runs out and they are released.

The Texas Legislature only meets every other year, so, in 2011, for the third time out of the last four sessions, Lone Star State lawmakers revisited criminal justice reform, trying to deepen past years' trends in lowering crime and incarceration rates.

Dealing with a massive deficit, lawmakers made $15 billion in cuts in the 2011-12 budget. Naturally, there was immense pressure to cut back on the funding given to improve the criminal justice system in 2005 and 2007. Instead lawmakers closed one adult and three juvenile lockups, the latter made possible by a major decline in youthful offences, allowing the state to reduce

Budget Board, January 2007.

[205] Garron Guszak, Legislative Budget Board, email, December 16, 2009.

[206] "Current Correctional Population Indicators," Legislative Budget Board, April 2011.

[207] "Adult & Juvenile Correctional Population Projections Fiscal Years 2011-2016," State of Texas Legislative Budget Board, January 2011.

[208] "Statewide Criminal Justice Recidivism and Revocation Rates," State of Texas Legislative Budget Board, January 2011.

[209] "2007 Annual Report," Texas Board of Pardons and Paroles; and "2010 Annual Report," Texas Board of Pardons and Paroles.

reduced the number of juveniles in state institutions by 52.9 percent. In addition, legislators reduced housing allowances for top corrections officials. The money saved allowed them to prioritize the proven cost-effective alternatives to prison and in-prison treatment programs that have paid for themselves since being implemented.

In 2011, lawmakers also passed, and the Governor signed into law, three important bills.

- SB 1055 builds on 2005's reforms by allowing counties to opt for performance incentive funding based on reducing commitments to prison of low-level offenders while also reducing recidivism, increasing the share of probationers making victim restitution, and increasing employment among probationers.

- HB 1205 creates a positive incentive for probationers to pursue self-improvement by allowing judges to award time credits for good behavior, such as earning a degree, fully paying restitution, and completing treatment programs.

- HB 2649 incentivizes state jail inmates, the lowest-level, nonviolent offenders in state lockups, to complete educational, treatment, and vocational programs and exhibit good behavior. Judges can require those offenders who demonstrated such exemplary conduct to spend several months of their sentence on probation. Formerly, most state jail felons had no opportunity for probation or supervision upon release. Transitioning exemplary state jail inmates upon re-entry to probation holds them accountable to an officer, directs them to find a job and housing, and requires parolees to comply with restrictions such as drug testing, curfews, and avoiding anti-social peers. The new law is projected to save $49 million.

Summarizing these criminal justice system reforms, Texas lawmakers implemented them without lowering the penalties for any offense. To the contrary, they lengthened sentences for sex offenses against children and for repeat auto burglary. Rules for parole, for which 28 percent of eligible inmates are approved today, compared with 79 percent in 1990, were also left unchanged with the exception that the most serious violent offenders are no longer eligible for parole. Nonviolent drug and property offenders who might have a chance at rehabilitation now won't be attending advanced criminal studies in prison from a murderer or rapist "professor." They don't go free, but they're under control in a separate system.

So, Texas has managed to be tough on crime while simultaneously being smart on crime.

Juvenile Justice Reforms[210]

How a state approaches juvenile justice—the time at which most criminals make their first contact with law enforcement authorities—will often determine whether a person becomes a productive citizen or turns to a life of crime. A landmark 2006 University of Cincinnati study of 1,500 youths found that the likelihood of reoffending increases when a juvenile is incarcerated as

---

[210] Research in this section derived from previous work by Jeanette Moll of the Texas Public Policy Foundation.

opposed to being diverted to non-prison alternatives.[211] Similarly, an August 2009 study that followed male juvenile offenders for 20 years found that incarceration or residential placement increased the rate of reoffending vs. restitution to the victim or community.[212]

In 2007, the Texas state Legislature put these concepts to the test, with Senate Bill 103 stopping the practice of sending youthful misdemeanor offenders to institutions run by the Texas Youth Commission. Further, the bill provided counties with $57.8 million for these youthful offenders, representing half of the costs the state would have incurred had those youths been sent to Texas Youth Commission facilities.[213]

With savings mounting from the new, more effective approach to juvenile crime, lawmakers cut the Texas Youth Commission budget in 2009 by $115 million. Most of the savings was generated from closing two prison sites. This allowed a redirection of $45.7 million into juvenile probation, improving diversion funding for juvenile probation departments provided their judicial oversight boards agreed to reduce the number of youthful offenders they remanded to the Texas Youth Commission. The diversion funding supports programs proven to reduce crime, such as nonresidential (non-custody) treatment, community service, and strengthening the family.

Senate Bill 103 became effective in mid-2007 and started diverting misdemeanants from the Texas Youth Commission, contributing to a 10.3 percent decline in juvenile adjudications from fiscal year 2008 to 2009. From 2006 to 2009, the population of young offenders in the Texas Youth Commission system dropped 52.9 percent.[214]

A Dallas County detention bed for juvenile offenders runs $54,955 per year to operate, more than double the cost to house an adult inmate in Texas.[215] But growing bodies of evidence suggests that mingling low-risk youths in the juvenile justice system with hard-core cases while disrupting schooling and family life increases the risk of reoffending, setting the young person spiraling down.[216] Yet nationally, some two-thirds of youths are being detained for non-violent

---

[211] "Specific Deterrence with Juveniles: Does Incarceration Reduce Recidivism?" Paper presented by Catherine Arnold, Christopher Lowenkamp and Paula Smith, at the annual meeting of the American Society of Criminology, Los Angeles, CA, October 31, 2006, http://www.allacademic.com/meta/p125046_index.html.

[212] "Iatrogenic effect of juvenile justice," by Uberto Gatti, Richard E. Tremblay, and Frank Vitaro, *Journal of Child Psychology and Psychiatry* 50:8 (2009), 991-998, December 21, 2009, http://www3.interscience.wiley.com/journal/122201997/abstract.

[213] Senate Bill 103 Fiscal Note, May 22, 2007, http://www.legis.state.tx.us/tlodocs/80R/fiscalnotes/html/SB00103F.htm.

[214] Texas Youth Commission Population Trends, November 17, 2009, http://www.tyc.state.tx.us/research/growth_charts.html.

[215] Dallas County FY 2010 Budget, September 22, 2009, http://www.dallascounty.org/department/budget/documents/FY2010ApprovedBudgetDetail_000.pdf.

[216] "Iatrogenic effect of juvenile justice," by Uberto Gatti, Richard E. Tremblay, and Frank Vitaro, *Journal of Child Psychology and Psychiatry* 50:8, 2009, December 21, 2009, pgs. 991–998, http://www3.interscience.wiley.com/journal/122201997/abstract; "The Dangers of Detention: The Impact of Incarcerating Youth in Detention and Other Secure Facilities," by Barry Holman and Jason Ziedenberg, Justice Policy Institute, Oct. 16, 2006, http://www.justicepolicy.org/images/upload/06-

offences and detained juveniles are some three *times* more likely to be committed to expensive long-term residential facilities.[217] Further, placing a youthful offender into detention does not result in restitution to the victim. With all this in mind, it makes sense from both a budgetary and a criminal justice standpoint to carefully weigh options in this arena. Texas lawmakers appear to have done so, in spite of severe political pressures to "get tough on crime"—even if "getting tough" makes matters worse.

Another example of Texas' success in this area, proven with statistics, is the Dallas and Harris counties Juvenile Detention Alternatives Initiative, in operation since 2007. In the first two years of operation, Dallas has reduced the beds in its youthful offender system by 48, generating savings of $1 million per year.[218] Harris County closed a detention center, reducing its operating costs by 25 percent, with an exceptionally high 95 percent of Houston area youths diverted from detention showing up for their court date.[219]

Juvenile Detention Alternatives Initiative uses a data-driven, objective risk assessment instrument to more accurately predict whether youths will miss their court hearing or re-offend, rather than a subjective guess. Factors weighed can include the most serious alleged offense, number of charges, prior adjudications, and any prior instances of failing to appear before the court. The detention alternatives deployed in Dallas include a day reporting center, in-home probation officer visits, GPS monitoring, and home detention. The statistics indicate success for this program in Texas' largest metro area: 4.5 percent of Dallas juveniles in the alternative program reoffend prior to the court rendering a decision vs. 10 percent of youths in the traditional system.[220] A nationally-tested program, the four Juvenile Detention Alternatives Initiative sites across the country saw juvenile arrests falling between 37 and 54 percent after implementation.[221]

Texas has a well-deserved reputation as a no-nonsense state when dealing with criminals. This reputation may have given officials the confidence, when confronted with a series of stories of abuses in state juvenile lockups, to fix the broken system, establishing protections for juvenile offenders, reducing crime, and saving taxpayers' money. From 2007 to 2011, the Texas juvenile justice system experienced major transformations. These initiatives have contributed to a historic decline in the state's youth incarceration rate, during the same period that crime rates fell to their lowest levels since 1973. The much smaller number of youths that still remain in state facilities

---

11_REP_DangersOfDetention_JJ.pdf;

"Bad Crowd: Why Juvenile Detention Makes Teens Worse," by Maia Szalavitz, *Time Magazine,* August 7, 2009, http://www.time.com/time/health/article/0,8599,1914837,00.html.

[217] "Detention of Juveniles: Its Effects on Subsequent Juvenile Court Processing Decisions," by C.E. Frazier and J.C. Cochran, *Youth and Society* 17:3, 1986, pages 286-305. "Florida Juvenile Delinquency Court Assessment," Office of State Courts Administrator : Office of Court Improvements, Tallahassee, FL, 2003.

[218] Mike Griffiths, Dallas County Chief Juvenile Probation Officer, email, June 15, 2009.

[219] Nancy H. Baird, M.Ed., Site Coordinator, Harris County Juvenile Detention Alternatives Initiative, email, August 31, 2009.

[220] Pernilla Johansson, PhD, Research Manager, Dallas County Juvenile Department, email, September 16, 2009.

[221] "Detention Reform: An Effective Public Safety Strategy," Annie E. Casey Foundation, September 17, 2007, http://www.aecf.org/upload/PublicationFiles/jdai_facts2.pdf.

are now safer and have access to more effective programming, and verified abuse complaints have fallen significantly: 69.5 percent from 2008 to 2011.

As a result of these changes, state incarceration of juveniles plummeted to record lows, and is now reserved for offenders who truly pose a risk to public safety. This saves taxpayer dollars and achieves better results by keeping more youths closer to families, churches, and other sources of community support.

From a public safety standpoint, the lower incarceration rates have not resulted in higher crime rates: in August of 2011, 9.1 percent fewer criminal cases were pending against youths as compared with August 2007, and the juvenile arrest rate has fallen substantially from 2007 to 2009, the most recent year reported.

These reforms show that Texas' juvenile justice system has moved far beyond its storied, if checkered past; with an often skeptical *The New York Times* declaring Texas' reform efforts, "impressive strides."

A Link Between a Strong Economy and Crime (Not What You Think)

Some criminologists link the overall employment picture and crime. Interestingly, the persistently high national unemployment rates of the past few years have not seen a significant increase in crime nationally.

But, for people already touched by the criminal justice system, gainful employment is a big deal. Texas, having a better jobs climate than most states, also does better at reintegrating ex-offenders into the economy, making them productive citizens. Employed ex-offenders are far less likely to re-offend and most Texas parolees are working. Job placement and training for parolees has been enhanced since 2007 through closer ties between parole offices and local workforce centers. Some 65 percent of Texas parolees are employed. In contrast, 80 percent of California parolees are unemployed. This impacts recidivism—the rate at which former inmates return to prison.

Texas and Capital Punishment

Texas has a national reputation for tough, frontier-like justice: if you murder someone in Texas, you might forfeit your life. Critics claim that Texas executes too many criminals. The truth is more nuanced.

According to the anti-capital punishment Death Penalty Information Center, there were about 3,260 inmates on death row in 2010, with 14 years being the average time in prison before execution. In 2010 California had 695 prisoners on death row, Florida, 400, and Texas, 335.

It takes committing a murder to face a death sentence, but not just any kind of murder. Texas law specifies eight kinds of murder which may result in a death penalty: murder of an on-duty public safety officer; murder while committing another felony such as robbery or arson; murder for hire; murder will trying to escape prison; multiple murders; murder of a child under ten; murder of an officer of the court or a jury member in retaliation for a court case; and murder while already incarcerated if one of the three is true: if the victim worked for the lockup; if the inmate was already in prison for murder; or if the inmate was serving a life or 99-year sentence. Convicted murderers who are minors or mentally disabled can't be executed, as is the case nationwide.

Until 1976, a U.S. Supreme Court ruling stopped state executions of inmates on death row. Since then, Texas, the second-largest state, has executed 464 convicted murderers. California, with more than double the number of prisoners on death row, has executed only 13, with no death row inmate having been executed there for more than five years.

Looking at four five year periods, from 1991 to 1995, Texas executed an average of 13.4 death row inmates every year; from 1996 to 2000, 27; from 2001 to 2005, 23.3; and from 2006 to 2010, 21.8. So, the rate of executions, after hitting a post-1976 high in 2000 when 40 death row inmates were executed, has slowed in recent years. In the past five years, an average of 11 convicted murderers get placed on death row every year while an average of 5.8 are removed from death row, while 1.6 die awaiting execution. There were about 318 prisoners on death row in Texas in 2011.

Perhaps because judges and juries know that Texas is serious about the death penalty, Texas has a lower rate of death penalty sentences than do other states. A 2004 Cornell University study found that Oklahoma sentences 6 percent of convicted murderers to death, Nevada, 5.1 percent while in Texas, 2 percent of convicted murderers receive the death penalty, below the national average of 2.5 percent.[222] Further, the study found that states that use defined objective criteria for the death penalty, such as Texas, assign the death penalty in 1.9 percent of murder convictions as opposed to states that use subjective criteria such as the heinous nature of the crime which set a death penalty 2.7 percent of the time.[223]

A year after the Cornell study was completed, Texas changed its penal code to make criminals convicted of capital murder and sentenced to life in prison ineligible for parole. This change was made with the intent of reducing the pressure on jurors to apply the death penalty; the theory being that if they knew that the convicted murderer would never be set free, they'd be less likely to use the death penalty. Facts validate the intent of the law. In the ten years prior to 2005, an average of 35.8 people were sent to death row by juries. From 2005 to 2010, the average number of people placed on death row dropped by a third to 11.7 per year.

So, a murderer is less likely to be placed on death row in Texas than the national average, but more likely to be executed once placed there.

---

[222] "Explaining Death Row's Population and Racial Composition," by John Blume, Theodore Eisenberg and Martin Wells, *The Journal of Empirical Legal Studies*, Cornell University, March 2004.
[223] Ibid., rates for the 22-year year period from 1977 to 1999.

CHAPTER NINE—THE AMERICAN DREAM

There's been on ongoing battle to define the American Dream. In a sense, this battle has been with us since our beginnings as a nation. During the Revolutionary War, Patriots and Tories were evenly divided, with the former believing that King George III had "a history of repeated injuries and usurpations" against American rights while the latter remained attached to the Crown and vast majority in the middle just wanted to live their lives. The Civil War was as much about whether all Americans had "certain unalienable Rights" as it was about states' rights or the established rights and privileges of slave owners.

But, in the midst of America's battle against Nazi German and Imperial Japan, President Franklin Roosevelt promulgated a "Second Bill of Rights." His was a summary, a gathering together of the vanguard of progressive, liberal thought. To some Americans, it represented the next step in the process of perfecting the American project. To others, it was a willful break from the Founder's vision of a limited government whose chief object was securing liberty for a naturally free people.

During Roosevelt's State of the Union address on January 11, 1944, he declared America's old "political rights proved inadequate to assure us equality in the pursuit of happiness." That mere "rights to life and liberty" weren't enough "if some fraction of our people—whether it be one-third or one-fifth or one-tenth—is ill-fed, ill-clothed, ill-housed, and insecure." Roosevelt told Congress that every American had a right to good paying job to provide "adequate food and clothing and recreation"; the right to a "decent home"; to "adequate medical care and the opportunity to achieve and enjoy good health"; "the right to adequate protection from the economic fears of old age, sickness, accident, and unemployment"; and "The right to a good education." 67 years later we hear Roosevelt's economic bill of rights echoed in the cries of the "Occupy" movement and its supporters from President Obama to former Speaker of the U.S. House of Representatives Nancy Pelosi.

Roosevelt's 1944 speech declaring liberty inadequate owed its pedigree to a line of political thought that took hold in the French Revolution and was developed by thinkers such as Jean-Jacques Rousseau (social contract theory—rights come from Man, not God), Germans Georg Wilhelm Friedrich Hegel (historicism, a belief that political philosophies are rooted in their times, meaning that the ideas of the American Founders are now obsolete), Karl Marx (class warfare), and Friedrich Nietzsche (the will to power and the primacy of the state) and by American progressives Frank Goodnow ("The rights which [an individual] possesses are... conferred upon him, not by his Creator, but rather by the society to which he belongs.") and Woodrow Wilson, before and during his presidency (a "living" Constitution that can adapt in a Darwinian fashion). In 1848, Marx himself set out ten demands in his Communist Manifesto, many of which Roosevelt in 1944 and Occupy today approve of: a heavy progressive income tax; a strong national bank having control of credit; government control of development (called "smart growth" today); and free education.

Political theorists have had more than 200 years to discuss, implement and perfect their dreams of a classless society. While nice sounding in theory, practice has been more than a disappointment, with hundreds of millions killed in the name of the "New Soviet Man" or the "Cultural Revolution" in places like the former Soviet Union, the People's Republic of China, Cambodia, Cuba, and North Korea. Even in nations that have walked the path of soft socialism, such as France, Spain, and Greece now find themselves in deep financial difficulty, with rhetoric unable to match reality.

The practical problem with Roosevelt's call for an economic or second Bill of Rights is this: who determines and who pays? Who decides what "adequate food and clothing and recreation" is? Who decides what a "decent home" is and who gets to live there? What do we do if the person to whom we've given housing doesn't take care of it? What's "adequate medical care"? How much is enough? Since Men are mortal and get sick and die, who decides when to ration care? All the money in America can't keep everyone alive forever! How does government ensure that we all have "the opportunity to achieve and enjoy good health"? Does it mean passing laws that make it mandatory to use seatbelts or wear helmets when riding a motorcycle or bicycle? What about laws against smoking? What about higher taxes for "unhealthful" snack foods? Or bans on large sugary sodas as is the case in New York City? Does a "right to a good education" mean that people who didn't study hard in high school should have access to a free college education? Who makes that choice? And, just as important, who pays for all these promises?

Among the 50 American states, the closest thing we have to a state run by the "vanguard of the proletariat" is California. Yet even in California, income inequities are growing[224] and the unemployment rate remains stubbornly high, leading California's governing left to call for more taxes, especially on the state's most productive people. In this, California is the template for both the unrealizable future and the failed past; where the dream never dies of big government giving people a free college education, a "living wage," saving the global environment, building government-run trains with borrowed money, and trying to advance human history through a myriad of detailed laws and regulations, where utopia is always just around the corner if only we tax ourselves more.

By sharp contrast, Texas spends less, taxes less, sues less, and secures for their people the liberty to earn a living, keep more of what they earn, and live where they want. Is it any wonder that for more than ten years, Americans have been moving to Texas while Californians have been fleeing as fast as they can sell their home and pack?

So, Texas and California represent two opposing versions of the American Dream, one based on liberty, the other, government. Figure 36 looks at how these competing dreams stack up using objective measures, showing conclusively that, if it can be influenced by public policy, Texas is better than California. Texas epitomizes the classic definition of the timeless American Dream realized by hard work in a climate of liberty while California's poor numbers speak for themselves.

---

[224] "How California Creates Greater Income Inequality for Itself," by Steven J. Balassi, *Journal of Business and Public Affairs*, Volume 2, Issue 1, 2008.

Vital Statistics for Two Competing Models of the American Dream	Texas	California	Difference
Net Domestic Migration, 2000 to 2010	781,542	-1,965,599	2,747,141
Change in Nonfarm Employment, 2000 to 2011	1,093,600	-519,600	1,613,200
Economic Growth, 2000 to 2010	65%	44%	48%
Increase in Per Capita GDP, 2000 to 2010	37%	31%	19%
Cost of Living Adjusted Poverty Rate	16.1%	23.3%	-45%
State Taxes as a Percent of Income	4.1%	5.9%	-44%
Local Taxes as a Percent of Income	3.8%	4.7%	-24%
Per Capita State and Local Debt	$8,968	$9,370	-4%
State and Local Government Employees per 10,000 People	491	504	-3%
Public Education Employees per 10,000 People	295	252	17%
Public School National Standardized Test Scores for 4th & 8th Grade Math, Reading & Science, 6 Categories Avg.: 216.7, 2009	0.7 above U.S. avg.	10.4 below U.S. avg.	11.1
Average Electricity Costs per Kilowatt Hour in 2011	$0.0970	$0.1383	-43%
Average Price of Gasoline per Gallon in 2011	$3.12	$3.72	-19%
Cost of Living Index, U.S. = 100	90	132	-47%
Lawsuit Cost Per Capita (Low-end estimate)	$529	$1,121	-112%

Figure 36—In ways that count, Texas realizes the American Dream while California has become the American Nightmare.

With such a large difference in the outcomes in America's two largest states, what's remarkable is that there is still an argument over what policies produce the best outcomes. Perhaps it's the elites' desire to hold power, and *do* something with it that keeps them and their supporters blind to the consistently poor results they generate. Or, maybe they justify their constant expansion of government power by telling themselves and the rest of us that, with just a bit more time and a little more power, they can improve our lot, lift up the poor, bring down the wealthy, and make people more equal in the material goods and services they enjoy. The problem is history shows that we never quite reach the utopia they promise, getting only bigger government consuming more production and limiting our liberties in the bargain.

Big government doesn't produce the benefits it claims, but it is a tempting target for influence. As government commandeers more resources from the productive sector, people who have learned to make a substantial living off of government figure out new ways of enriching themselves at the expense of those who are less well-connected. Whether it's Members of Congress trading off of inside information that would send the average citizen, or even Martha Stewart to prison,[225] or large portions of the financial sector enjoying taxpayer bailouts because they're "too big to fail," big government looks after its own.

Even Social Security and Medicare, those two sacred entitlement programs that together consumed $1.2 trillion of the $3.5 trillion Federal budget in 2010 have, contrary to myth,

---

[225] See Peter Schweizer's excellent "Throw Them All Out," Houghton Mifflin, 2011.

actually *increased* income inequality by taxing younger, poorer workers, and transferring their wealth to an older generation that is wealthier and living longer than at any time in U.S. history. In fact, these income transfer programs have done more to enrich the rich and impoverish the poor than the combined effect of both the Reagan and Bush-era tax cuts.[226]

That the cornerstone programs of American liberalism work at cross purposes to liberals' frequently expressed desire for equality tells much about both the state of liberalism and government.

We've made the case that the American Dream is rooted in liberty; that, when people are left alone to pursue their own definition of happiness, the greatest good for the largest number of people results. Beyond any utilitarian notion of tangible success, liberty itself is a prize worth pursuing.

As for those for whom success seems to pass by, we can take solace in the fact that most people aren't forever stuck at one income level, with 58 percent of Americans in the lowest quarter of income in 1996 rising to a higher level by 2005 as they get educated and more experienced at work.[227]

Even so, it oughtn't to be government's job to ensure the same outcome for all. James Madison, writing as "Publius" in The Federalist No. 10 predicted this would be a trying issue for the new Republic back in 1787 when he outlined the pressure, driven by envy, to curtail liberty in the pursuit of material equality. Admitting that differences in wealth lead to political factions, Madison nonetheless said that government had to protect the liberty to pursue "unequal faculties of acquiring property." And that, curtailing liberty to achieve equal outcome "was worse than the disease (of political faction caused by unequal wealth). Liberty is to faction what air is to fire, an aliment without which it instantly expires. But it could not be less folly to abolish liberty, which is essential to political life, because it nourishes faction, than it would be to wish the annihilation of air, which is essential to animal life, because it imparts to fire its destructive agency."

Were Madison alive today, he would observe the Occupy protests and be wholly unsurprised, telling us, *Deal with it. We did in our day. Remember, liberty begets inequality of outcome which begets the pressure to curtail liberty. Resist it. Liberty must be your object.*

---

[226] "Entitlements, Not Tax Cuts, Widen the Wealth Gap," by Michael Barone, *Washington Examiner,* Nov. 28, 2011.
[227] Ibid.

EPILOGUE

As the Great Recession began to impact state budgets in 2009, America's two largest states, California and Texas, both faced major budget challenges. But, elected leaders in Sacramento and Austin took divergent paths to solving their shortfalls.

California's money problems had their origins in massive increases in spending, as well as salaries and benefits for unionized state workers during the heady days of the Dot.com bubble. Sales and car taxes were also reduced, but only by a fraction of the new spending obligations.

When the bubble burst in 2000, California lawmakers used a series of budget gimmicks to paper over the red ink, pushing the accumulated debt into the next fiscal year, culminating in a budget shortfall of $34.6 billion in 2003 out of a final budget of $76.3 billion.

This fiscal meltdown, combined with a government policy induced electricity crisis in 2000 and 2001, led to the second recall of state governor in U.S. history in October, 2003.

California's new governor, Arnold Schwarzenegger, ran for office on the promise to "cut up the state credit cards." He didn't. Rather, one of his first acts was to push a ballot initiative to paper over half of his inherited debt with $15 billion in bonds. With the pressure for deep cuts and government restructuring ameliorated by the new line of credit, California state government spending soared more than $26 billion in four years, reaching a peak of $103 billion in the 2007-08 budget, an increase of 35 percent.

As the recession began to take hold, and with issuing additional debt made more difficult by Schwarzenegger's prior borrowing, budget writers were forced to spend less—spending declined $12 billion to $90.9 billion in the fiscal year ending in June 2009. Still, the cuts weren't enough, and the governor, with Democrats a handful of Republican votes, pushed through the largest state tax increase in U.S. history, a two-year, $24 billion hike in sales, income, and car taxes.

Throughout California's budget difficulties, the focus remained on government: how it could get more revenue. Lawmakers sought a multitude of ways to tax more, proposing higher taxes on income, sales, oil, the Internet, and even porno films. Lost in the discussion were business and jobs. It was as if taxes could be raised in a vacuum, with people just forking more money over to government without any impact on investments to create new enterprises and payroll to hire more workers.

Some 1,600 miles away from Sacramento, lawmakers in Austin, Texas were making different decisions.

In 2003, Texas, like California, faced a large budget shortfall. The price of oil had dipped in 2002, shaving about one percent off of Texas' total economic output. Lawmakers had to make painful decisions to close a $10 billion, two-year deficit out of a budget of $60 billion. Instead of borrowing to cover the major portion of the deficit, as the Californians did, legislators in Texas used "zero-based" budgeting to tear the budget apart and carefully examine its components. The easier alternative, used by California, most states, and the Federal government, is to simply take the current year's budget as the base, then add to it an increase for workload and inflation. This government spending on autopilot absolves lawmakers of the responsibility to perform oversight on government programs that may have long since outlived their usefulness or that have become grossly inefficient.

Tough decisions taken by Texas in 2003 not to raise taxes or borrow money allowed the Texas Legislature to enact property tax cuts in 2006 as part of a school finance reform package, saving Texas taxpayers $16.4 billion.

By 2009, when California was enacting its $24 billion tax increase, Texas approved a budget with no new taxes and a $9 billion Rainy Day Fund.

Led by their governor, Texas lawmakers kept their focus on jobs and the economy, understanding that the private sector generates the resources needed to run government.

By 2011, the deteriorating economy caught up with Texas as well. But, rather than raise taxes and rely heavily on budgetary gimmicks to close an estimated $25 billion two-year shortfall, the Texans once again tightened their belt—not an easy task in a state that already had the lowest per capita state spending in the nation.

Over time, policies regarding taxes and spending, as well as regulations, increased the competitive gap between Texas and California. By the time the recession hit in full force in 2009, the exodus of labor and capital out of California had grown from a trickle to a flood. The one-way cost to rent a U-Haul moving truck from San Francisco to Austin reached $3,236 in 2009 while so few people wanted to move out of Texas to California that the fare for moving west was only $399.

Mindful of their deteriorating job climate and its impact on state finances, a delegation of 12 California lawmakers, including the Golden State's lieutenant governor, Gavin Newsom, the former Mayor of San Francisco, left Sacramento for an unusual destination on April 13, 2011: Austin, Texas. Their mission: learn why Texas was creating jobs while California was losing them. As one visiting legislator said, "From 2008 to 2010, Texas added more than 165,000 jobs. During that same time period, California lost 1.2 million jobs. In terms of creating jobs, Texas is clearly doing something right and California is doing something wrong."

The Californians met with Texas Governor Rick Perry, their counterparts in the Texas legislature, former California Governor Arnold Schwarzenegger's first finance director, and business owners who made the decision to relocate from California to Texas.

Governor Perry assured the Californians that, "We want California to succeed. The fact is we need a strong California in this country."

But, as the delegation was wrapping up in Austin, bad news arrived from home: word that 69 companies relocated all or part of their operations out of state in the first three-and-one-half months of 2011, the highest rate since tracking was begun in 2009. Texas was the beneficiary of 14 of those corporate moves, creating more than 2,000 jobs at California's expense.

California business relocation expert Joseph Vranich listed several reasons why firms decide to leave California: soaring energy costs caused by "green" regulations mandating greenhouse gas reductions and renewable energy; high and unfair tax treatment; heavy regulatory burden; unfriendly legal environment for business; and uncontrollable government spending.

Of course, this California-based business analyst focused on the negatives of California. Left unsaid were the positives of Texas: low taxes, a light and predictable regulatory regime, and a business-friendly legal climate. None of which just happen—elected representatives have to work to enact then defend these policies against a vast array of competing interests.

The California lawmakers flew back home April 15. Tax Day. Had they wanted to look for extra meaning in that day, it wouldn't have been hard to find. According to the Tax Foundation, a national non-profit group that's studied tax policy since 1937, Tax Freedom Day, that day when an average taxpayer has earned enough to pay off their total Federal, state, and local tax bill for the year, came on April 7 for the citizens of Texas in 2011. In California, it arrived nine days later, on April 16. This nine-day difference translates into billions of dollars in profit that businesses invest in new equipment and hiring new workers. It adds up. And, over time, it leads to higher economic growth in some states, such as Texas, while others end up lagging behind.

ACKNOWLEDGEMENTS

As with any project of this nature, there are many people to thank.

First of all, I am in deep debt to my wife, Diane, who has participated in my public service and, despite personal sacrifices too numerous to catalog, still says it was worth it. I also must thank my long-suffering daughters, Jennie and Amy, who also bore the burden of service while I was out trying to save the world from itself, both in uniform and in a suit and tie.

Brooke Rollins, President and CEO of the Texas Public Policy Foundation deserves great credit for seeing the need for this book and applying the resources to make it happen. Without Brooke I might still be in California trying to salvage a state far beyond my very limited means to rescue it.

Josh Treviño, resident visionary at the Texas Public Policy Foundation requires mention as the man who dreamed up this book, then convinced the powers that be that I was one to write it. It was Josh, a native Texan, who first broached the idea of our family decamping to Texas, allowing this Washingtonian by way of California to say, "I wasn't born in Texas, but I got here as fast as I could."

The Hon. Arlene Wohlgemuth, Executive Director at the Foundation as well as the Director of the Center for Health Care Policy and The Hon. Talmadge Heflin, Director of the Center for Fiscal Policy, both accomplished veterans of the Texas House of Representatives are excellent purveyors of Texas hospitality. They greeted me less as a pitiable political refugee from a failing state and more as a survivor of California's political equivalent to the Alamo.

The wonderful policy experts at the Texas Public Policy Foundation deserve praise as well. They were quick to welcome me and point me to their prolific work. Special acknowledgement needs to be made to authors of the various Foundation studies and reports from which this book liberally borrowed including The Hon. Kathleen Hartnett White, Distinguished Senior Fellow-in-Residence & Director, Armstrong Center for Energy & the Environment and, for six years, the Chairman and Commissioner of the Texas Commission on Environmental Quality; Bill Peacock, the Vice President of Research and Director of the Center for Economic Freedom; Mario Loyola, Director of the Center for Tenth Amendment Studies; Marc Levin, Director of the Center for Effective Justice; and, The Hon. Joseph M. Nixon, former State Representative and our in-house expert on tort reform. In addition, policy analysts John Davidson and his predecessor, Spencer Harris (health care), James Golsan (education), Tom Lindsay, Ph.D. (higher education), Jeanette Moll (juvenile justice), Josiah Neeley (energy and the environment), James Quintero (fiscal policy), and Vikrant P. Reddy (effective justice) all had a part to play in this effort coming to fruition.

Special thanks is due to Nancy Druart who, through the wedding of her daughter, year-end sickness, and many competing requests for her artistic skills, created the book's cover art, without which it would not be in the reader's hands today.

The Foundation's crack development team is also worthy of mention. The Foundation's many papers, commentaries and reports sell themselves—figuratively, not literally. We need people who ask for the resources we need to keep operating so we can craft and send our message far and wide. For that we have Shari Hanrahan, Sarah French, Mike Joyce and Geoffrey Tahuahua to thank.

For any organization with many moving parts, smoothly running operations are a must. Greg Sindelar and Rikki Risinger (to whom we say, "Gig 'em Aggies,") as well as Jeremy Kee, make it all come together on a daily basis.

Our hard-working communications team in the windowless "bat cave" are worthy of especial mention: Kristen Indriago, David Guenthner, Brendan Steinhauser, and Travis Speegle.

Also, Billy Fickling, a Foundation policy intern, spent his last week with us reviewing this work and uncovering many needed edits.

I see all the Texas Public Policy Foundation's staff as keepers of the citadel of liberty in the Lone Star State.

Any mistakes herein are mine while kudos are to be directed to the Foundation.

Chuck DeVore
Dripping Springs, Texas

Made in the USA
San Bernardino, CA
23 February 2013